I0771271

The Best of Gowanus II

More New Writing from Africa, Asia and the Caribbean

Edited by:

Thomas J. Hubschman

Gowanus Books

http://www.gowanusbooks.com

The Best of Gowanus II
More New Writing from Africa, Asia and the Caribbean

© 2007 by Thomas J. Hubschman

Cover art by Eric and Issac Black

Published by:
Gowanus Books
473 17th St. #6
Brooklyn, NY 11215-6226

ISBN: 978-0-9669877-7-5
LCCN: 2007931754

Printed in the United States of America

http://www.gowanusbooks.com
info@gowanusbooks.com

Contents

Introduction

By Thomas J. Hubschman

I didn't know after I brought out the first *Gowanus* anthology (*The Best of Gowanus: New Writing from Africa, Asia and the Caribbean*) if it would be possible over the next five years to equal the quality of the short stories and essays we had published between 1997 and 2001. In a sense, that question was out of my hands: I only edit and publish. I depend on other people, scattered all across the globe, to provide content—writers who are strangers to me until they discover *Gowanus* and choose to submit their work. What I *could* aspire to was a table of contents that was even more representative of the peoples living outside the "West" than we had already published.

The first five years of Gowanus turned up a quantity of remarkable writing from the Indian subcontinent and the West Indies, but not as much as I had expected from Africa, particularly "black" Africa. My emails to African newspapers and universities seemed to bear no fruit, just as to this day my attempts to solicit material from the Middle East have been largely unsuccessful. Back in 1997, I naively imagined that the Internet had made a global village of the planet, with little regard to economic or social status. I know now that writers require more than an Internet connection to flower. Some introduction to the world of letters is also essential. That means education, and education usually means the kind of income we associate with a middle-class life. I had been thinking and making assumptions as an American, knowing that much of the world subsists on a dollar a day but not realizing what a statistic like this means on the ground in a place like sub-Saharan Africa and in so many other parts of the world.

I realize now that to a large extent what I experienced was a consequence of numbers: India is a nation of more than a billion people, about a quarter of whom speak English. That's roughly the population of the United States. Out of an English-speaking population that size, of course there will be many who have the education and leisure time to write. In Africa it is quite another matter, and I should not have been surprised that most of the submissions I initially received from that continent were from writers with European last names—excellent material that I was happy to publish and subsequently include in the first print anthology, but not what I had expected. Africa's indigenous middle class, at least that portion whose ancestry predates European colonization, is tiny by comparison with the middle class of India.

And so, it took a while for Africa to find *Gowanus*. But it was worth the wait. Once it happened the stories and essays were all that I could have hoped for: a contribution from a seasoned Nigerian journalist; a story from the member of a Ugandan women's writing collective; another story, liberally peppered with Zulu phrases, from a South African, to name just a few.

Meanwhile, the rest of the world had not forgotten us. The writers who made such a success of the first five years of Gowanus—Anjana Basu, Abbas Zaidi, Anthony Milne, Raymond Ramcharitar, Viktor Car, Rasik Shah—continued to delight our readers with their work. And new talents continually emerged, some from South America, thanks to help we received from Vicente Revilla, enabling us to realize our original goal of publishing material in both the writer's native language as well as in English.

Dana De Zoysa, truly a citizen of the world if that epithet means anything, provided us with a steady stream of superb reviews and essays. Mita Ghose, Lila Rajiva, Mohammad Nasrullah Khan and Marlene Amero and a host of other new names whose work is represented in these pages, guaranteed that the second half-decade of *Gowanus* would be at least as successful as the first.

For that success I have first the writers to thank. But without the help of Ellen Larson, my co-publisher, the volume you are reading would not have come into being. I am likewise obliged to Isaac and Eric Black for the cover design, and to Isaac especially for his continued moral support. My wife Luella already knows that without her there would be no *Gowanus*.

I also have to thank the tens of thousands of readers who have swollen the monthly statistics of the *Gowanus* website to a number any publisher could be proud of. Thanks also are due to the many academic and public libraries, as well as individuals, who have purchased the first print anthology of *Gowanus*. The reviews for that volume—starting with *Publishers Weekly* in May of 2001—were without exception gratifying.

Thomas J. Hubschman
Brooklyn, New York
tom@gowanusbooks.com

Preface

By Kenneth Ramchand

Professor of West Indian Literature (Emeritus), University of the West Indies; Professor of English (Emeritus), Colgate University

"The truly noble writer does not publish." None of the authors in editor Thomas J. Hubschman's engrossing second Best of Gowanus anthology would subscribe to this pronouncement by the apparition in Viktor Car's "Pessoa's Ghost." Most of the writers from Africa, Asia and the Caribbean whose work appeared in the first collection, The Best of Gowanus (2001), continued to publish in the e-magazine afterwards, and many other writers from these same countries made their debuts, with a notable increase coming from the African continent. In addition, authors from Latin America began to appear; and writers from Australia, Canada, Europe, and the USA felt enough of an affinity with their colleagues on other continents to join the chorus.

Tens of thousands of readers visit the Gowanus website annually, and each can post a response to what they see there. This can mean immediate feedback to the writer and hence a dynamic relationship between readers and writers. If I were one of those writers I would regard publication in Gowanus and elsewhere on the net as an opportunity to make instant contact with a new generation of readers on their own terms. Not critics or reviewers, but the kind of persons I write for or about. If I were one of those writers I would be happy to sift through the e-mails I receive from readers who want to enter into a dialogue about writing, about the world as it impacts upon us and about life in general--readers who don't need to go to the trouble of using pen, paper, envelopes and stamps to make themselves heard.

The present collection brings together in conventional book form a selection from the work of writers from all over the world who have been published in Gowanus. Putting this published work into old-fashioned print is a good thing. Only someone who has not enjoyed the touch and smell of leaf and spine or who has not lugged around and slept with "real" books can contemplate a reading life in which the only books are e-books. Also, while readers of an e-zine can focus on particular countries and writers, the cross-section found in an anthology encourages a more catholic approach. No one reading this collection can fail to recognise that although Gowanus is global it is a forum for a distinctive group of writers not necessarily bound by race, nation or ideology.

A quick look at two literary movements in the second half of the twentieth century helps us to see something new shaping up. In the 1960s and 1970s a group of writers emerged from the English-speaking West Indies (V.S. Naipaul, Derek Walcott, Edward Brathwaite, Edgar Mittelholzer, Wilson Harris, Sam Selvon, Austin Clarke, George Lamming, John Hearne, V.S. Reid, Roger Mais), to name a few, and made the world take serious notice. Two of them became Nobel prize-winners and a third, Wilson Harris, surely cannot be denied for much longer. No region in the world at that time could show anything like this group of writers. After that it was Indian writing in English, certainly in prose fiction, that became a major force in the world. Although it was not a national literature in the same way as the West Indian output of the 1950s and 1960s, the Indian contribution has been strong.

The writers in the present collection come from many countries, including India and the West Indies. I suspect that they first discovered one another's work in Gowanus and that the majority have not met, e-mailed or spoken with one another. But they have a lot in common as human beings, and more specially, as people who do not belong to the mainstream in the so-called developed, usually

Western, world.

Gowanus authors live in or come from countries whose need for self-representation and whose problems of self-representation (needs closely connected with their struggles for survival and identity) stem from similar historical or contemporary experiences. In the "The Donkey-Man" (Khan and Amero) the point is well taken that slavery and oppression heartlessly deny the humanity of the enslaved. In "Childhood Pleasures," Pumla Dineo Gqola of South Africa evokes a world in which custom and ceremony, the child's respect for elders, and a sense of community still exist. The older folk declare they have no one and nothing to go back to the rural areas for, and the young narrator is left trying to figure it out: "Their words surprise me, because they like to reminisce about their youth and how things were back then. But maybe all they want is to remember, not go back." More understated but no less about conflicts of this kind are Padma Prasad's love story, "A Family Business," which charts the drift of two ethnically disconnected characters towards each other, and Joanna Shireens's "Mr Gurupadam's Affair," the story of an exile with an empty heart awaking in middle age to the possibility of romance.

Disruption is also implicit in Rumjhum Biswas's delicately expressed "Sunset in the Hills." A grandson comes from Calcutta with his family to visit his grandmother in a rural area. She has schooled herself to accept their living in the city where prosperity and security await; but when it is time to go, Biswas makes us feel the wrongness of these brave choices. And then we are left with the grandmother, again alone: "The car jerked forward. The sun slipped out of the sky, pulling down the light with it. And then she couldn't see them anymore."

Andrew McKenna, an Australian, writes movingly about Koreans wilting under Japanese occupation and about both peoples being subjected to US weapons of mass destruction in Hiroshima and Nagasaki ("A Dark Place"); a writer from the Ukraine grieves over the loss of her friend, a victim of the unending standoff between Israel and Palestine engineered by powers with interests of their own

("Ali's Pictures," Veronica Khokhlova); a Croatian, identity stripped away by recent wars and travels, seeks answers: "I am forty years old and I live far away from Croatia and my mother; it is as if I have abandoned them." ("Pessoa's Ghost," Viktor Car).

These writers record the modern-day massacre of the innocents. They also register their worlds' encounters with what is new, including the consequences of global consumerism. They are appalled by cover-ups of the dark sides of family life. But they play their themes straight and without pretension. They are readable, they care about living, they don't care to theorise about whether they are modern, post-modern or post-anything. Good fiction is something so felt and true, they can't be distracted into meta-fiction. They write about the realities peculiar to themselves. And, even while they try to render convincingly external circumstances and the daily grind, they want the literal and material to convey their innermost thoughts, feelings, dreams and nightmares.

Their countries are fragments of empire or mutations from colonialism rife with poverty, internal strife, cultural repression and misprision in the highest degree, child abuse, gender inequalities, the dissolution of communities, personal trauma as well as traditional and modern forms of tyranny. In "The World Bank Has a Lot to Learn," Dana De Zoyza details how institutions like the World Bank impose meanings and patterns on cultures and societies about which these institutions have little knowledge, understanding or experience. In "The Last Colony," Richard Czujko shows how with the coming of the native tyrant Mugabe the people of Zimbabwe learn the Third World lesson that oppression does not end when foreign colonialism recedes. Abbas Zaidi reflects that although none of the Ayatollah's crimes even remotely compare with Hitler's, the Nazi leader gets a better press in the First World, where judgment of Khomeini is conditioned by the opinion that he "brazenly" defied the West("Ayatollah Khomeini and His Tormentors").

The inclusion in the anthology of seven non-fiction pieces is more than justified by the ways in which these essays and reviews establish referents that enhance our appreciation of the fiction that accompanies them. Lila Rajiva's "Missing Women, Missing Selves," discusses the shocking prevalence of female infanticide and selective foeticide in India, admitting there are economic and cultural factors involved but pointing to the culpability of "husbands, in-laws, neighbours, priests, tradition" who stand "tangled in a poisonous web of complicity." The subject of Hanifa Deen's Broken Bangles (reviewed by Dana De Zoyza) is the inexorable encirclement of Bangladeshi women by marriage and domesticity and their descent into poverty and worse when the husband/protector dies and the bangles are broken. The burden of women in Hindu and Muslim societies and the determination of women to take up their case for themselves are then contrasted in De Zoyza's review of Indelible Imprints: Daughters Write on Fathers.

Women writers from Asia dominate this collection, and the non-fiction referred to in the paragraph above enrich our responses to and understanding of the emotions their fiction expresses about family, the interaction between men and women, fathers and grandfathers, mothers and daughters and about child abuse. After reading about female infanticide we cannot take lightly the following sentences from "The Flame, the Amulet and the Scarlet Bras" by Anjana Basu: "Her mother had never wanted her in the first place. She told her that sometimes, in between slappings." "The Flame, the Amulet and the Scarlet Bras" and Mita Ghose's "Grey White Yellow" are well-constructed stories charged with emotion about the destructiveness of failed marriages both for the spouses and for the girl children trapped in storm or stasis. The evil truce between husband and wife in Ghose's story exposes the child to the nightmare of a predatory grandfather; the vain exhibitionist and sour mother in Basu's story reduces the daughter to a pathetic creature incapable of bringing anything but abject self- surrender to a relationship with a man. Abha Iyengar's "The High Stool" is built on a foul conspiracy between husband and wife which turns a young servant woman into the husband's private prostitute and forces her into a brazen but, hopefully, ironic acceptance of her "elevated" status.

Mr Hubschman has put together a balanced selection. The stories, essays and reviews in this anthology complement and reinforce one another exceptionally well and form an integrated whole full of fact and feeling. This is a book book worth reading and worth keeping.

Trinidad & Tobago
December 2006

The Donkey-Man

By Mohammad Nasrullah Khan and Marlene Amero
(Pakistan)

Every night on my way home I pass a dark corner and encounter a donkey lying there, a donkey that has worked very hard over the years to carry his master's load. His front legs both seem broken. At first, I tried to avoid him because he reminds me of our common destiny. He tries so hard to get up. He tries to go on laboring for his master, but he has barely any strength. One night I felt compelled to stop and watch as he struggled to stand. He managed to reach an upright position, but then his body began to wobble and he collapsed. He seems to know where he wants to go, but he only manages to move a few feet each day.

That donkey reminds me of Hussani, someone from my village who came from a very low-born family but for whom I couldn't help but feel pity. I also learned a lot through making his acquaintance. We may learn to recognize our common humanity by studying literature, but it was through mathematics that I learned how to determine Hussani Poweley's status in our village. It was when Father was testing me to see how well I had learned to count.

"Son, how many animals are in our courtyard?"

I was sure I had counted nine, but according to my father I was wrong.

"No, there are not nine, my son."

I thought Father was wrong and to prove it I started counting on my fingers. There were two cows, three goats, one mare, one donkey, one dog, and one Hussani, who I thought was also an animal.

Father laughed. "But Hussani is not an animal. He is a human being like us."

I disagreed. How could Hussani be a human being when he spent all his time with animals?

We brought our dispute to the court of my grandfather. The whole family was present and a decision was announced: Hussani was human. But even though I had lost my case I was awarded one rupee for making a strong argument.

It was hard for me to sleep that night because my tiny brain was not ready to accept the fact that Hussani was human. Questions kept flooding my mind: If he is a man, why does he not live like us? Why is he always with the animals? He even sleeps on the ground with them. In my dreams I saw Hussani eating grass, walking like a donkey and barking like a dog.

Hussani was the only servant of our large family. His big front teeth made him look like he was perpetually smiling. His complexion was like burnt stone. His mother died when he was only ten years old. No one knew anything about his father because his mother didn't want to reveal that secret. I only knew what I knew about him because of the stories Hussani used to tell me. After his mother died he was driven away because the village people thought of him as a whore's son. When they were driving him out of town it was my grandfather, then chief of the village, who brought him back to our house.

Our village lies at the foot of hot, dry mountains. Due to a very low water level, the land is not suitable for agriculture, and there is only one well in the village for a population of nine hundred. Hussani got up early each morning to draw water from it before he went out to graze with the animals, where he remained all day. At sunset he reappeared on his slow-moving ass, looking like a man from the Stone Age. As he rode through the dusty streets the villagers mocked him, saying he had an unacceptable relationship with the ass. They shouted, "Hey, Hussani, the ass moves like you put her to better use today."

Someone else cried from the tea-hut, "No, don't say that. The ass is Hussani's sister. How could he do it with his sister?"

Hussani was very much like that donkey I spoke of earlier—big-hearted. He always showed his big smile, hoping he could get people to smile back at him. Though he had no home and his clothes were ragged and worn, he was grateful. He had a mare, but because he was born to ride donkeys, he never rode her. Each evening as I stood at the big front door of our courtyard, I heard the melancholy chimes, like tragic music in an old film, as Hussani made his way down the Black Mountains with his slow-moving animals like a ragged line of retreating troops. He always brought back something for me—wild fruits, flowers, mushrooms. But better than all these, he had stories to tell. Stories of wolves and other, fantastic creatures.

Thursdays and Fridays were Hussani's good days. Those were the days the simple-minded villagers cooked special dishes and left them under the thick trees of the fields, thinking ghosts lived in the trees and the only way to please them was to offer sweet dishes. Hussani secretly ate as much as he could, thus reaffirming the villagers' faith.

I and my friends became young men. Our grandparents died, elder brothers became fathers, but Hussani never changed. His responsibilities only increased; he had to lift even more water on his feeble shoulders.

My elder uncle became the head of the family. He was very strict and often beat Hussani. Then, rather suddenly, Hussani's personality began to change. He started to dress differently. He used to wear only one set of clothes that he washed scarcely once a month, but now he began washing them every week. This new fastidiousness did not long go unnoticed, nor did the reason for it.

Hussani had fallen in love with the village beggar's daughter. But the villagers did not approve, because they thought Hussani lived too much like an animal and was a disgrace to them all. Too, beggars lived outside the village and were even more detestable than the servants who where lodged inside it. Hussani also had some status by being the servant of the village chief.

Soon the news of the disgusting love affair reached my uncle.

"Who can love such a donkey—someone who has always lived

with animals?"

He could have punished Hussani for such a presumption, but he decided to make of the news an entertainment for the nobles of the village. For, no one thought Hussani was worthy of any woman's love. The issue was to be decided in the presence of an aristocratic assembly. One night all the headmen gathered in my uncle's big sitting room. Hussani sat on the ground in the center of them.

"Well, Hussani, is it true you are in love with the daughter of a beggar?" asked Uncle in his heavy voice.

Hussani sat with his head bowed, not saying a word.

Another voice remarked, "His mother was also a great lover." Everyone laughed, and there followed an interlude during which they all told dirty jokes about Hussani's mother.

"She was the teacher of our youth. She shared the violent burden of our puberty."

Hussani's love wilted and died under the stinging laughter. When he rose from the meeting, he felt free of love's burden. His mother had taught him how to live, but she had never taught him how to dance with death. He resumed carrying his water pitchers and went back to doing his other chores as though nothing unusual had happened. After that no one ever saw him near the beggars' huts again.

I left the village in search of a job. When I returned many years later to attend a cousin's wedding, I could not find Hussani anywhere. I was told he was living outside the village, suffering from tuberculosis and that the disease had almost finished him. I knew no one would take him to a doctor because it would be humiliating to be seen with the donkey-man.

I found him lying alone in a dark, cold hut. I was barely able to stand the smell. For a few minutes he did not recognize me. When he did he began to weep. He tried to speak, but each time the congestion in his lungs prevented him. It was difficult for him even to breathe. "Hussani," I said, "don't worry. Tomorrow I will take you to a doctor. You will soon be all right."

At the door of the hut I looked back and saw the shadow of death on his face. He called me back and whispered, "Khan, life will go on whether I wish it to or not."

He died that night and was buried the next morning. There was no ceremony, because no one knew what religion he was. I still wonder why the villagers allowed his body to be interred in a graveyard set aside for human beings. He had certainly never been treated as one in life.

He was still smiling when they laid him in his grave. He seemed incapable of abandoning that smile, even if he had severed his ties with this life. It was as if he was saying to us all that death isn't as horrible as we think.

Now, after so many years have passed, this dying donkey has brought back to me these memories of Hussani. And I again asked myself, "Was he a man or a donkey?" But this time I have no hesitation answering the question. Would God that we all could be such a man.

The Black Tongue
(from the novel)

By Anjana Basu
(India)

Women are not born witches. Life makes them turn that way. If you want the truth of what I say, look at the facts: there are no young witches, no child witches. All the women torn or hacked to pieces in the columns of the newspapers are old. Some of them are not even witches at all. Perhaps just women like me who discovered the gift of a black tongue when everything else had failed them. I didn't know I had a black tongue until all the pieces started falling into place. And not even then.

We are not proud of our gifts. Pride is dangerous unless you have the strong-armed power to support it. A battalion of young men with smuggled machine guns whom you can let loose at night to make your predictions of disaster come true. Men who obey your commands without question or regret. Or a rich *thakur* husband with *izzat* four centuries long who can unleash death and destruction if one of his subjects just looks at him in the wrong way. A woman with a black tongue is nothing unless she has men behind her.

Otherwise she exercises her gift in secret, utters the dread word in anger in the dark. A black curse whispered on a black night that goes straight from her mouth to God's ear. If she does not do this, then the same dark night can bring her destruction. Actually, why night? The burning noon can explode in flame and consume her. How many times have you read of women being stripped and dragged through the fields till the skin is raked off their bones and the blood spatters the growing corn? Once every month? Every week? Ten men dragging a woman half their weight till the screaming thing that they drag becomes nothing human or recognisable, not someone's mother or wife or grandmother, just a thing that had to be killed.

And behind them, egging them on, is a witch finder. She can be a she—a powerful she with a tongue so black that it is hard to withstand its power. But her tongue, she says, is white and she uses it to protect. Nirmala Barui is one of those and I know her, though she does not know me. Very pleasant for a witch finder—she has *kajal* around her eyes, lips that she reddens with *paan* juice and a flower tucked in her sleek oiled hair. You can hire Nirmala to find you a witch if you pay her enough—I don't know what she charges, but her witch finding has bought her a colour TV and her son-in-law a new lorry. She's the most successful witch finder in the whole of Midnapore, she says, and I believe her. We've drunk tea together often, and she's boasted of her accomplishments while showing me her new teacups. "It's so easy. You just have to have the gift." The teacups came to her from money that she got for hunting down a witch in Patharpratima. That one was seventy-five, a grandmother whose three grandchildren had died one after the other. The doctor said it was malnutrition, chicken pox, a virus, but everyone in the village knew better, it was witchcraft. However, the men said, let us be fair, let us have a trial. So they tied the old woman to a pole in the middle of the village in the burning Jesthya sun and sent for Nirmala.

I'm told her technique is very impressive, unlike that of many other witch finders. She has to wait for the auspicious hour, when she will cast the bones and blow the conch. I must be fair, she said, sitting at the foot of the pole while the sun drew the life out of Nanibala. She cast the bones three times and got, she told me, the same answer. The old woman was undoubtedly a witch. So they left her tied to the pole for three days without food or water—no violence, Nirmala told them, do not raise your hands to her, who knows what will happen—till the sun that May did their work for them.

Yes, you have to have the gift. A gift for hatred. I don't know how Nirmala came by the gift or why she uses it against other women, but

I do know that a woman taught me how to hate. She is the one who put the black into my tongue. Oh, a very different woman from all these. She lives in the city, in a tall house, with a tall husband and a son. She has a red Maruti car as bright and shining as a tomato—no, she *had* a shiny red Maruti, I used to drive in it once, twice, I've forgotten how many times. Had—the Maruti is gone now. I don't mean to say that things are different in the city. The difference is only on the surface—because you have witches and witch finders in the city too, though they don't always behave in the same way there.

She had everything, this woman, when I had nothing at all. And she took everything from me—my home, my future. And she left me my life. In a village that much would have been enough to doom her—if I had been powerful enough. I would have summoned up a witch finder and said, "She is a witch, she has cursed me." But in those days I didn't know any of this. I sat in my place of exile and brought her face into my mind and thought of all the things that I wished her, one by one.

This village, our *desh*, is a small two-TV-set village. When I got there it only had one TV set, and the *panchayat* would meet under the banyan tree and debate how to collect money to build a meeting hall. That was less than my shantytown *bustee* had. When I climbed out of the train all those years ago, there was no one to meet me at the station and the station itself was just a shed in the middle of wide flat plain with the sun beating down out of a faded blue sky. The tracks stretched in both directions, running out of my sight, one set I knew crossing the border, the other going to the city where I belonged no more.

The second TV set now is mine—earned after years of writing letters for the village and filling in for the village schoolmaster. Whatever letters leave the village leave it in my handwriting—love letters, mother-sick letters, lies, truths, curses and all. It will continue to be that way until one of the children from the school is interested enough to take my place. I started writing those letters from the day I set foot in the village, because that was the idea that lurched into my father's head.

That was twenty years ago. If I had known when I stepped out of the train that I was exiling myself for twenty years, I would have tied a pitcher round my neck and thrown myself into the nearest pond. But I didn't know—so the ponds around our village remained flat unsympathetic bodies of water, furred over with hyacinth leaves. Twenty years. If I stuck my tongue out at that sheet of water it would probably reflect black at me. But I don't—someone might see and send word to Nirmala. You never know when someone might see.

Of course, I have been careful. The others who were accused had tidy little homes and money. They stood in someone's way—a nephew, a son-in-law, a brother. My father is still alive—barely. If you come to my hut, you will see a sack lying in one corner of the porch, a large blackened leather sack, and you will wonder what I keep in that sack and why it lies exposed to the open air in all weathers. You will wonder until the sack moves and groans. My father, always drunk, always looking for money to be more drunk.

When my mother was alive, she sent money—more after I came here, knowing that I would hide it away. That is the other thing I cannot forgive. The first time she came down we had to meet in secret, because if Baba saw her he might turn violent. She sent me a message from the station by one of the other women who knew the whole situation and we sat under a tree and talked. "When can I go home?" I asked.

She turned her face away. "I don't know," she said on a sigh. "I told your *boro bhai*. He says that it is best you stay here."

"Here!" My disgust took in the flat plain and cows with their bones sticking out like ploughshares near their hips. "To do what? Learn to plough?"

"There are worse things," Ma answered. "If you had only studied as I told you." She sighed again. "I thought you were dead. We all thought you were dead!"

"And I might as well be dead! That woman—I hope she's miserable!" The word welled out of me on a gush of hate and spattered the blue cotton-wool air. I almost expected the sky to turn black.

"*Omni boltey neyi,*" Ma said. "You shouldn't talk like that."

"But she should pay."

"She will pay. Your *boro bhai* is seeing to that. It might mean that

I will be able to send you more money."

She told me what they were doing, though in snatches, hastily, looking over her shoulder. There were always people to carry word to Baba. "Aren't you going to see him?" I asked.

"Not this time," she answered. "Here." She pushed a bundle of notes at me. "Bury it under a tree. Just make sure that your Baba does not find it."

The day I came to our *desh* was the day I uttered my first curse. And that was the day that I started collecting and hiding the money. Not all of it, because it would have made Baba suspicious, but bit by bit. I didn't know that I had uttered my first curse, but that night I had a dream. I dreamt of a house surrounded by people carrying sticks and stones. And I saw *her* standing on the rooftop with her husband drowning in that sea. When I woke up, my string bed shook and I heard the birds cawing and screaming outside. The earth had turned in its sleep and shaken the village. My bed shook once, twice, thrice. Then the birds settled again and the conchshells blew from the small temple. My rage had shaken the earth, I thought, and knew that the power was in me.

Nirmala told me, "I discovered my first witch when I was sixteen. Shaila, an old woman who had no family. I was taking mangoes from her tree—you know, young green mangoes to eat with chillies"—she licked her lips as she said that with her fat red paan stained tongue—"and the woman came out screaming and throwing stones. I climbed out of the tree as fast as I could and started to run. Believe me, my way was clear, but my foot turned and I fell on those hard green mangoes and was bruised all over. What would you call that if not witchcraft?"

"And then?" I asked.

"I fixed her. She overreached herself. Too many people were dying all around her place, in her fields. Four years later I threw a fit by the tubewell and said she had bewitched me."

"You have the illness that causes fits?" I asked, meaning epilepsy.

She laughed pityingly. "It's easy to throw fits. You rub soap in your eyes and chew some of it so that you foam at the mouth—

washing bar soap. I screamed her name over and over again." She looked at me with her sly small eyes. "It's so easy."

Was that what I should have done? Chewed bar soap and rolled around? Not that that occurred to me when I was going to *her* house. "What happened to the woman?"

"She was a witch—what do you expect happened to her?" Shaila was denounced and stripped. Her son-in-law gave Nirmala the woman's best sari and told the village that she should be cherished. "They said the goodness ran so strongly in me that it could not tolerate the presence of evil." She looked at me consideringly. "You never know—it might run strongly in you as well."

"How do I know whether it does?"

"You ask your dreams. You walk in the fields and let the wind talk to you. And you pray—always you do *puja* for guidance." That I would have guessed: her two-room brick hut reeked of incense and husks of coconut shells rolled on the ground outside, brown coconuts, the symbol of human sacrifice. "Prayers to Ma Kali, queen of the night." She dropped her voice, "And of course you must learn some spells of your own, so you can combat theirs. Nothing too complicated, and it must be done secretly, very secretly." She sat back and laughed, her cheeks pushing up and creasing her eyes shut. "But be careful, or people will think *you* are a witch!"

"Why are you telling me this?" I asked.

"Because you're the village letter writer—you know everyone's secrets. And because if you tell anyone that I said this I will denounce you as a witch. And no one will believe that you are not. It's so easy!"

The power ran through me as she sat there, and I thought shall I call out my tongue, shall I let its blackness out to mar this woman's life as she has marred hundreds of other lives? But the anger was not there. I did not hate the woman as I hated the other one. "You're safe," I told her. "I wouldn't have said anything anyway."

I walked out of her home hearing her self-satisfied laugh. She was rich—that *pukka* house must have cost her a *lakh* or more. How much money had she made for all those men for whom she had hunted out witches? Chillies and coconuts could be used for good as well as evil. Chillies burnt to blind the eyes of evil and coconuts used to trap the human soul. I didn't know any of that when I began my cursing. I ran *her* name round and round in my head. I traced it with my finger on the running water so that it would ebb away. I wrote it on the pond side in mud as black as my hair and trampled it flat.

The other girls wondered what I was doing, and then I realised that I had to be careful. Especially after the first *daini* call spread like wildfire through our village. I saw the woman being dragged out of her hut before I knew what was happening. She was a young woman who was having an affair with the carpenter. Even I, new as I was to the village, had heard about the affair with the carpenter—they met in the farthest field where the *palash* trees grew thick and showered the grass with their flame flowers in summer. Even her husband knew—he could not have helped it. Finally, he was the one who denounced her. "Who is she?" I asked. "What's happening?"

"She's a witch, a *daini*. Come, come, let's look!"

What was there to do beyond wash clothes, run through the household chores, write letters for other people and make sure my father ate something through all the liquid that he consumed? We ran after the men, listening to the screams and watching like we watched the monkey man and the *chhau* dancers. No one thought of lifting a hand to protest—and in any case, we were just more women. What would we have done? But I thought as I ran, if something like that can happen to a woman who is not a witch, it could happen to me— and I *am* a witch. So I honed my tongue and mind in secret, waiting for my mother's visits to tell me whether my hatred had struck.

The Other Sex
A Review

By Dana De Zoysa
(Sri Lanka)

Broken Bangles
By Hanifa Deen
Penguin Books India
324 pages

Hanifa Deen is an Australian of Bangladeshi descent who returned to her ancestral home in 1995 with the idea of writing a book about how women live there. But she wanted to go beyond the usual accounts of women in Islamic societies. To her it seemed most people's perceptions of the Muslim woman were "centred on the Middle East, yet there are more Muslims in South Asia and Southeast Asia than anywhere else in the world." She points out that "religion is just one of the many building blocks that shape women's lives: colonialism, history, nationalism, economics, gender, culture, and patriarchal values make up a litany of influences embedded in the psyche of each country."

Like many of those who study the women of a culture from afar, she did not anticipate the complex, self-concealing, nuanced, diverse reality she met. From her home base in the Kiplingesque Mona Lisa Hotel in a rumpled-shirt neighborhood of Dhaka, she met women from all corners and byways of Bangladeshi society, from her masseuse living on the edge of survival to Dhaka's rich and famous.

Her book is an antidote to the perception of Islam as monolithic, backward and violent. Islamic developing countries are not mere forges of fundamentalism. Fundamentalists, conservatives, middle-of-the-roaders, liberals and a far left exist in any Muslim society in about the same proportion as they exist in non-Muslim societies. The main difference is what one identifies as middle-of-the-road. Deen shows how feminist utopianism can survive in a land where liberal is what middle-of-the-road is anywhere else, middle-of-the-road is conservative, and the religious right is Mussolini without the brown.

For example, in Bangladesh (and many non-Arab countries) the *burqa* that so outrages some Westerners is a largely middle-class garment, and there is a class component to *purdah*. Village Muslim women are workers first and foremost; they often wear only the simplest of head covering because drapy cloth gets in the way as they labor. On the other hand, upper-class women of the cities can wear stylish headgear because they have the wealth and power to not be bound by Quranic face- and hair-covering rules.

Deen paints Goyesque you-are-there portraits of her trips into the Bangladesh and Pakistan hinterlands, some regions of which are bastions of fundamentalist misogyny. She finds that religious fundamentalists are every bit as cruel towards women as portrayed abroad, but for reasons less related to contempt for that sex than for economic gains to be had by frightening women into giving up their money and land. The nexus of local mullah, politico and money-lender allied for mutual financial gain plays a far larger role in the issuance of religious *fatwas* than does blasphemous female behavior—what Ms. Deen calls the Fatwa Industry. One result is a litany of widow horror stories; another is a myriad of tiny one-woman revolts that the author describes with delicious piquancy.

Suppressing women for financial gain is not a uniquely Muslim phenomenon: it happens in Buddhist Sri Lanka, Hindu India, and post-Maoist secular China. Children are no better off, being exploited for labor, sex and marriages of alliance all over the region. The common thread is economic inadequacy resulting from the refusal of power-holders to encourage a strong middle class. Almost everywhere in Asia that one looks, there is a correlation between the size of the middle class and the rate of both social and economic advance.

There is also an unseen cultural component to fundamentalism. Fundamentalists want to impose their version of purity on a very old and peculiarly Asian version of Islam which blends legalistic Arab Islam with pre-existing Hindu, Buddhist and animist traditions. The ghosts of Hindu gods and Buddhist *devas* (almost-gods) inhabit a world of spirits both good and malign, animal totems, divinations, dreams and visions. These ancient feudal institutions exploit Islam, Hinduism, and Buddhism to hold on to power. Indeed, one must grant Islamic fundamentalists a certain respect for their relatively temperate handling of this mix: Christianity burned thousands at the stake trying to stamp out the ghosts of Cathars, Druids and forest spirits.

But Ms. Deen also demonstrates how fundamentalists actually tend to come out the worst because of their stridency. To the pragmatic city-dwellers who hold a country's economic purse-strings, bigoted shock tactics do not introduce any lasting change. Instead, they just bring about alienation. Even in the parts of Bangladesh considered their power bases, fundamentalists consistently do poorly at the polls.

"Reading about poverty, illiteracy and malnutrition from academic texts never prepares anyone. You sit watching television documentaries from comfortable armchairs, Chardonnay in one hand, pizza in the other, and you delude yourself. Everything is at arm's length and poverty, disease, and death become sanitised. You know nothing—you realise that later. Nothing prepares you—how can it? Your cocoon is shed soon after you and the distance between you and a world crowded with pain is instantly reduced. You develop a protective veneer just to get through the day, and you hate yourself for doing this."

The picture the author paints of NGOs (non-governmental organizations, a fancy term for not-for-profit charities) is an eye-opener to anyone who has ever seen the ads by organizations trolling for money with pictures of starving waifs. In all too many cases the first thing the money goes too is a huge Pajero with fat tires. The second is a luxury office in the capital (leaving just enough left over for some properly mediagenic, poorly furnished outposts in the countryside). The third set of cheques hires all the family members the local manager can get away with. Only then does the cash buy anything that ends up in the mouths of hungry children.

On the plus side, NGOs do bring international attention to things governments should be doing themselves, even if the end result is the NGOs taking over a government's responsibilities. The politicians are delighted: it translates into more of the country's economy going into their own pockets.

Ms. Deen's ability to elevate the particular to the level of the general without directly saying so raises *Broken Bangles* to the quality of a good novel. Readers acquire insights into developing-country thinking and customs that do not appear in any travel literature, and rather little of it even in mainstream subcontinent literature. For example, she describes the hidden nuances behind passion in subcontinent Islam: "In Bangladesh, little is what it seems. People do not express themselves as much as enact their feelings. Stage-drama behavioral expectations find their way into religious and political culture." Just about every high-sounding ideal is an admission of low self-esteem. Men say they are protecting their women, but in fact they are protecting themselves against their own insecurities.

Asian and Middle Eastern thought processes are very different from those in the West. To the Islamic mind there are conclusionary mechanisms more powerful than reason. Westerners tend to think in networks, with linkages and threads in many directions. East Asians tend to think in a silo or in the vertically integrated clan-based model first codified by Confucius. Most Indians' context is three-layered: a specific caste level communicates one level up or down from itself but rarely much higher or lower. Also, Islam is a prophetic system: knowledge is revealed and received rather than arrived at. Muslim thinking can be visualized as a single, vast, flat sheet of equality and unity based on the principles of *umma* (the brotherhood of believers) and *tawhid* (unity with God). Underlying all this is a view of one's place in the world that explains why forcing democracy and a market economy on people results in the kind of cultural rejection whose extreme is Osama bin Laden.

But, surprisingly, Islam has no significant economic argument with the West. The Qur'an is pro-capitalist—Mohammed was a merchant. And, like the West, Islam urges uplifting one's moral character through vigorous self-effort. It is salutory to visit a bookstore in Dubai, India, Malaysia or Indonesia and see Muslim self-improvement guides addressing the same concerns as the *Seven Best Habits*.

The big difference is that most Asians, and Muslims in particular, see the world not as a market but as a courtyard. Courtyard culture arose from the use of worshipping places as common grounds. The courtyard is a socially cohesive unit founded on religious identity, bound on one side by market stalls, on another by the prayer hall, on the third by the codes of class and station, and on the fourth by secular power in the form of police, army and tax. The focus is on leaders, not institutions; function, not reason. The governing principles of decision are *muafakat* (collective council) and *masyarakat* (concordance).

Imagine for a moment what would happen if Asian and Arabic proselytizers from a country where these notions predominate were suddenly to arrive on Western shores informing the inhabitants that their society is hogwash, that Eastern ways are better and, by the way, everyone should switch to Arabic and Eastern food and fashions, too. Welcome to *Broken Bangles*.

A woman's bangles are given to her by her in-laws on her wedding day. Occasion by occasion she adds to them, sometimes for pleasure, sometimes for obligation. Over the years her bangles acquire social baggage: the symbol of marriage, protection of husband, dependency, adornment of self. And then slowly, inexorably, they become symbol made reality: encirclement, fear of the whisper, the prison of the hearth. Romantic feelings are a luxury of the privileged; guilt is an indulgence enjoyed mostly by the middle classes. For most, marriage is desperation packaged as property. The glittery bangle binds.

A woman breaks her bangles when her husband dies. Islam does not impose on widows the banishment that rural Hinduism does, but a woman without a protector (the husband's role as seen in Islam) is not much better off than a woman without a god (the husband as seen in Hinduism). Bangladeshi wives become excellent misers, hoarding every *taka* coin for the day when their protectors are gone. Unless she is rich, self-deprivation links hands with social deprivation.

Ms. Deen's etchings of these women are the writer's version of Goya's "Los Caprichos." But the broken bangles in her title are something far worse than Goyesque grotesqueries. You must endure them yourself to understand. Thanks to Ms. Deen's book, to a great extent we do.

Grey White Yellow

By Mita Ghose
(India)

Grey

Baba drops the telephone receiver into its cradle with a sharp click. "He's not coming home this year either," he mutters.

Ma's tone is shrill. "I don't understand that wimp of a principal! How can he allow a teenage boy to dictate to him?" Her voice breaks and the words tumble into the crack. Beneath her blusher her cheeks are sunken, the colour of ash. Ma's using make-up these days. Lots of it. She's also started wearing saris in shades that hurt the eyes. "Tarty colours," she called them once. They make her look old, older than Baba. "That boy needs a few lashes of the cane to teach him what's what!" she snaps. "Why doesn't that imbecile of a principal understand?" Her pale palms lie upturned on her lap, forgotten, useless.

"Personally, I think it's immensely reassuring that Father Bryant understands his boys so well. He realizes that bright, promising youngsters like Rono wouldn't fib about something so serious just for the hell of it."

"You don't for a minute believe...?"

"Of course I do."

"That miserable wretch wouldn't dare say such a thing!"

"Oh, yes, he would. My son dares. Unlike his sorry mess of a father."

"You swine!" Ma's voice is a hiss of steam as her body uncoils from the sofa. "How *dare* you insinuate there's even a jot of truth to the filth the boy's been spouting! And about his own grandfather!"

"He caught the bastard at it, didn't he?"

"Don't *you* call *my* father names! That son of yours needs psychiatric treatment! What did Babai ever do but show love for his grandchild? Everyone knows he dotes on her!"

"So he does. And I can't sleep nights wondering what really went on in that house in Deoghar when he took her there on holiday year before last!"

Ma's off the sofa now. "You sanctimonious bastard," she whispers. "Who are *you* to point fingers? What about the scandal you've created in your own home? And with scum from the gutter! Your beautiful "widow" in white! You think I haven't figured out what that bitch's fainting fits are all about? How about telling Rono that he just missed having a bastard brother or sister to play with? I'd love to see what he thinks of his precious Baba then! What was it, by the way? A bonny boy? Or a cute little girl who would've followed in her mummy's footsteps?"

Baba's large body looks weightless as it spins in her direction. His hand rises like a saw. No. Please, God. He stops. He's noticed me on the balcony where I've been polishing his shoes for the last half-hour. Back and forth goes my brush. Right to left. Left to right. I can't make my hands stop. "Hey, that's enough for now, Babe!" Baba calls to me. "You don't want Kalidas to pack up his kit and go back to his village to starve, do you?"

As though I were going to earn my living sitting at the gate of our apartment complex like our *mochi*! So what if I love polishing shoes? It's just a hobby—ther-a-peu-tic, as Ranjan *Da* says—like reading, painting or playing the guitar like Rono, my Dada, my big brother. I'm actually going to be an astronaut, with my own spaceship that'll take me far away to another planet. Mars, Jupiter…Ur-an-us. But I know what Baba means: "This is a war zone. Get out."

I feel his eyes on me cold as the North Pole as I put the brushes, rags and tins of polish back into my shoebox. I carry the box carefully to the closet next to the front door. My hands are shaking. I have to go to the bathroom. I keep my thighs squeezed tight as I place Baba's shoes neatly on the rack beside Ma's new grey leather pumps.

Grey like her hairline which used to be black last year. Grey under the angry red henna she now uses. Next to the red is her face—a dead grey, like the haunted house down the street with its windows shut forever. Baba's hair is grey too, all over, as grey as the papery skin under his eyes. The rest of him is golden brown like a sponge cake that's just come out of the oven. It makes his teeth look white as the toothpaste ads on TV. Sneha too, is grey these days, a soft, mushy grey that melts into the walls which used to be white many years ago. I wonder how that could be, because her skin is soft pink, her eyes green-brown and her saris white as Baba's teeth.

Once inside the bathroom I slam the door shut and slap down the lid of the potty seat. It's cold to the touch, cold under my flattened thighs. As cold as Darjeeling so many years ago when Dada pinched his nostrils and whined, "Ohhh, my sinuses!" just like Ka in the *Jungle Book* movie. It was he who said when he left for Darjeeling last year, "I hate you all. Especially *you*," to Baba, who flinched. Dada who now won't come home from school. For my last birthday he handed me a sheet of lined paper with a drawing of a stick figure on it, its braids standing up like horns, the mouth a big round "O." That was me bawling my head off. I didn't know till that moment that I loved my Dada almost as much as I love Shah Rukh Khan.

Dada, who's always at Ranjan *Da*'s when he's not studying or playing football. Dada, who hates to be home. If he has to stay in, he's restless, like those bats zooming up and down the stairwell at night in the house in Deoghar. When he gets that way, I can't stand it. He has this thing about rapping his knuckles on the glass of my aquarium to watch bug-eyed Rambo, my fighter, go crazy. He knows it'll start me shrieking, "Stoppit! Stoppit! You *shala haramjada shuorer chhana!*" Ranjan *Da* taught me those bad words, and I love them. Dada uses those words all the time. He knows exactly what makes me cranky, what makes me cry. So he can chant, "Skinny Minnie, crybaby! Skinny Minnie, rave rave rave! Skinny Minnie, rant rant rant! Skinny Minnie, sob sob sob."

Idiot. "Minnie"! As though he doesn't know my real name. And I have so many, more than him, more even than Ranjan *Da*, who's Khokon, Dadababu, Chhorda and Shubhoranjan to different people.

I am many people, all at the same time. Ma calls me De-bo—a double karate chop that makes my brain soggy like cold noodles when I hear it. To Dada, I'm Hulo, a tomcat yowling all the time. Ranjan *Da* calls me Bonty. To Keka, my friend at school, I'm Debbie. Keshto *Da* calls me Puchkey. I'm Chhoto Mem to Kalidas and Khoki to Bansi, Mr Kanodia's *durwan*. To Miss Tomkins, I'm "the Terror." And Sister Paula calls me Devleenah, with her voice going all the way up on "nah" like Sister Braganza's cre-scen-dos, when Miss Tomkins reports me for disrupting the class. Sneha, whose job is to look after me. She calls me Shona-mona, and to Baba, I'm Babe. Both mean darling, sweetheart, honey, love…. They said so. All lies.

De-bo-li-na is the Cobra's name for me. Debolina, his wife, my Dida—Ma's mother. She died just before Ma's fifth birthday. Her picture on the bedroom wall of the house in Deoghar is grey, a flat dead grey, as though she was never there, even when she was alive. De-bo-li-na. The moment I think of it I see the Cobra's yellow eyes, yellow teeth. I hear the sound of his yellow nails, scraping. It's De-bo-li-na's fault that Ma threw her Big Fit and Baba threw his after Dada caught the Cobra red-handed. It's all because of De-bo-li-na that Dada is now at boarding school. Because of her he needs a few lashes to teach him what's what. De-bo-li-na is a *shaitan*. "De-bo-li-na" will always hurl me back to the day I vomited when the Cobra asked me if I wanted to go with him again to Deoghar and Ma said, "Why not? It'll do her good."

Why am I always thinking of De-bo-li-na? There are so many other me's to think about: Hulo. Bonty. Debbie. Chhoto Mem. Khoki. Even the Terror and Devleenah. Babe. But, no. There's no Babe now. Not anymore. And Shona-mona is gone too. Even if Ma's words keep bringing those names back to me and everything they once meant. Ma's words. "Your widow." Dada with a bastard to play with. Baba's beautiful widow. Baba and Sneha. The Cobra and me. *Shaitans*. And Dida's dead grey eyes looking down at us from her dead grey face in the picture. Dirty grey. Dirty.

There's a rap on the bathroom door. It's beginning to open. I hurl myself at it and slam it shut again. Why didn't I lock it? I lean against it with my whole body and slip the bolt across. I'm sweating and shivering. My nails scratch at the wood. Scratch, scratch, scratch. Black nails, not yellow.

"What's wrong, baby? Are you ill? Why have you locked the door? Open up, Shona." Sneha's voice. Far away.

Sneha. Baba. Ma. Dada. All far away. De-bo-li-na alone. Alone with the Cobra.

The Cobra smoothing the hair back from De-bo-li-na's face with his yellow nails, hissing, "Shhh…shhh…" as she lies shivering and crying. Crying all night for Baba. But Baba never hears. He's far away, clasping Sneha's soft pink hand, smoothing the hair back from her face as she lies, her white sari crushed on the floor. In our grey house. But no dirty-grey picture of Debolina on the wall. Debolina is dead.

Baba's bunched fist. Ma screaming. Dada gone. Just Sneha. Baba. Ma. Cobra. De-bo-li-na.

Cobras right inside our house, our grey house with no grey picture on the wall. Cobras lying together, tongues flicking, locking and unlocking slowly, like in the English movie Ranjan *Da* was playing for Dada in his flat once when I went up to fetch him because Ma wanted him to come down and do his homework. De-bo-li-na sees, from inside my mind, the cobras lashing their gleaming tails, soft pink and golden brown, rippling and slithering before coiling together in a tight throbbing knot that looks as though it can never be untangled. Cobras curled together, wrapped in each other, trembling in a close dance, not shivering and crying. Just hissing softly, deep in the throat, like a purr that turns into a moan. Pink mouths opening and closing, moaning deep in the throat, ah, ahhh, ahhhh, the sound filling my thumping heart with terror. Then silence. The cobras half-smiling at each other, still entangled, green-brown eyes drooping, teeth bared sparkling white like in a toothpaste ad, ready to strike anyone who disturbs them.

The bruises on Ma's face turning purple. Sobbing all day. De-bo-li-na, curled around her pain, crying all night. Debolina staring down, blind. Seeing nothing.

"Shona?"

"Go away." De-bo-li-na's voice, all splintered.

"Please, Shona-mona! Open up. I can tell you're ill…."

De-bo-li-na spits into the washbasin. The bitter taste stays in my mouth. De-bo-li-na turns on the cold-water tap and splashes my face with water. Splash splash. She rinses out my mouth. The bitterness is like a furry grey leech on my tongue. De-bo-li-na stares into the mirror. She sees my face. Flat. Blurred. Grey. Like the face of the other Debolina. Dirty.

"Shona, please open the door. You're scaring me! *Please,* Shona-mona!"

From the bathroom ceiling I hear De-bo-li-na's screams explode in my ears. "Get away! GET AWAY FROM ME, YOU SNAKE!"

White

"Why does Sneha wear white?" I ask Ma.

"Stop bothering me," she says, stepping into her shiny new heels with a grimace. I notice a new strip of Bandaid just above the back of each shoe. "I'm late for work already." She snatches up her handbag.

"Baba, why does Sneha wear white?"

"She's a widow," he says, not looking up from the suitcase he's packing.

"Widow-shidow. My foot!" says Ma. "All those yards of white are just a bad cover-up for a tart fallen on hard times." She looks at Baba sideways, sharp as a knife.

"Can't keep that cobra's tongue in check, can you?" Baba snaps.

I shiver.

Ma sniffs. "Pure as the driven snow, is she? With those looks? Well, Daddy knows best, doesn't he." She's looking at me, but I know she's talking to Baba. She does this all the time.

Baba stabs Ma with a stare. She stabs right back.

"What's a tart?" I ask.

"Never mind," Baba says. "No school today?"

I catch Dada on his way out, dragging his schoolbag. He's in a hurry and one of his shoelaces is undone. He'll trip and fall. Then I'll laugh. "Why does Sneha wear white?"

"What?"

"Why does Sneha…?"

But Dada's already out the door. "How should I know?"

I corner her in the kitchen. "Why only white, Sneha?"

"Drink up your milk fast," she says. "You know your Ma."

My eyes stray to the pickle jars on the shelf I can't reach. "I want the tamarind one."

"You can want all you like. The last time I gave you some, you came out in a rash and your Ma bit my head off."

"Please, please, please!"

"No."

"You're a stupid tart!"

Sneha's eyes freeze over like ice cubes. They remain frozen all day.

At four o'clock she braids my hair, tugging it tight. She changes my frock and gives me milk in my favourite mug with a smiling tomato painted on the side. She sprinkles dry Bournevita on top. She knows I like to tease the granules with a spoon. She's still not speaking to me. I don't care. I'm not speaking to her either. Stupid tart.

That's why I go to Ma instead of Sneha just before dinner and tell her, "I feel funny."

"You're not going to start that again?" Ma says, her eyes on the TV. She's watching Shah Rukh Khan dancing with Kajol. I love Shah Rukh more than anyone. I watch him turn Kajol upside down. Doesn't she feel giddy?

"Besides," says Ma suddenly, "there's your favourite capsicum chicken and orange-flavoured *kheer* tonight. Made especially for you." But when she turns to look at me her face changes. "Oh, God!" she says. "Why can't you fall ill when your father's in town?"

"Work, work and more work," she says. "Your Dad's one helluva busy man. Busy as a beaver—the older, the busier. At home and abroad." She turns to stare at Sneha. Her laugh's like a sharp knife: You don't know you're cut till you notice the blood welling up.

But I don't know what she's talking about. I just want to crawl into bed and stop the Bournevita from coming back up. I run towards the bathroom, but I don't make it. Out it all comes on the threshold.

"Yuck!" says Dada, standing at a safe distance. "Yuck, yuck, yuck!"

I puke all night. In the morning Sneha raps on Ma's bedroom door.

"What a mess! And what a stink! Clean it up, will you, Sneha? I'll call the doctor before I leave for work. What timing. Her Dad's girl all right. I can't take a day off. Year-closing and all that."

The doctor's specs glitter, so I can't see his eyes. I dive under my blanket, cling to it and shiver.

"Come on, let go," says Ma in the kind of voice she puts on when visitors are around. "Doctor Uncle needs to have a look at you."

"No," I say. "I'm cold."

"Don't give me a hard time!" she snaps in her normal voice. "My ride will be here any minute."

"No!"

She yanks off the blanket and whacks me hard. The doctor is shocked. He picks up my wrist as though it's something dirty and jabs my chest with his ice-cold snaky stethoscope. Then he takes out a syringe from his black bag, and I immediately start to bawl.

Ma stares at me and I abruptly stop. When the needle goes into my arm I don't even make a peep. I sleep the rest of the day.

Sneha lays her cool palm over my forehead. "A little soup," she cajoles. "Just a sip."

Sometime in the night I wake up. The Cobra is standing over my bed. His tongue flicks out and licks my lips. It nudges its way into my mouth and coils tightly around my tongue. "Baba!" I try to scream, but my tongue is locked. "Baba!" I scream again as the Cobra's tail lashes out and coils around my tummy and legs, thick, blue-black, glistening, thrashing and squeezing its way in, hurting, hurting, hurting. I see Baba walking down a dark, narrow tunnel. Walking away from me, getting smaller and smaller and smaller. "Baba, Baba, Baba!" I scream. He doesn't look back. Gone.

I wake up sweating. My heart's trying to jump out of my chest. I look for Sneha in the dark. She's not there. I start to cry.

"Here I am. Silly girl!"

"I saw the Cobra," I whisper.

"Just a bad dream, Shona." She won't believe me if I tell her he was right on my bed. She wipes me off and dusts me down with talc. She covers me up and opens a window. Then she stands by it, staring out. In the moonlight she looks as white as her sari—a ghost.

I'm too scared to tell her I'm scared.

"What are you looking at?" I ask just to see if it really is Sneha.

"My life," she says.

"I'm scared."

She doesn't hear me.

"Please, please, please! I'm so scared!"

She gives me a long look as though she doesn't remember who I am. Then she comes and squats on the floor by my bed. "My baby," she whispers, her hand trembling on my blanket, "my poor, dead baby!"

"I'm not dead, Sneha," I say.

She buries her face in her white *pallu*. Her shoulders shake. I've never seen her cry.

"I said, I'm not dead!"

"Shhh…. I didn't mean you."

"Aren't I your baby?"

"Of course, Shona-mona."

"Don't you love me?"

"What a silly question!"

Stupid tart, I think. Crying for nothing. She rubs her face hard with one hand and gives me the other so that I can hold on to her little finger. My eyes close, shutting out the ghost in white.

Yellow

It's Saturday.

"Ah!" says Baba, looking at the newspaper he's just unfurled, smoothing out the creases with a lot of crackling sounds. "Saturday.

Time for the Cobra to strike again."

Ma turns and stares at him, her jaws clenched like fists. Baba doesn't look up. If he did he'd turn into a pillar of salt, like Lot's wife. Sister Celine told us about Lot's wife last week in Scripture class.

The Cobra comes to visit every Saturday. Except when he's away in Bangkok on business. Or on holiday in Deoghar. "King Cobra, up to no good in his Black Hole," says Baba. "All those little girls the lonely old widower employs from the neighbouring village to cook and clean and fetch for him, far away in his country home. All those unsuspecting little girls," Baba murmurs.

"Love to wallow in all that concocted filth, don't you?" Ma spits every time Baba talks like that.

It's Saturday, when my parents don't go to work. Saturday, when they have lots of time to fight. Saturday, when everything goes wrong.

I remember the Saturday morning when Ma read aloud the bit from a newspaper about a well-known nursing home dumping hospital waste in its backyard. Blood-soaked bandages. Gangrene-infected arms and legs. Dead foetuses. Sneha, who had just finished serving tea, suddenly turned white and keeled over. Thump. The tray slipped out of her hand and landed beside her with a clatter, clatter. I could hear it long afterwards, long after Baba knocked over his teacup as he sprang out of his chair to attend to her where she lay sprawled on the floor, her long hair fanned out around her, her *pallu* flung from her body. My ears were still ringing with the sound as Baba knelt feeling for her pulse and smoothing her hair back from her chalk-white face. His own face was grey. His hands trembled.

Ma didn't budge from where she was sitting. Her face was stone, her unblinking eyes fixed on the Sneha. And I saw what I had never seen before: how fair and silky the skin was where Sneha's hip dipped sharply into the hollow of her waist, how deeply her belly button dimpled, so high above her petticoat string. I saw her big dark nipples straining against the thin white of her blouse, the two top buttons gone, sweat crawling like a worm down the hollow between her breasts. I saw Ma's eyes on Baba and Sneha. Back and forth. "Oh, not to worry," she laughed, a sound like glass being scraped with a knife. "She's alive all right. But just to be *absolutely* sure, shouldn't you call the doctor? Better than just sitting there holding her little pink hand…. But maybe there are warmer, more promising places your hand would rather be."

I was home when Baba caught Ma by the hair and slapped her hard, slapped her and slapped her. I was home when the doctor came to look at Sneha, home all day to hear Ma's sobs leaking out from under the locked door of her bedroom. Because on Saturdays I don't have school. I don't have school on Sundays either.

On Saturdays I get to polish shoes. Mine, Baba's and Dada's too, until Dada left for boarding school. Ma doesn't let me touch hers. She sends them down to Kalidas, the *mochi* who sits at the entrance to our apartment complex, next to the gate of Mr Kanodia's big white house. Kalidas has been polishing shoes all his life.

"Keep your paws off my footwear," Ma warns when she catches me eyeing her shoes. She has so many. Black, burgundy, chocolate and white. Navy blue, bottle green and cream. Silver and gold and bronze. But no reds. No yellows.

She scoffs at Baba when he tells her that I do a better job than Kalidas. I've watched Kalidas brush the shoes clean of dust and caked mud, then smear polish on with his finger and let it "air" before attacking the leather furiously with a second brush. Then he takes an old soft rag and, stretching it in a taut line, skims it back and forth over the leather the same way I've seen Keshto *Da*, the sweeper, rub his back dry with his checked red *gamchha* after a bath. Then he adds his finishing touch—a gob of spit—and swipes the rag back and forth across the leather till it gleams like nobody's business and you can see your face in it.

I want a kit like the one Kalidas has. You should see all those brushes, the little cans of polish, the collection of tins full of shiny little needles and nails, the strips of black and brown leather. And the spools of thread, the shoelaces in black, white and brown, the rags, all stained, some darker than others. The only thing I don't like in that kit is a bright yellow square of polishing cloth he recently bought. "Get a red one next time," I tell Kalidas every time I pass him on my way in or out of the gate. He grins up at me with his lovely *paan*-stained teeth. I asked Baba to get me a kit exactly like the one Kalidas has, and he laughed. Then I asked Kalidas where I could buy one, and he laughed too. Finally I asked Sneha.

"Hush!" she scolded. "Don't let your Ma hear you. A *mochi's* tools? She'd throw a fit."

That would be nothing new. Ma throws fits all the time. "Item numbers," Dada calls them. The biggest was on my last birthday, just before she sent Dada away to boarding school.

"He's gone crazy!" she screamed, spit bubbling at the corner of her mouth when Dada told Baba, late at night, about the Cobra, and Baba told Ma. She slapped Dada with the back of her hand, cutting open his cheek with her ruby ring.

"Stop it, you crazy bitch!" Baba yelled, pushing Dada out of the way.

"Oh, my God!" Ma dropped onto a sofa and sobbed into her hands, her smeared *kajal* making her look like a weeping panda. "It's all that scum's fault! That *friend* of his—that pervert in schoolboy's garb—Ranjan Whatshisname! I keep telling you, but you never listen! You're too *busy*! We have to get him away from that bastard or he'll end up a delinquent himself! Or in an asylum like your Aunt Jharna. God help me, what shall I *do*? *What* shall I do?"

It happened on a Saturday.

I know what day of the week it is today when Ma orders Sneha to marinate the chicken in milk and cook it with poppy-seed paste. I know it has to be Saturday when she tells Sneha to let the milk simmer for at least half an hour so it's thick and creamy before she makes the *kheer* with *kaju* and *kishmish* ("That's cashew nuts and raisins," Miss Hendricks corrected me last month during English period. "Don't you Bongs know the language at all?"). Ma usually doesn't bother about what's being cooked in the house. When she does, I know it's Saturday. Especially when she tells me to wear the lemon-yellow dress the Cobra gave me on my last birthday.

"No," I say.

"What do you mean, no? I made Sneha let out the hem."

"Not that dress."

"Why not? It's from Mademoiselle, and it's more than *your* father could afford. That's real Brussels lace on the collar."

"I don't care. I hate yellow."

"We'll see about that as soon as I'm out of the kitchen."

Yellow. The colour of egg yolks. I spat them out on my breakfast plate at the hotel in Darjeeling where we had gone on holiday when I was three. Ma walked me all the way to the traffic policeman at the junction and told him what I'd done. The policeman looked down at me from his yellow box, his eyes like slits, and told me it was a very serious offence to spit out egg yolks. That if I did it again, he would be forced to punish me with his stick. I was too scared to cry.

Yellow is the colour of my report card in which Miss Phillips wrote last year, "Inattentive. Does not apply herself."

Yellow is the colour of the jaundice that laid me flat for two whole months, year before last. Right after I came back from my grandfather's house in Deoghar. The Cobra's Black Hole, where the silk curtains in the bedroom are shiny yellow.

Yellow is the colour of the Cobra's eyes burning into mine as he sat in our drawing room last year, alone with me on my birthday. Alone, while Baba was on the phone and Ma was in the kitchen. Dada was in the bathroom, and my best friend, Keka, hadn't arrived yet. Sat alone, breathing in and out, in and out, deeper and deeper, staring at me as I sat shivering in my yellow birthday dress.

Yellow is the colour of the Cobra's topaz ring. Yellow is the colour of his nails, crawling, stroking. Up and down, up and down, as he told me in a blurred whisper how pretty I looked. So, pretty, so pretty....

And yellow is the colour of my vomit when, two hours later, I threw up my slice of birthday cake along with my lunch.

Yellow, yellow, dirty fellow, Dada teased when Ma unwrapped the dress the Cobra had bought and made me wear it. Before Dada came back out of the bathroom and saw what the Cobra was doing. Before he told Baba about it that night. Before Ma threw her Big Fit. And Baba threw his—the only time Baba ever threw a Big Fit.

But Baba shut up soon afterwards. He shut up after Ma screamed, "*You* dare talk? You think I don't know what's going on in this house?

Maybe you"d like me to tell your son about *that*—your mixed-up fool of a son? And you believe him, instead of whipping him straight like you should!"

Not a word from Baba.

And he's back again today, the Cobra. As he is every Saturday. The box of sweets he's brought for us, wrapped in gold paper, lies open on the table. Ma is arranging them on a big plate with a gold border. Big, yellow *laddoos,* silvered over with foil. Yellow *sohan papri,* sprinkled with slivers of almond. Fat yellow *kamala bhog,* swimming in syrup. I struggle to keep the vomit down. Ma's made pulao. Lemon-yellow, flecked with *kishmish* and half-moons of *kaju.* I swallow and look at Ma's face, pink and shiny, hovering around a smile. She doesn't make a sound, but I can tell she's humming inside.

I look at Sneha setting down a jug of chilled water on the table. Her eyes meet the Cobra's, and she turns red. She looks at Baba, then whips back to the kitchen. I look at the Cobra. He's staring at the door through which Sneha has just left, his eyes gleaming with a yellow light. Then I look at Baba. His eyes are on the Cobra's face, and his face is tight as if it's going to burst. The skin where his collar cuts into his neck is bright red.

"De-bo-li-na?" says the Cobra suddenly, smiling with his yellow teeth. "Want to go for a l-o-n-g holiday with me to Deoghar this summer?"

"Why not?" says Ma, spearing each ball of *kamala bhog* with a toothpick. Jab. Jab. "It'll do her good. She's been looking peaky after that bout of typhoid last month. And she hasn't been to Deoghar for years."

"You won't keep crying for your Baba this time, will you, De-bo-li-na?" murmurs the Cobra. His yellow nails won't stop playing with the stiff white folds of his dhoti. Up and down they go, up and down. "You're a big girl now, aren't you, De-bo-li-na?"

Baba stiffens in his chair, his fists bunched. But I can't wait to see if he'll stop the Cobra from taking me away again to his Black Hole. I don't even hear the crash as my chair overturns. I'm in too much of a hurry to get to the bathroom.

Time Must Wait

By Crispin Oduobuk
(Nigeria)

In that lacklustre way which characterises most of the world, Forneeso seems to be in a state of perfect monotonous normalcy when Assak begins to speak of his Awakening. That is to say, the inhabitants of this small road village with a reputation for producing gasoline blackmarketers are, as usual, busy spying on each other and swapping bits of gossip while the occasional hapless motorist who runs out of gasoline in the vicinity gets cleaned out—amidst many sympathetic tongue clicks—for a few adulterated gallons of fuel.

Though no immediately discernible change has taken place, Assak's Awakening is soon on every lip. While some folks saunter over to his home to see and hear for themselves—their reactions being as mixed and as varied as their dietary preferences—others stay away jeering, and eventually deriding, Assak's Awakening as his Maddening.

A thin, generally likeable shopkeeper of mild manners, Assak has had little formal education. However, he has broadened—or narrowed (his fellow villagers cannot agree on which)—his mind with wide reading. Whether because of or in spite of this, he welcomes all to his home, even those who clearly visit merely to mock him.

To such visitors—and we should place ourselves in this group on this occasion—the "awakened" Assak, on a typical evening, is never at a loss for words. We meet him now as he holds court in his front yard, his four-year-old daughter bouncing happily on his knees.

"Subject to his interpretation, either from within or without, there is always evidence before man. And the more significant evidences reside within men, where they really live. Denying the presence of evidence is a futile effort, as it will out, given time and circumstance."

That is how it goes with Assak. He makes many unsure whether it's the language or the topic they do not understand, though, it must be admitted, there are those who are certain it's both. Some consider this the stuff of genius. For others, grotesque images of the madhouse present themselves. This babble of reactions, while silencing most, has quite the opposite effect on Kapsak, a gasoline blackmarketer neighbour of Assak's.

"I had no idea they awarded degrees in the shop or on the farm, Assak," Kapsak teases. "Or is yours a home-grown kind of professorship for which no degrees are needed?"

Bent on delivering his latest piece of wisdom to his small audience, our divinely inspired host (how else shall we put it?) carries on as if Kapsak has not spoken at all. Or, perhaps, he does take Kapsak's words into consideration.

"Since evidence reveals itself sooner or later, it is only a matter of time before everybody becomes aware of it."

"What evidence are you talking of?" Kapsak queries.

This time some of the other neighbours in attendance glare at the impertinent Kapsak. "Why don't you listen first?" comes from Awadamoto, the only car owner in the village and a taxi-driver in New Town, twenty minutes drive away.

Dahsang, Assak's closest friend, heaves an exaggerated sigh in Kapsak's direction and wags his head. Kapsak swallows hard as Assak, gesticulating slowly, continues his lecture.

"Consequently, the awakening of a man to the importance of some thought-provoking or life-defining experience is of significance in itself, for itself. Perhaps quite as significant as the original happenstance. This is much in the same way as when a curious student seeks out the underlying reason why a teacher decides upon a particular experiment to illustrate a point. Some men come to this realisation easily. Some labour over it. Some even deny it, though, curiously, being in denial has never destroyed evidence.

"Therefore, realisation—the Awakening—is a deep-seated aspect of life which no circumstance can permanently put off."

Now we learn that for Assak realisation has not come with the heart-shattering suddenness of bad news. Neither has it arrived with regal slowness like the kaleidoscopic rays of early morning sunlight. Nor has it materialised in the manner of a witch doctor's mumbo-jumbo predicting the imminent return of the longed-for rainy season, which anyone could have made with less fuss. Rather, realisation has come very much in the way of a tiny ant starting out at a man's foot yet bent on stinging only the fleshiest part of his buttocks.

What Assak does not tell us—but we learn nonetheless with a little snooping—is that with realisation, or Awakening, as he prefers to call it, has come this new fad of his to go off on a tangent that no one—not even the dramatic witch doctor—can predict. Interestingly, curious solitary brainstorming sessions usually precede these rather unscientific extrapolations.

The often-opinionated folks of Forneeso are no longer arguing over how, when or even where the whole matter is going to end. While they're all agreed that some conclusion will cap the issue, scoffers and admirers alike have silently decided to wait and see what strange creature Assak's Awakening will give birth to. Some wait in well-articulated anticipation.

"It'll be nice to have tourists asking to be taken to meet Assak, 'the Philosopher of Forneeso,'" says Awadamoto, his mind on potential fares.

"More likely it'll be Assak 'the Madman of Forneeso' we'll end up with," Kapsak cracks. "I assure you, no tourists would want to meet him."

"Let's just wait and see!" Dahsang snaps.

So Forneeso is in waiting, drearily seated under the tropical sun as if it were in mourning. However, while they wait the villagers still marvel at Assak's new-found tendency to drop bits of unfamiliar sayings from out of nowhere into ordinary conversation or into the suspicion-laden silence of a full room. Inexplicably, Assak keeps bringing up some touching—and some not so touching—issues, everyday matters that come and go.

"I feel tears in my eyes even though I know I'm not crying," Assak points out to his wife one breezy evening. "I wonder why, and eventually it dawns on me that even though I may not be aware of it, a part of me, I'm sure it's the soul, is crying. And it must be for some unjust happening."

His wife nods silently and hastens into the kitchen. As far as she knows, weeping souls can neither cook dinner nor be of help in any practical way.

Dahsang, being the new philosopher's best friend, also has to put up with quite a bit.

"Infamous schemes to keep crooked politicians in the mainstream of events always stick out like sore thumbs," Assak says to his friend one clear night while they're observing the stars in the sky.

"What has that got to do with anything?" Dahsang replies.

"I don't know. It just came into my head."

"Hmm. Assak, all this thinking, has it been able to tell you what tomorrow will bring?"

"No," Assak replies truthfully.

"See there? No one knows what tomorrow will bring, so stop thinking so much."

"Empty promises that will sail with the dust."

"What? Is that what tomorrow will bring? Or are you talking about politicians again?"

"Huh-huh-huh! No, it just occurred to me. I—well, come to think of it, politicians do make empty promises that sail with the dust. And tomorrow may bring just that."

"Assak! You've started again. What does 'sail with the dust' mean?"

"Just think about it and you'll see."

Dahsang thinks. And he does see. Much to his amazement. And, thenceforth, he too takes to thinking, much to his own wife's chagrin.

"I don't like this at all," she complains. "That crazy friend of yours has got you thinking like him. Very soon you'll be talking nonsense too."

"Assak is not crazy," Dahsang declares. "He's just got the Awakening, and I think I'm getting it too."

To ensure that he really gets it, despite his wife's scoffing, Dahsang recalls some of Assak's sayings. "If I could define with certainty my purpose here on earth, I believe that would empower me more than a landslide victory at a presidential election."

But this only angers his wife the more. "Now I don't know who's crazier, you or Assak!"

"No one is crazy," Dahsang assures her, imitating Assak's quiet way of talking. "It is in the nature of the mysteries that govern this world that one day the sledgehammer will bounce off the back of the ant and return to smash its wielder," Dahsang quotes, glad to have said it just the way Assak would have.

"You see what I mean? Now I truly don't know you anymore."

Dahsang shrugs and wonders what Assak would have said next. Probably nothing.

Our survey of Forneeso in the days of Assak and his Awakening continues with a visit to his home on another day. For our friend of the unusual philosophical persuasion, this is a day of environmental sanitation. We bear witness as Assak begins to clear the small bushy area behind his house.

"Don't stand behind me," he says to his daughter as he begins to work.

But the thwack-thwack sound his machete makes as he cuts through the dried-out shrubs and grass excites the young girl so much that she walks around him in order to get a better view. Unfortunately, she walks straight into Assak's return stroke. The heavy farm tool splits her fragile skull and the young girl goes down without uttering a sound.

"Oh, my God!" Assak cries as he turns to see blood gushing from his daughter's head. "God, help me! Please, help me!" as he tears off his shirt and tries to stop the bleeding. Wrapping the shirt around the gash, he picks up his unconscious offspring. Already moving, he thinks fast. By this time of day Awadamoto would have left for New Town. Kapsak has a scooter. But besides Kapsak being Kapsak, it is said that he uses only heavily adulterated gasoline, so the scooter runs for a hundred meters and then has to be pushed for the next hundred.

Assak begins to run. Barrels flat out. It's the race of his life. His only chance is to get his child to the local dispensary as quickly as possible. Seconds later, he blows onto the narrow main village road and races on.

Like an ancient locomotive, he puffs through the village square at leg-breaking speed. Unintentionally, he knocks Dahsang's wife—who's returning from the market—out of the way and cuts off into the bush. The dispensary is four miles away. Staying on the road will take him longer to reach it. Cutting through the bush should shave off a mile or so.

Dahsang's home. We find him totally relaxed in the comfort of an easy chair in his living room. His head is slightly bowed. He is obviously in the middle of a mind-expanding meditation. Presently his wife barges in, breathing hard.

"Didn't I say it? Didn't I say it? That crazy 'awakened' friend of yours has joined a cult!"

Dahsang looks up at her slowly. Interrupting him in the middle of a mind-expanding meditation—he has said this many times—is a clear case of his wife's failure to grasp the fine points of the art.

"He has joined a cult!" his wife insists.

"My dear, would you please calm down? What is this talk about a cult?"

Even so, Dahsang is slightly worried. He knows his wife, and her excited state can only mean she has happened on some troubling discovery. But Assak cannot be a cultist. Not Assak.

"I saw him just now running with his daughter into the bush. I think he's going to offer her as a sacrifice."

"Don't be silly! Assak will never do such a thing!"

"I saw the blood myself! It seemed as if he'd violated her too, though I won't say so since I didn't actually see that. He pushed me down and ran away with the girl. She may already be dead by now. And I know it's all because of his silly Awakening!"

Dahsang jumps to his feet. There are things a man should see for himself.

His lean frame surprisingly strong against the wind, Assak blows on. He jumps over shrubs, dips slightly to avoid a low tree branch and powers on, determined to save his daughter.

He fords a shallow stream and puffs up the muddy bank, oblivious of the blood oozing from a cut on his right toe. He clutches his daughter's body tightly as he tears through the bush with the fury of a lion bent on overtaking its prey.

If only time will wait, Assak tells himself as the thought crosses his mind that he might not make it to the dispensary soon enough.

"Time must wait!" he suddenly cries. "Time must wait! Time must wait!" To make time wait, he reaches deep within himself and finds extra strength to increase his already amazing speed. Over an anthill he goes with a leap that would impress even an olympic jumper. Uneven ground sends him plunging to the earth, but an unseen force steadies him as he repeats his battle cry: "Time must wait!"

"Time must wait! Time must wait!" The words echo over and over through the bush. Yet we are silent witnesses as time continues its destinationless journey, unwilling to halt a course set down long before the days of such as Assak.

With Dahsang's wife re-enacting her knock-down experience in slow-motion to all comers, it happens that the girl actually passes on, and all of Forneeso has heard that Assak's daughter is dead, and that "he sacrificed her, you know, that Awakening thing of his."

Assak returns from the dispensary limping from the big cut on his toe. Still in shock, we hear him barely manage to tell his wife and Dahsang what happened before delayed hysteria intervenes.

Meanwhile, legging about the village, Kapsak has launched a new career explaining precisely what sort of ritual Assak has performed on his late daughter.

"It is a devilish sacrifice for wealth and knowledge," he declares to a family that lives near his home. Deciding that the news is worth dining out on, he walks some distance to a wealthy palm-wine merchant's, hoping to get some fresh wine in return for his analysis.

"You'll see how rich Assak is going to become now," Kapsak, forerunner of the TV/Radio news analyst, declares between gulps of sweet palm wine. "It's the blood, you know. They use it to perform the ritual, and then money starts pouring out of a hole in the floor. But I tell you the end result is always madness, you'll see."

While he is still holding forth in his new area of expertise, a mighty explosion rocks the village and forces everyone outside.

"I wonder what that blood-thirsty Assak is up to now," Kapsak muses in a tipsy voice.

"What makes you so sure the explosion had anything to do with Assak?" his host, who's always been fond of Assak, asks.

"I tell you, I know these things! It's part of their rituals!"

Just then an over-excited boy comes running by and is besieged for news. "It's Assak's doing, isn't it?" Kapsak growls, making us wish fervently we weren't here merely as observers, so that we could smack him on the head to shut him up.

"Let the boy talk!" his host snaps. "Come, boy, tell us, what happened."

"Fire," the breathless boy says. "Then it went boom!"

"Where?"

"Assak's house?"

"No," the boy begins, then stops and stares at Kapsak.

"What is it, boy?" Kapsak says, his eyes swimming in alcoholic frenzy. "Did you see the ghost of the dead child?"

"Come on, boy, where is the fire?"

"It's…it's at *his* house," the boy finally manages, pointing at Kapsak.

"Where?" Kapsak screams, his wine gourd dropping with a splash. "I'll kill Assak! I swear I will!"

Since the whole village is now heading in the direction of Kapsak's house where an inferno is threatening to flatten everything, it makes sense for us to make our way there too.

"What a day of tragedies," a toothless old woman cries while struggling to keep up with a group of much younger women.

"They say it's all Assak's fault. The gods are angry. They're going to punish us all."

"How can that be? Assak isn't the one who kept gasoline at Kapsak's house."

"So it's gasoline?"

"You mean you didn't hear?"

"Aye, but I thought it happened in the bush."

"Yes, it's in the bush but it is still close to the house. They say Kapsak's first son wanted to burn the garbage and he chose a spot too close to the gasoline cans his father hoards to sell to stranded motorists."

"I hope he's alright."

"Who, Kapsak or the son?"

"The son."

"That shows how little you know about gasoline."

"May the gods have mercy on us!"

"Will they? I thought you just said they're angry and out to punish us."

By the time he reaches his burning house Kapsak is in no state to kill an ant. Drunk and stupefied by grief, when he sees the 'awakened' Assak at the head of the human water line, fighting a lost battle to save his friend's house, he merely crumbles into a heap and begins to weep.

Pessoa's Ghost

By Viktor Car
(Croatia)

Jose Saramago, in *The Year of the Death of Ricardo Reis*, informs us that, after his death, the writer Fernando Pessoa regularly visited Ricardo Reis. Maybe it was because Ricardo Reis was part of Fernando Pessoa himself. Reis was a doctor and a poet, and he died in a confusion of love. Pessoa wrote:

"Time! Time past! Something—a voice, a song, a chance fragrance—lifts in my soul the cloth from the mouth of my memories…That which I was and will never again be! The Dead! The dead that loved me in my childhood. Evoking them sends a chill across my soul and makes me feel exiled from hearts, alone in the night of myself, weeping like a beggar before the close silence of all doors."

Years have passed since I died in Claire's heart. I can't shake off the moist spray of that cool morgue, and the substitute love of passersby does not heal.

I live alone in a small apartment in Toronto. I earn a good living without much effort. The owner of the firm is sympathetic, looks favorably on my frequent excursions. More than my death in Claire's heart hurts the love that does not issue from me. I must appear lonely to someone who peeks through my window and sees me at this table for the third day in a row, not saying a word, not hearing anything but Preisner's music. Zbignew Preisner must have loved Krzyszt of Kieslowski, I conclude as I listen to his *Requiem for My Friend*. Without longing for love, Michel Houellebecq could never write *The Elementary Particles*. Jose Saramago must have craved love, otherwise he could never so subtly and precisely portray Lydia's love for Ricardo

Reis. Lydia is also a symbol of Reis's muse; he was blessed with talent as well as love. Not recognizing this love, he insulted his talent as well. Fernando Pessoa must have had some answers that I need. I am forty years old and I live far away from Croatia and my mother; it is as if I have abandoned them.

Pessoa writes:

"I don't remember my mother. She died when I was one year old. My callous and scattered sensibility comes from the lack of that warmth and from my useless longing after kisses I don't remember. I am spurious. It was always against strange breasts that I woke up, fraudulently lulled.

"Ah, it's my longing for who I might have been that scatters and staggers me! Who would I have been if given the affection that comes from the womb and the kisses planted on an infant's face?"

I too am often fraudulently lulled against strange breasts. When I wake up, at first I feel like crying; but despair dissipates with the light. Once, I was held against my mother's heart, but unlike Pessoa, I feared definition. By choice, not by destiny, I have abandoned my mother. Or is it my motherland?

I travel and I write. Pessoa knows why: "To create, I've destroyed myself; I've so externalized myself on the inside that I don't exist on the inside except externally. I am the living stage where various actors act out various plays." Destiny deprived him of identity; fear made me strip mine away. I understand Pessoa well, and obviously he understood me. He died in 1935. Saramago wrote convincingly about the dead Pessoa meeting one of his own heteronyms, Ricardo Reis.

I read, pace about my apartment, read some more. By Sunday evening, after not talking since Friday, I can hear Pessoa's voice.

I don't do laundry, I just buy new clothes. There are mounds of moldy garments in the corners. I can cook—light Mediterranean meals or hearty Hungarian stews—but don't. I lie in bed, and there is nobody to turn off the light after I fall asleep. In the morning I long for coffee, but there is nobody to share it with. I befriended Preisner, I befriended Saramago, and they also visit me in my dreams. Preisner arrives accompanied by sad musical themes. Saramago's voice is soft and slow. He likes to talk about architectural detail, about Manuelism visible everywhere in the facades of Lisbon. I also once befriended Raban, but he doesn't visit any more. My old editor from Croatia sends me emails from time to time, reminding me to keep writing so my talent doesn't wither and die. He also asks about my health. My American editors never call, never ask if I write, never ask how is my health. We immigrants are a cheap commodity here. Hence I must inform you: my cholesterol is under control; my alcoholism recurs biweekly; and, since I have died in the heart of a living person, I am light as a ghost.

That is why I believe I shall meet Fernando Pessoa.

The other day I started seriously thinking about hiring a nanny—I even wrote down a list of tasks she'd have to do: read to me in Portuguese; have coffee with me in the morning; drive me to work, maybe; turn off the light when I fall asleep (and stop the agony welding through my eyelids); have meals with me; fold laundry, do dishes, open rejection letters and throw them away. After I made a list in bullet form I realized I was not being rational. I am very proud of being rational; after all, I am an engineer. I thought some more about the idea of the nanny and gave my head a shake. Idiot and fool, how could I ever have conceived such a ridiculous idea? The logical answer is not a nanny, of course. Clearly, I must go immediately to Lisbon and see Fernando Pessoa.

I rent again the *Double Life of Veronique*, and Preisner's music drills itself straight into my bone marrow. It begins to seem perfectly logical that twinned souls do not necessarily have to exist in the same time-frame. Reassured that I will find Pessoa in Lisbon, I phone Alena, my travel agent. I tell her get me to Lisbon as soon as possible. "You're sure it's not Paris this time?" Very sure, Alena, Lisbon. I have a meeting there. I can hear her typing, and she chuckles. She is young, Czech, models on the side, and sometimes we flirt and then don't talk for months. As she types she says, "So, who will you meet there?" Fernando Pessoa. Maybe Ricardo Reis, I tell her, but they are really not very different, and she says, "Oh, I see." I add, Zbignew Preisner assured me I will see them, and we both giggle at this absurd exchange. She finds me a ticket for $399 to Lisbon for that Thursday. To be picked up at the airport. She already has my

Mastercard number, so I'm all set.

It takes some phoning to book a hotel—in the end, it is the Albergaria Pax on Rua Jose Estevao. Ten thousand escudos a night is not cheap for Estefania, but I comfort myself with the thought that Graca and Alfama are not far away. I inform the boys in my office that I will be away for a couple days.

At the airport, waiting in the bar for my flight, I read more Pessoa:

"Ah, let those who don't exist travel! For someone who is nothing, like a river, movement is no doubt life. But to those who think and feel and are alert, the horrendous hysteria of trains, automobiles and ships makes it impossible to sleep or to wake up. From any trip, even a short one, I return as from a slumber full of dreams—in a torpid confusion, with one sensation stuck to another, feeling drunk from what I saw. I can't rest for lack of health in my soul; it's not movement I've been denied, but the very desire to move."

I murmur, Of course I don't exist, I died in her heart, and ever since I have never stopped traveling. You are some brother, Fernando.

Those who travel are those who cannot feel. That is why travel books are always so woefully lacking as books of experience, worth only as much as the imagination of the one who writes them. And if the one who writes them has imagination, he can enchant us with the detailed, photographic description of landscapes he's imagined just as well as with the necessarily less detailed description of the landscapes he thought he saw. All of us are near-sighted, except on the inside. Only the dream truly sees when it looks.

You'll hear from me, Fernando, I can't wait to meet you.

I order a beer, and then another. There are some Portuguese sitting beside me, also waiting for the plane. "I haven't been home for sixteen years," one of them tells me. Why not? "Oh, I forgot who I was, but time has reminded me. And you?" I am going to meet a friend. "In Porto?" No, Lisbon. Beside my interlocutor sits a middle-aged woman. She smiles, talks, orders rounds of drinks, asks like a little girl "Are we there yet?" and we all smile, continue to talk about Portuguese food and the gentle ocean air. There is the subtle excitement of home-coming, seeing loved ones again. When our flight is finally announced we all start moving in the same direction together, and I feel included.

Up in the sky, through the darkness over the Atlantic, we travel very fast back to where Vasco da Gama started off so slowly. I read, study the city map, memorize a couple of Portuguese words. In my hand luggage I have a notebook to write in, Pessoa's *The Book of Disquietude*, a map of Lisbon, a tour guide of Portugal, a little camera, passport, plane ticket, hotel confirmation, some money. I am well organized—in the side pockets of my little backpack I have my cholesterol drug, aspirins, a spray to clean my eyeglasses, tissues, two pens and a highlighter, a pack of cigarettes and a lighter, two rolls of film. I didn't even forget a bottle of water. I read about Portugal and the dream co-ops even the street names ("Only the dream truly sees when it looks."), the various quarters of the city, the ancient kings. Dom Sebastiao is dead and they still wait for him, it is a sorrowful thing that he is not back from Morocco, well, already six hundred years. Ines de Costa was murdered. Still, the prince who loved her, once he took power, posthumously married her and she became a queen. Fernando Pessoa visited Ricardo Reis many times. Being dead is not a major hurdle in Portugal, I assure myself, and it should be even easier for two people to meet if they are both already dead, I consider. As I am falling asleep the thought crosses my mind, Zbignew Preisner must frequently be meeting the dead Kieslowski in Warsaw.

Sliding down the seat beside me, my well-organized backpack falls to the floor. Dreams and reality mix like broken glass and soil. My last thoughts before falling asleep are like careless feet walking through broken glass—there is the vague awareness that it is better to step around it, but my legs have a mind of their own; they continue down the dangerous path, somehow landing between the shards in a soft red soil. Maybe it is my own Croatian soil; but whose are these tiny, barefoot legs? Maybe I am a child; maybe a dead grown-up reverts to childhood. That would entitle me to a nanny and small feet. I should remember to ask Fernando Pessoa.

The plane's motion is sedative. The simple joy of a child exploring a friendly forest, the broken glass, are gone. Now the tiny feet step across thick moss covering massive roots. I am still aware of the plane's buzzing, my motion in the present, no memory involved, no future. Sliding down in my seat I probably snore, my jaw falls open and saliva drips on my sleeve.

A new dream. Not a child any longer. A plaster corpse standing on the southeast corner of Bloor and Bay Street in Toronto observes the faces of passersby. The corpse hopes to rekindle itself back to life if a spark can be caught from those passing eyes. From a distance I realize that I am the corpse. People come and go but do not notice. Failing to attract their attention, I see detail: cheap shoes, pudgy faces. I hate how they look, but I also neglect my own appearance. I pity their unhealthy obesity; but I am fat too.

Then, as only happens in dreams, I am suddenly in a pub. I despise the miserable divorcés with urine stains on their crotches. Yet, as I leave the washroom a couple of drops of un-drained urine drip onto my pants. I pull my shirt out to cover it, then notice the dirty toes in my worn-out sandals. Only the dream truly sees when it looks.

Everyone looks away. Not a single pair of human eyes looks at me. Hence, the casuistic loop is closed: the corpse remains a frozen corpse, and it is its own fault.

The noise of the airplane fractures the dream, inserts flashes of reality and bits of the previous dream. There is understanding in the thoughts of the half-sleeper: the corpse might meld into a child through warm sleepy eyes. Fernando is omnipresent in Lisbon. He'll spot me. I will walk on thick moss again.

Lisbon

It is still dark. I see dreamy tired yellow street lamps, regular loops and lines, the lights of ships in the ocean. Or is it the Tagus? I am not sure. The plane drops closer to the ground, and I can see the odd car moving slowly. It is about 6:00 a.m.; we land softly. The dawn is dawning as I walk through the airport, wait for my luggage, light a first cigarette, draw some 15,000 escudos from the bank machine and realize that is much more than I really need; clear passport control. The sunlight is now at full blast, people are moving in different directions. I join a line and after a much shorter wait than in much shorter Canadian lines I get my strong, aromatic, double espresso and sip it slowly.

I smoke, like everyone else. No rush, it is only 7:30 a.m. For a while I speak with a clerk at the tourist information booth. Her English is excellent; she is bubbly, not in a rush, we take our time. She warns me that espresso is stronger than American coffee. Oh, I know, I am from Croatia, I am familiar with the beverage. She shows me the city map, and with lots of charm and smiles talks about the Lisboa Pass that will get me, if I buy it, on public transportation and into churches and museums.

I wonder if Fernando Pessoa ever visits such places, maybe to make fun of the tourists. The girl stops me from buying a three-day pass, recommends I take only a two-day because on Sunday everything is free anyway. I thank her for being so considerate of my budget; if only I were so considerate of it myself. We talk a little longer, about the weather, my Portuguese friends over in Toronto named Araujo. Oh, she knows some Araujos but, I smile, Let's not get into the gossip yet, I have just arrived and I have screwed up enough already where I live; allow me a fresh start. We both laugh. She teaches me to pronounce a couple Portuguese words. I look into her vivid, playful, dark eyes; her teeth could use some work. I am ashamed of myself again; God knows what kind of shape Fernando Pessoa is in after more than sixty years in the same soggy suit. I look straight into her eyes and she doesn't look away, no, she smiles back at me, You seem to be looking for someone in me. I quickly turn my eyes away. I murmur, Forgive me. "You are as pale as if you saw a ghost." I hope, I hope to find him. "Oh, it is him." Yes, I need to find him. "Don't worry, we look for our ghosts or they haunt us; with ghosts it is easy, there are no missed appointments." She smiles again. I thank her and, afraid I'll faint, walk out of the airport building. She manages to call after me, "Careful with those espressos!" The sun is bright and there are palm trees; the morning air is soft, I smell the ocean in it. Just outside I stand for awhile with closed eyes, ochre and orange light piercing the lids.

As a proud owner of a Lisboa Pass, I walk to the bus station to wait for the number sixteen, as she told me, the bus that will take me to Alfonso Enriques, the metro to Anjos and the walk to Rua Estevao. I repeat these simple directions, but as the number sixteen doesn't show I walk back to the taxi station. There is a long line there, and while I am standing on it the number sixteen passes by, stops where I had been waiting and goes on its way.

My taxi glides through the light morning traffic. My driver is in his fifties. He is small, has a belly, but is not fat; broad features, tanned, slightly furrowed face. His eyes are relaxed, he is not nervous because we can't converse; he knows all he needs to know about where to take me. And yet I manage to get a few words out of him: How is Figo playing this season in Barcelona? "So-so." Who is leading the league? "Ashamed to admit, but Porto." How are Benfica and Sporting doing? "Well, they'll play this coming Sunday." Here in Lisbon? "Yes, at Benfica's." Really? "Really."

At the hotel I pay him 2,000 escudos (about $15); I also give him a tip, not much, but enough for a warm smile and a nod. He taps my shoulder and drives away. At the hotel, of course, my room is not ready, No, I don't need to go in right away, let me just leave my luggage here at the desk. No problem, says the older man, pudgy, hair gray but thick. Now, don't tell me later this afternoon that you never saw me in your life; I like this bag. He laughs heartily, waves to me as I leave. It is not 8:00 a.m. yet, and I am out again, carrying my small, well-organized backpack.

The air carries the aromas of the city—the ripe linden canopies that arch over Rua Passos Manuel; fresh pastries and bread, that bread that no other city in the world can produce, soft but not puffy; crispy, glazed crust. As I walk toward Avenida Amirante Reis my feet feel springy on the *empedrados*, the sidewalk mosaics that invite you to discover their intricate patterns. The day is now warm, but with a breeze. I pass by Rossio and, taking Gold Street, pass under the arch, and at Praca do Commercio I am blinded with light. I sit by Dom Jose's horse and politely greet them both. But suddenly I need some shade. I find it in a nearby bar, where I drink a double espresso and order a shot of grappa. They give me a very generous shot. It is as tasty as Croatian grappa. I scribble some nonsense in my notebook, and the waiter brings me a couple of freshly fried balls of *bakalau*—a mixture of potato and cod. He smiles, says, "Try it, it will do you good," and pours me another generous shot of grappa. I nod, say, I like it a lot, and light a cigarette. The waiter is discrete, brings me more *bakalau*. I am exhaling cigarette smoke as if I am letting it go after having held my breath for a long time, too long. In the corner, by the bar, sits a tall good-looking woman in business attire. She eats a small pastry without hurry, sips her cappuccino, then in a slow elegant walk, leaves. The waiter smiles, he saw me observing her, and with another discrete nod says, "Lots of ministries around here, good government jobs, no rush." I am slightly tipsy and start to feel the loss of sleep.

Walking up the hill I see freshly roasted piglet and just-baked bread in a shop window. I buy a sandwich. It is good; the taste of warm pork reminds me of Croatia, especially Christmases there. As I chew I walk amongst tram cars up steep streets and eventually find myself at the church that looks like a fort: Se Patriarcal. In front there is a small area with benches and couple of trees. Sitting on a bench on Largo da Se I eat my sandwich, observe passing tourists and tram cars, but I am seeing winter in Croatia, a piglet roasting on the spit, then cooling off in the cold storage alongside hams and home-made salamis and rings of garlic and a small oak barrel filled with our own burgundy. There is also a barrel with sauerkraut, the planks on top held down by a big granite stone covered with white cloth. Every time I entered the cold storage to bring more wine or another salami or plate of roast pork (because the feast would continue whenever guests dropped by, morning, noon or night) I couldn't resist removing the cloth, as if it hid some mystery. I'd look at the stone, touch it and restore the cloth and the mystery.

The crenellations at the top of the church towers, in contrast, conceal no mystery. Faith is a battle, church a fortress. I go inside just to briefly greet, as I have always done, the Princess in Stone. She lies there reading, perfectly straight and comfortable, on her simple marble slab. Two stone pillows firmly support her head. I feel maybe

I should fluff them up for her, it has been so many years since I last saw her. I touch her face and realize how warm my own palms are. The princess is anonymous, but for some reason I call her Ines. She lies there reading, a book supported in her gentle hands, her fragile wrists slightly bent. Her robe is folded at her stony feet. As I put my feverish palm on her cold forehead, an older man who has been standing silently behind me says in a low, gentle voice:

"Do you come here often?"

Without actually turning around, seeing him more or less out of the corner of my eye, I reply, "Every time I am in the city."

"So you are a tourist too. Do you have family here?"

Now I do turn around. His face is laced with almost invisible creases, not entirely unlike those in the stone I have just been touching. His skin is a pale yellow, like old marble in the sunset.

"No, I have no family," I say as, looking down, I wonder where he could have picked up those traces of loam on his shoes.

"Me neither. I came here for the first time after the funeral of my wife. She really loved me, you know."

"It is better when we die in their hearts, I think."

"Frankly, I don't know. I felt a kind of sweet relief when she died, as if I had been relieved of the obligation to love her back. It can be a burden."

"Are you not nostalgic?"

"Well, you see, I am a writer. And, when you think about it, nostalgia is a literary sentiment. We remember external things, we remember love through images. But maybe that was some other woman? Or our childhood—we remember it through images of a child, presumably ourselves. But it could be some other child, maybe this very stone princess, running through cold dew on a misty morning. So, what is our nostalgia but a longing for such scenes? Why should these scenes necessarily contain our selves? After all, someone else's childhood can move me as much as my own does; both are purely visual phenomena from the past. They move me, yes, but because I see them, not because I remember them. For instance, I can clearly see this stone princess's childhood, I am moved by it, and I come to visit her every day. Usually I place my palm on her forehead, but today you did so instead."

"In my own case, I died in her heart and I will also disappear from her memory. To live is to have sentiments. I have them if I live in the memory of others."

"We are but passersby of everything, our own souls included. We belong to nothing, desire nothing, are nothing—abstract centers of impersonal sensations. And, by the way, can those 'others' whose memory you need to inhabit be unknown to you?"

"Yes, I think so."

"Write, then. But do not bother publishing. Someone will read you, probably after you die. The truly noble writer does not publish."

"How do you know I am a writer?"

"Don't be ridiculous. How do I know about the princess's childhood?"

"What is noble about not publishing? Why write at all, then?"

"Because you wouldn't be a writer if you didn't write, would you? Not exposing to others what you write is a spiritual dispensation. To write is to objectify dreams. The act of objectifying this interior world is in the nature of creators. To publish is to give this world to others. But to what purpose, if the outer world common to us and to them is the 'real' outer world, the one made of visible and tangible matter? What do others have to do with the universe that comes from inside us?"

"But I am sure your own books are published."

"True, but I am dead."

"Who are you?"

"You know me."

"Fernando?"

He smiled. "You must excuse me now," and put his palm on the princess's forehead. Then he touched her breast, smiled again and said, "If you fell out of a stone heart you may not be dead yet, you know."

Needing fresh air, I stumble out of the church and walk up Limoeiro, my eyes half closed by the sun. At Miradouro de Santa Luzia I sit under the *pergola* of grape vines and observe the Tagus. The sapphire lines of the river melt into the distant sky. Two policemen stand nearby talking and glance toward me. Two old men, the same as last time, sit on a bench in front of the big blue and white *azulejo* panels showing Praca do Comercio before the Earthquake.

Missing Women, Missing Selves

By Lila Rajiva
(India)

"You who bear your sons in laundered linen sheets and call your pregnancies a 'blessed' state should never damn the outcast and the weak: her sin was heavy, but her suffering great." —"on the infanticide marie farrar," Berthold Brecht

Matrubhoomi (*Nation Without Women*), Manish Jha's prize-winning feature film that debuted in Venice last year, tells the story of a widower who is forced to pay a woman to marry all five of his sons because there are no other females left in his village. The film dwells with unsparing candor on a topic that India's bubble-gum film industry refuses to touch—the shocking prevalence of female infanticide that has caused the sex ratios in that country to decline in some places to about 800 women per 1000 men, compared with a world average of slightly more than 1000 females to every 1000 males.

When *Matrubhoomi* was shown last year at the Toronto film festival, a part of India's sizeable émigré community there felt offended enough to walk out. The film obviously touched a raw nerve, for the truth is that, while affluent Indians may not need to resort to poisoning babies with oleander juice or smothering them with gunny sacks—as they do in the villages near Madurai, a cultural center of the deep south where the practice first drew national attention in 1986—they certainly are selective about their abortions, especially in the Sikh community, which is well represented in Toronto.

It is largely women—the mothers themselves, midwives, mothers-in-law or paternal grandmothers—who preside over the murders, sometimes with the stoic indifference of pagan goddesses, at other times with the limp desperation of sacrificial victims. They talk about the intolerable shame of not having produced a son or the unbearable future of daughters. And so they push a rice grain into the baby's windpipe, or shake it until its neck snaps, or drown it in a bucket of water. Until recently, people knew but did not talk about the practice. Now feminist activists are demanding that the guilty women be punished like any other murderers, to underscore that female life also matters.

Selective infanticide and its upscale cousin selective foeticide have led Indian feminists to take strange and disturbing positions. On the one hand, it's a woman's right to choose to abort her child, a right that asserts her value as a human being; on the other hand, what if she chooses to abort because the baby is a girl, a little miniature of herself? Does that devalue her as a woman? It seems most activists think so. But if choice trumps everything else, one can't help wondering why aborting a girl should be any worse than aborting a boy or, for that matter, aborting an unborn child with a handicap. But if such questions instinctively repel us, perhaps what is at stake is something more than a choice or a right; maybe there are relationships between people that don't lend themselves easily to a language of ownership and disposal—language ironically derived from the Anglo-Saxon system of law and property which in other places activists attack vigorously. There is in fact an Indian law passed in 1971 that flatly bans selective abortions—and is just as flatly ignored. Indians, oddly like Americans in this, seem to turn such moral imponderables into gladiatorial legal clashes between individual rights.

In the 1990s, despite the 1971 ban, economic liberalization introduced a grotesque entrepreneurial twist to the abortion story as private networks of doctors cruised villages with ultrasound vans, offering foetal sex tests. Billboards cried, "Better 500 now than 5000 later"—a reference to the cost in rupees of the average dowry needed to marry off a girl, the custom seen by many as a root cause of female foeticide and infanticide.

My grandmother, a Christian who for several years before her death ran a home for destitute women in Madurai, was proud that she had never asked for a dowry for her son, my uncle, who as a doctor could have commanded a premium price in the hilariously pragmatic Indian marriage bazaar where ads list the exact value of earnings, apartments, cars, brass cooking vessels and jewelry, describe the bride-to-be's "homeliness" (meaning domesticity), complexion ("wheat" being less fair than desirable) and, with almost palpable anxiety, her visa status in the US.

My friend Seema (not her real name), an engineer then completing her Ph.D. at an Ivy League university, deliberately kept finding something wrong with all the eligible "boys" directed her way by a conservative uncle. "Hey, yaar (buddy), the guy hung up on me when I told him I didn't have a green card," she told me, both rueful and relieved. "Anyway, if I keep saying no for another year, I'll be thirty and then it will be all over for me anyway." Although the "boys"—there are never any men and women in those ads—are catalogued quite as carefully as the "girls" (here and there the odd widower with "encumbrances" plaintively assures potential companions that "caste/creed is no barrier") men overwhelmingly seem to be the buyers, women the sellers, and the barriers are in fact formidable.

Rather odd this, considering the telltale numbers of what Nobel-Prize-winning Indian economist Amartya Sen calls the "missing women." One would think, with fewer women available, their price would skyrocket and men would pay for them at the rates they do in Jha's film. Actually, the decline of the female-to-male ratio in India, as well as in South Korea and China where it is also a major problem, has led to an increase in violence toward women from young, poorly socialized males acting out their deprivations, a scenario painted with lurid intensity in *Matrubhoomi*, which is laced with nauseating scenes of gang-rape.

For this reason, not everyone accepts the cultural explanation of female infanticide. Historians like Veena Talwar Oldenburg point out that dowry, after all, was supposed to give a woman a means of support that did not depend upon the benevolence of her in-laws and that before the British arrived in India it did just that. It was the coming of the British imperial economy that undermined the original purpose of dowry. Land that had been owned communally, and had given women a measure of security for that reason, became a commodity like any other to be rented, bought or sold. Cash flooded the market, turning owners into rentiers and pauperizing women who had been rich in just that agricultural wisdom that the new cash-based economy debased. It was at that point that dowry deaths—the practice of killing wives, usually in staged kitchen fires, in order to confiscate their dowries—began.

Anti-globalization activists like the physicist and environmentalist Vandana Shiva provide an update for the story of the missing women of today's India. For Shiva, the global market explains the logic of the marriage market. The green revolution of the 1970s that reoriented Indian agriculture towards the export of commercial cash crops for export and away from domestic needs, along with the arrival of Western multinational agribusinesses like Monsanto, has pushed laboring women out of the traditionally valuable sectors of the labor market—such as farming—into the most menial areas where they are exploited economically and sexually. The poorer they are, the more expendable they become in the garish modernization overtaking Indian cities. Since the first census under the British was taken in 1871, the sex ratio has continued to slide in favor of men (i.e. fewer and fewer females) for every year except one, so that according to UN reports, since 1901, 50 million girls and women have simply disappeared. World-wide, India tops the list for illegal abortions and female infanticides, and 90% of those abortions are of female foetuses. In one widely publicized study of a clinic in 1984, 7999 of 8000 abortions performed there were of females.

Cash or Culture?

There is a savage double standard in India. Real names and faces betray what is ignored by the language of rights and laws. I remember some of those names and faces from my college days—Shaila, a Kashmiri Rapunzel, forever tossing her heavy braids, prancing and lip-synching her way through the latest Hindi film in our all-girl hostel. When her strict Muslim family in the north discovered that she had been sneaking out and had become involved with a Hindu, they flew down, dragged her by the hair into the courtyard and stripped her of her gold bracelets, necklaces and anklets in front of the whole hostel. We never saw her again but heard she had been chlorophormed, taken home and married into a suitable family. Her Hindu boyfriend, though, felt no social consequences. She was married off; he simply got on with his life.

Hamsa, the servant girl of a well-known film director who kept open house for young artists, was like one of his family, running in endlessly with tea, scolding everyone good-naturedly and bursting into giggles when she dropped something in the kitchen. It came as a shock when I learned that she had had more than five abortions, although she could not have then been out of her teens. Why? Because when contraception is forbidden by society and family, abortion takes its place for some, infantcide for others. For poorer women, abortion is actually an easier recourse than contraception, especially as boyfriends or husbands rarely consent to the use even of condoms, let alone male sterilization. She gets the abortion, but his body must remain inviolate.

This is why discussing the issue of infanticide in terms of the law is ultimately pointless, for the law puts the onus of responsibility solely on the woman.

Another face from the past—Prema, who worked as a low-level administrator in an American university at the point I met her. After paying a sizeable dowry to marry into what she was told was a medical family, she arrived in America to find that her "doctor" pumped gas at a filling station and had a long-term illness and a learning disability. Twenty years and two children later, she is still with him, bearing her fate with religious resignation.

Supporting a cultural rather than economic explanation, studies have shown that in some regions infanticide tends to occur more among higher castes than among what are called "backward" tribes where women actually often enjoy a more equitable status than their upscale cousins. Among the higher castes, the key factors seem to be the tradition of family inheritance through the male and the prestige of having sons. In addition, among warrior tribes like Jats, Rajputs and Sikhs where the subjugation of women is reinforced by the ethos of the fighting man, hypergamy—the practice of women "marrying up" in order to increase their value—is a powerful factor in promoting the killing of females among families who cannot afford the huge dowries that marrying up entails but do not want the social stigma of marrying down. Culture presumably also explains both the Bermuda triangle of missing women in Punjab, Haryana and Uttar Pradesh and the greater prevalence of infanticide among Hindus than among Buddhists or Christians.

Other studies point to antique Sanskrit religious texts that deny property and education to women and virulently denigrate them. But there are no easy answers to the problem, for Indian history during the British, Muslim and Hindu periods alike is also filled with examples of women as scholars, artists and political leaders. Indeed, in contrast to America, India has famously flaunted women at the helm of state, from the medieval Muslim queen Razia Begum to the twenty-year reign of Indira Gandhi, and today India has one of the world's highest proportions of women in its professional work force.

Still, there is the inescapable economic reality. While the burning of eighteen-year-old Roop Kanwar on her husband's funeral pyre in 1987 in the ancient ritual of sati received widespread attention, there have been only 41 such deaths in modern India. Infanticide, foeticide and dowry killings are far more common and are clearly linked to both illiteracy and poverty nation-wide.

Of course, culture and the means of production can work in close harmony to endlessly create new socio-economic forms, some of which are viable. If globalization has marginalized peasant women, it has also created a new breed of female entrepreneur in the hub of India's high-tech revolution, Bangalore, as Western multinationals rush offshore to meet their need for scientists and engineers to India's vast pool of high-caliber professionals eager to work for pennies on the dollar. In Pepsi-colonial India, the market taketh away, but the market also giveth. And if patriarchy has given us such nostrums as "A woman is impure by her very birth; but she attains a happy state by serving her lord (husband)." (Tulasi Ramayana, Aranya Kanda, 5 A-B), it has also produced the chivalry of Manu's, "Where women are honored there the gods are pleased; but where they are not honored no sacred rite yields rewards." (Manu Smriti III.56)

The daughter-in-law whose early years in her husband's home are marked by rank servility eventually metamorphoses. Having borne and raised sons, she comes into her own and acquires a power and status within the family in her later years that more emancipated women might envy. From the Tantric Kali to the Vedic Saraswathi, the traditional goddesses offer forms of potent femininity more original than the masculinizing calculus of some forms of modern feminism.

But can Indian culture be singled out for unique blame? Don't most religious texts have misogynistic passages: the Talmud ("The daughters of the [heathens] should be considered as in the state of niddah [filth] from their cradle." [Avodah Zarah 36b]); Buddhist scriptures ("A woman's heart is haunted by stinginess...jealousy... sensuality." [Anguttaranikâya iv. 8, 10]); the New Testament ("the weaker vessel" [I Peter 3:7])? And, besides John Stuart Mill, has there ever been a canonical philosopher in the West who has thought of women in any way except as inferior? Yet, has there not also been praise for women in these same religions—the divine Beatrice, Sophia, Radha? Isn't it the case that the texts invoked—derogatory or adulatory—depend on the context of the socioeconomic status of the individual woman being judged? Religious pronouncements, in other words, tend to be post-hoc rationalizations of facts established within the power relations of a society.

Calls to criminalize female infanticide ignore such complexities. The laws so far passed—however needful—can actually exacerbate the problem. For instance, the Hindu property act, created to give the daughter her share of the inheritance, added a perverse incentive to kill young girls out of fear that they would take that inheritance with them into another family when they married. Similarly, the 1971 law allowing abortion was less about women's empowerment than it was about population control. Laws are necessary to signal what a society desires, but between desire and realization lies the complexity of reality. Making examples of infanticides fails execrably to halt the selective killing of female foetuses, e.g., it does not staunch the bleeding from the body politic but only foments a new hemorrhaging elsewhere.

Laws ignore the context and assume what should be questioned. Are, for instance, these Indian female infanticides actually individuals and bearers of rights in the Western sense? In interviews with the killers they appear not to believe such to be the case. Rather, they express feelings of desperation and overwhelming worthlessness, fears of social and family expectations, or violence from in-laws and of a hopeless future for the newborn. These are women with no control over their own bodies or even over their own desires, for whom shame is attached both to contraception and to conception, if the conception is of a female child. Caught between these two shames, these women do not see what they do to their children as an assertion of a right but as simple acquiescence to fate. They suffer guilt, trauma, remorse, but see no other way. Not finding their own lives worth living, they come to believe that the few minutes of pain their infant daughters endure is preferable to lifetimes of degradation like their own.

Consider the degree to which such women do not even have a sense of separate self-hood. Their lives are not demarcated as men's are into work-hours that bring status and leisure-hours that bring sociality. For these women, to breathe is to work. Constantly. At unpaid slavish chores that benefit others. The worth of such a woman is measured in terms of the male members of her family—her father, her husband and then her son. What other self does she have?

I remember a secretary, Malini, who worked from 7:00 a.m. to 7:00 p.m., every day. A painfully thin, plain girl, she scarcely had time enough to herself to eat the small tin of rice she brought with her for lunch. When there was a lull in her secretarial duties, she was automatically assumed to be available to do the boss's private work. Her time belonged to him. Her monthly pay envelope was handed over unopened to her husband who spent it on himself and his relatives, leaving Malini only enough to eat and clothe herself minimally. There was not one moment of her life that was her own, not one inch of existence from which someone could not demand her services. If such a woman kills, it is not out of choice in any sense that we normally understand, because the boundaries between her own identity and her daughter's, her husband's and her family's are porous in a way that we with our discrete individualized selves can scarcely fathom.

Even those powerful matriarchal figures who do wield domestic power over men do not derive it from any individual sense of their worth but from family structure. And men themselves, despite their privileged status, exist still very much as creations of the same family and social structure.

Misplaced zealotry calling for more law, more education, more this or that—all of which are of course necessary—does not recognize that so much of the answer lies in the balance of things: it is not just whether a woman is wealthy, educated or powerful but whether she is as wealthy, as educated or as powerful as the family she marries into. If not, she has no ground from which to hold her own. If not, no matter how well off she is economically and professionally, she is going to suffer the fate of the powerless everywhere.

The facts bear this out. In Kerala, the southwestern Indian state which has been home to generations of publicly outspoken literary women, from Kamala Das to Arundhati Roy, property passes through the mother, and infanticide, foeticide and dowry deaths are almost unknown. Not surprisingly, the sex ratio favors females 1036 to 1000. In patriarchal parts of the country like Punjab, which are relatively wealthy and where males control property inheritance and are also favored in the more basic standards of nutrition and nurture, the reverse is true. Studies have shown that the decline in the ratio of females to males in Punjab is not primarily due to female infanticide but to a general neglect of females caused by their low participation in income-generating activities. They simply do not contribute enough to warrant feeding and looking after properly—a tragedy of the everyday. By sensationalizing the unique aspects of the crime of female infanticide, we forget the commonplace nature of the most extensive crime against women, which is neglect.

Bride-burning accounts for about 15,000 female deaths a year in India, still too large a number but a small fraction of a population of over one billion. The real erosion of women's numbers comes from the denial of equal nutrition, education and opportunity.

By demonizing female infanticide we fail to see it as only another instance of this unequal distribution of power that is not specific to Hinduism or to India or even to women. We ignore our common human history, where the killing of children has been the norm, not the exception. In her 1978 book, Hardness of Heart, Hardness of Life: the Stain of Human Infanticide, Laila Williamson, an anthropologist at the American Museum of Natural History, cites the prevalence of child-killing in cultures as diverse as classical Persia, pre-Mohammedan Arabia and medieval Christian Europe. She points to its practice in colonial America, both among the settlers and the indigenous peoples and the existence of "stubborn child laws" which put sons of a certain age to death for disobedience. In fact, child-protection services in America came rather late and were modeled on the Society for the Prevention of Cruelty to Animals. Only the practice of legal abortion (more than 5 million in the West in 1988) has mitigated the practice of child-killing. Still, from 1982 to 1987, approximately 1.1% of all homicides were children under the age of one year. The US, in fact, leads the world in the murder of children between the ages of one and four and is ranked fourth in killings of children between five and fourteen. As in India, such killings are more frequent among the poor, the uneducated and the alcoholic and, again as in India, among children under one year. Parents, usually the mother, are the perpetrators. For children over the age of one year, non-parents, usually fathers, are the killers.

The plausible conclusion is that it may have been only advances in the technology of contraception and the legalization and practice of abortion that have reduced the number of infanticides. The law may have stated society's intent, but it was technology that effectively changed society's practices; technology that created labor-saving devices to lighten women's chores; technology that freed them to step outside the home. It would be ironic if anti-globalization activists now failed to see how the new information revolution and the home computer may themselves be the means for even the poorest women to find markets for their home-grown products, and it would be twice as ironic if feminists failed to see how the ideal of the home as enunciated by patriarchy could be modified to support a more original, authentic and indigenous feminism.

Neither the law that permits some women to abort handicapped children but will not indict men who threaten and coerce women into committing infanticide, nor the society that neglects and starves women to death, has hands clean enough to write the final verdict on those who consider their sex and the sex of their daughters to be handicaps from the very point of conception. Attempts to change a culture without changing its power relations end up making examples of the weakest link in a long chain and ignoring the culpability of all those others—husbands, in-laws, neighbors, priests, tradition—who stand invisibly in the dock beside her, tangled in a poisonous web of complicity. Where exactly is the fine line where "choice" becomes murder, which shelters the affluent émigré in Toronto but pillories her famished sister in the arid plains of the Deccan? It is not mercy that pleads that these women not be penalized, it is justice that demands it.

The Flame, the Amulet and the Scarlet Bras

By Anjana Basu
(India)

Her mother bought bras as emerald green as poison, as scarlet as passion or greed. She remembered their screaming brightness against the dismal yellow wall-papered flat. There, in her imagination, it always rained, so that the lights burned the whole day long and the paraffin stove panted occasional gusts of oily breath.

Her reason told her there must have been sunny days when she skipped down the hill to school, but her imagination allowed her no such comfort. In her mind, the brightest thing in those dreary London days was the bras. "Don't tell your father," her mother warned her, flashing a sliver of lace in the mirror. Later, she was to realise that the warning was because they had no money; that her mother scrimped pennies from the weekly shopping and put them together in a shower of black and emerald net. She, jealous of all that colour and brightness, thought her mother was buying those bras to flaunt at another man, so she always did tell. And inevitably, beatings followed.

It was a scene set for violence, the peeling yellow wallpaper with the rash of red coin spots, the garish bras, the dimly burning electric bulbs and the shrieks that were her mother, shrieks that melted into her own desperate sobbing. Her mother had never wanted her in the first place. She told her that sometimes, in between slappings.

"Once upon a time," she later told Ravi, "when I was born, they invited six fairy godmothers to the christening...well, the rice ceremony. Three of them were good and three were wicked and whatever one said the other immediately cancelled out." One gave her chiselled features, the other said, "chiselled like wood." One gave her length of limb, the other said, "and she will be fat." And the two last were the worst of all. One said, "She will be her father's pride and joy…" and the other pronounced, "…so her mother will do nothing for her." The good fairies promptly twittered together in indignation and tied a silver talisman around her neck to prevent this. "But," her mother told her, viciously yanking a comb through the knots in her hair, "you chewed it out of shape, so I took it off and look what happened!" Her mother wanted a sugarplum daughter to wear pink ballet dresses and turn on her toes. Someone who would be a credit to her own looks. "Instead, you turned out to look like your father." And her mother would turn in mid-yank to the mirror, her lips moving to kiss the reflection that swam out of the silver lake. White swan, white swan, let my mother grow feathers and swim away and forget me sitting here with my hair around my ears. But her mother never forgot: she did her duty with wire brush and twisted black clips, until the little girl was turned out with aching head and flaming slapped cheeks.

"No," Ravi told her, ruffling her black head, "you're not ugly." And he said it every time she asked for reassurance.

Perhaps the six fairies hadn't really existed, perhaps she dreamt them out of her mother's six old aunts. But there *had* been, it seemed, a Brahmin who timed her birth with a stopwatch and forecast her life on withered parchment and cast the talisman into the bargain. Afterwards, her mother hastily tied its battered silver lump around her neck again. "And all that did was keep you alive!" She would finger that lump as if it could keep the beatings away, but it never did. The only thing that worked was the mirror and the bras. "Look, Ma, there's a new one," she would point out as they walked down the High Street. It was the only time her mother's face melted into a smile. "Yes, you're right, yes, that's a new one. I wonder how much…." And they would walk into the shop and her mother would turn the slither of satin over and over in her hands until the girl thought it would grow wings and fly away in protest. She imagined a beautiful woman wearing humming birds brighter than the brightest bra.

They said her mother was beautiful. Everyone turned to look at her in the High Street, a splash of colour through the grey London day, trailing silks. She tilted her face this way and that in a plate-glass window reflection, even in a puddle, then she would catch sight of the girl and the beauty darkened. People came up to talk to her mother: lots of "Loves, what are you doing tonight, darlings?" No, not "people," men of all shapes and colours, black, white and pink. "I'll tell my father!" she stamped, when she dared. The jealousy eating her was the terror wolf in her mind. She was afraid of being left alone in that damp yellow flat—things might come out of the TV set, a pair of hands to chase her behind the cupboards and fasten around her throat. Her mother kept leaving her alone. "I'm only going to the cinema on the top of the hill. Look, you can see it from the window. Only there." She couldn't bear being alone—she would walk round and round the maroon carpet for hours and finally burst out of the door onto the grey landing, there to peep out of the window to see her mother or someone coming home down the hill.

The top of her mother's curly head would appear at the bottom of the window frame which was as high as she could see on her tiptoes. The moment she saw her, she would duck back into the flat, knowing the hands hadn't got her this time and she could watch Andy Panda in safety. Her mother flowered at the top of the grey stairs, her red mouth curved into a smile, one hand patting the lacquered hair in place. The girl was stupid, she never knew enough to shut the door, she always got caught. "It isn't safe," her father had thundered, one of his rare storms. "Don't open the door!" but she refused to be locked in the flat with the Hands. But for her mother there was always the saving grace of the mirror—she would walk into the flat prepared to explode, catch sight of her ghost in the glass and melt. Such a pretty ghost, such a bright-flowered-chiffon-and-roses ghost lost in the fogs of London.

Her father was as grey as the stairs and the smog that swirled on the winter pavements. He seemed to bring the colourlessness with him out of the streets to smear on the wallpaper. The child was always scared for him, as if her mother's flame would burn him out. At night, she slept in her mother's bed—her father had ordered it when, after a fever, she awoke terrified of the darkness—but when her mother was asleep she tiptoed over the froggy slime of the linoleum to the guest bedroom door to see whether she could hear her father snoring. If she could, then the fire hadn't burnt him for that day and he would awake safely in the morning. Very often, the night held nothing but the screams of police sirens, and then she would sit outside the bedroom door, clutching the knob while the cold seeped through her brushed nylon pajama bottoms. There would be a beating for her the next morning and no father to save her from that.

Later, stupid with love, she wondered how she had kept her parents apart for even a night, whether it was her fault. She asked Ravi once if he thought that she was the reason why it had all gone wrong between her parents. It was a blue day and she was walking back with him to the office after lunch. A red-flagged procession was chanting its mechanical way down the lane. Light-hearted, she twirled her flowered parasol at it in salute. "No, I don't think you could have been to blame," he told her, laughing at the salute.

"You spoil everything!" her mother stormed after she had asked, "Where's *baba*?" for the sixth time in a row. Later, her mother returned from shopping with her arms full of paper packages and a man trailing behind her. Uncle Samir, he offered her a wooden golliwog puppet with a smile as painted as the white slash on the puppet's face. She resented him being there, as she resented the puppet. He came more and more often, and *baba* was never home when he came, though once, one rare evening, her mother brought him home in the evening and he and her father sat and drank cheers together while she claimed her place on her father's lap. "She's getting far too old for that," her mother complained. "You both spoil her! Samir brought her such a lovely puppet." And the golliwog was brought out and Uncle Samir made him dance for them—he was good at that, she always got the strings tangled.

All happy families are alike, unhappy ones are unhappy in their own special way. Her mother was on the phone more and more often. "Oh, I'm not wearing anything," she would giggle. "No, I mean not wearing anything special, silly!" She danced and wriggled with the heavy black instrument fixed on her ear like a bloodsucker. Her ear was red when she lowered it. "That was the police," she told her father when the girl complained. "They wanted to trace a man, so they made me talk to him." She saw her mother in black and white cut out of the TV screen, all her colour bled into her bra. She didn't know why she was so afraid of her mother going away, when it was her mother who beat her. Locked themselves both up in the small bathroom so no one could interfere while her father rattled the knob and demanded to be let in, rattled and rattled until finally the door caved in and she was safe again behind his back. "Why won't you go! Both of you!" her mother screamed while the witch who lived upstairs thumped on their ceiling in protest.

"Men never go away," her mother maintained, until the day her lover left her. Her father wasn't the one who left.

"Your mother's so pretty," the old ladies cooed to her outside Tesco. "You must look like your father." She cringed behind her mother and felt the slim curves swell in appreciation.

"What was the talisman for?" Ravi asked. He didn't use the word "talisman." He used the local Bengali word, *maduli*—it was one of the problems her family had with him.

The talisman was a hard lump of silver that had its matching magic in a purple stone worn by her mother. "So that her stars will not eat up the child's," the Brahmin had said. Her father told her the story whenever she wanted to know why her mother hated her so. Her mother's tiger stars chasing her fleeing deer with emerald green eyes that burnt holes in the night. "You should forgive her, she is, after all very beautiful." There was a look on his face as if he had something bitter in his mouth when he said the words.

She showed Ravi a picture of curly hair and a dark brown mouth that he politely shrugged at. She took the picture away feeling a fool: it was old-fashioned, too much lipstick, the hair crimped and sprayed into ordered curls.

"*He* says I move like a song!" she heard the lips declare. "What do you know? Do either of you appreciate me?" At seven, she already knew more words than she was supposed to—she brought them out with the proper BBC accent that had her father's relatives oohing in amazement.

Ravi was a man with the boneless grace of a puppet and a face that was a cross between a pirate's and an eccentric professor's. Every time she looked at him a little ball of gold burst fire inside her and she wondered whether her mother had ever felt that way. Her own underwear was the plainest she could find, stark whites and blacks with not a trace of wanton greens. "I can hear it shrieking under my clothes," she told Ravi before he had even set eyes on her underwear. The mirror showed her with white strips tied around her breasts and loins. He never said she moved like a song. In fact, love made her clumsy, all left hands and feet, and doors opened so close they hit her in the face.

Her mother was a woman trapped in a cage of mirrors. Wherever she turned she found a mirror. One of the fairy godmothers came to visit—she looked like a walnut with as many folds—"Mirrors will be the end of you, Ira," she murmured, and her mother clutched at the purple stone while the little girl involuntarily reached for her silver lozenge. "I won't do anything Ma does," she told herself again and again, but the gesture was automatic. Her mother's mouth had crooked, and she played a little part on the end of the long maroon sofa, stretching and pretending she was a cat in the sun. At least, the child thought that was what she was doing, rather than acknowledge the truth of the mirrors. Behind the bedroom door clung the rose satin animal her mother had hooked there—when the godmother was gone she would drape her cat length in it. Hard lace claws and glittering sequin eyes frightened her asleep and then, in her dreams, the door would open and the wolf come in. He paused on the threshold with a growl before he sprang. It was like being tumbled by a wave, being caught up in a thunderstorm and rolled in grey cloud paws. "You were dreaming," said her mother, the morning sunlight splintering around her in the mirror. She would look around, stunned by the brightness and see an empty room, pink rose satin rumpled across a stool. Her father was no wolf.

"You must give him time to finish his studies," the godmother pleaded. "Then he will have more time for both of you."

"My father was studying law," she told Ravi. "He had those hours to complete. I thought she drove him away so she could beat me."

"But why did she beat you?"

A frustrated woman stranded among her satins in a city she didn't know. There had been no one to tell the child why. "You look like your father," she repeated. The words had set her staring at herself every time she looked into a mirror. "There's nothing wrong with your face," Ravi told her, over and over, how many times over again, holding her hand, kissing it sometimes in a stray quaint gesture. Her mother would never have believed that she could achieve a Ravi—she looked too like her father, after all. "Your father doesn't deserve me," dragging her home from shopping, a bursting brown paper bag clutched in the crook of one arm and smiles on her red mouth for all the men she passed. They fell around her, offering to carry the bag—occasionally she let them.

The godmother fussed around for a few days, inspecting the ring and the talisman in an aura of incense, making the whole flat smoky with it and floating through the haze as if she really had fairy wings. The child's father slept on two sofa cushions on the drawing room carpet. Fairy or not, the godmother's presence eased nothing—anger flared up and down the yellow walls on the occasions she was out shopping. "Why do I have to entertain your relatives? How long is she going to stay here? She has your father's ugly face," she told the child and, bewildered, the child told her father, as she told everything that confused her.

Her mother kept secrets—she smiled slyly into her mirror and locked her bottom drawer. While the godmother was there she was smooth and sleeked down with no trace of the rose-pink or emerald-green animal. "Hypocrite," the child would have spat, if she had known the word. That purple talisman ring, perhaps the only person it had worked on was her. A blonde plumber came home with them from Vanger. He hung around the bathroom making suggestions and chucking the child under her chin—she hated being chucked under her chin, her whole neck instinctively curled in protest and he laughed and did it again and again until her mother warned him, "You'll break the child's neck, Tony."

Tony, with the cup of golden hair turned upside down on his

head! She refused to call him "uncle." The godmother brought a brief truce to the wars. After she left they broke out again—her schoolwork suffered. One day she cried and cried in class until they had to call in her mother and send her home.

"I can't deal with this! How do you expect me to deal with this? I'm only...." How old? Twenty-five, twenty-six? She imagined her own useless self at twenty-six, locked behind a face she hated to meet in the mirror. Dealing with a child and a student husband in a strange city was unimaginable, and her frivolous legend-of-a-beauty mother must have found it even more unimaginable.

There was an old suitcase upstairs. If you lifted the lid the satin would slither out. Ravi didn't want to see it. "No," he protested and, "No," again.

"You don't want to understand me," she accused.

"What has understanding you got to do with looking at your mother's underwear?" The underwear was important to her, but whenever she tried to explain, the words tangled her tongue. He would look sadly into her eyes after one of those frustrated sessions and walk out of the house. "You're useless," she could hear her mother say. "Not one ounce of my sex appeal." Not that her mother would have used those words—she would have talked of beauty and elegance, the *bhadro bangali* terms that went so badly with the black lace and scarlet sequins.

Ravi quit his job, only telling her long after all their friends knew. And even then his eyes never released hers for an instant. She wrote him a whole series of poems, cries for help, which he took with him. They made love one last time after that—he came to her house one evening when there was no one home. He held her so tight she thought her bones would break. He's holding me, she told herself, I'm not holding him.

She was losing him, he was losing her. Loss spiralled into loss, though who lost whom was difficult to say. She had the feeling that she was being left out of a secret.

"Where are you going ?" she had demanded when either of her parents left the flat, and they would give her everyday answers like the grocer, a matinee, the college, all the places she knew they went to, but she would not believe them. "What's wrong with you!" her mother exploded, exasperated, shaking her off her bristly fur cuff. "Go inside and wait. You know your father will be back by three. I'm only going to the matinee. And don't open the door to anyone!" Sometimes, when she was by herself in the flat, the phone rang and she picked up the crooked black receiver and held it carefully to her ear. Once she heard a man's voice say, "Are you alone, darling?" before she let the black thing fall out of her hand. It was Tony, it had to be Tony.

She had been sure her mother would never come back—she paced up and down the landing, hugging her desolation to herself. Once, the huge Alsatian who lived in the next-door flat came and licked her nose, a warm sloppy lick that made her laugh, but no one else came until her father dragged his briefcase home and then she was all around him, trying to protect him from the black phone.

"I'm not your mother," Ravi said. "I think you try and make me your mother. I can't be her."

"I have to get him back into bed with me," she thought. She bought herself underwear as dark as her intent and looked at the limp bras in the mirror, but all her eyes showed were flashes of red and green, fresh drops of blood on a sheet or new young grass, a little yellow, a little hungry, more cat's eyes than grass. Tony with the sweat trickling down his muscles—why did her mind run on Tony unless it was because he tried to tickle her—and how on earth could her mother have let him? The point was, she didn't know.

One evening her mother never came back from the movies. She remembered that evening because while she was pacing up and down the little silver talisman slithered down and fell at her feet. She was terrified. It meant she'd broken it, how could she tell anyone it had just fallen off of its own accord? The fact that it might have fallen off by itself, that it might have been a sudden act of God, added to her panic; she picked it up waiting to feel her mother's hand curl around her hair. Instead, the sky turned as silver as the talisman, then blackened. The shadows on the landing clustered thicker and thicker until the grey was black with them and behind her yawned the open mouth of the flat door—she had stupidly forgotten to switch on the light—and she stood lost in all that blackness, hoping to become a shadow herself, until a bulb abruptly flicked light into the place. The old gaffer who looked after the building was downstairs, so he hadn't died and shrunk into his huge rubber gloves. There was someone alive somewhere. And then the phone rang.

She had almost forgotten Ravi sitting there, his eyes politely glazed with boredom—when had that started? He used to look at her with a little sparkle in them as she tilted her head and told him stories, and she said to her mother's ghost, "See, I can enchant a man, see!" Ravi shuffled those long gazelle legs of his—did gazelles wear white baggy trousers? "I have to go," he said and folded himself upright like an umbrella furling.

"When do I see you...?"

She hadn't meant to say that. Night closed on his face. "I thought you knew. I'm getting married next month."

Next month? When had that happened, after her mother didn't come back from the movies or before? He held her tight and let her go. "I can't be your mother." He had said that before, the time he held her so tight she thought their bones would fuse together. As he was leaving he turned once, reluctantly, he couldn't help himself, "I suppose she came home. Something must have gone wrong at the film."

"No, she never came home."

It was too late for the truth then. Her father found her shivering on the threshold of the flat clutching the broken talisman in her hand, staring at the ringing phone. "Your mother's gone away," he told her, hefting her up and taking her inside. The next day there was a godmother by her side who explained very carefully that her mother had gone to heaven. Angels in scarlet bras? That was all she could imagine, expensive wax shop-window angels with compacts in their hands, powdering their noses. Then the wax ran molten down her cheek. Hot wax, when she'd expected relief at being spared more slaps.

Her mother had opened up a black hole in her life that all the satin in the world could not fill. Ravi was standing at the threshold staring at her before he went away to get married. "You never told me that. What happened."

"She was running away with one of the men she met. They were killed in a car crash. The police were trying to ring us to get hold of *baba*."

A crumpled car stubbed like a cigarette against a concrete pillar in a dark night, the red fire of the tail lights still glowing, the boot forced open, spewing satin. She never saw it—though the godmothers said it had been flashed on TV: a silk lady and a fast life. Who had Tony been—the plumber, or even Uncle Samir? Her mother, her father told the older child, the grown woman, had been a nymphomaniac who slept with any man she could find. Did she want to follow in her mother's footsteps? That was in another country when he had caught her rummaging through the silk ruins of the trunk. She remembered his words the first time she slept with Ravi.

Sorrow, so much sorrow—they had never talked about love or grief or any of the things lovers in books talk about, just gazed lost into each other's eyes or created a ritual of flesh on flesh. Was that all it had been about? Underwear? "You failed," her mother said, powdering her nose in her mother-of-pearl compact. "I knew you would."

Childhood Pleasures

By Pumla Dineo Gqola
(South Africa)

I get off the minibus taxi and begin the short walk to my grand-parents' house. This has been my routine for two years now, ever since I left lower primary school. Every Sunday afternoon I board a taxi headed for kwaLanga for a visit. Grandfather will be sitting outside on the *stoep* of the house with Tatomkhulu uNgwevu, his old friend, both men basking in the sun, smoking pipes. I inhale the sweet tobacco smell along with the laughter shared by the two men, interspersed with the teasing that is so characteristic of warm February Sundays. As I open the gate they notice me at once, switching from whatever topic is on their lips to that of my arrival. Grandfa-ther calls out to Grandmother inside the house to come see me. He always announces my arrivals as if he is pleasantly surprised by them, although I cannot imagine why he should be so.

"Tyhini! Tyhini! Mamfene! Uthi mawuke uzosivakashela namhlanje!"—"So, Mamfene, you have decided to pay us a visit today!" they be-gin.

I smile and offer a greeting as I walk towards them, closing the gate behind me. After kissing them both on the lips—for Tatomkhul' uNgwevu is as good as family too—I stand on the *stoep* for a while telling them this and that. Sometimes they say how I have grown, and we all laugh because only a week has passed since my last visit. It is all said in good fun, and I know I am not to take anything literally. Then they ask about other people back home, although, to be hon-est, they see those people often enough too. Finally I announce that

I will go and say hello to my grandmother and am just about to enter the house when she comes outside herself.

"Oh! I see that you have only come to visit your grandfathers here, neh?" she teases.

"Hayi, Makhulu"—"No, Granny, I was just about to come in to you."

Grandfather calls me Mamfene, my family name, never Thembela, my given name. I do not mind, though. In fact, I rather like it, even though when I was a younger child I found it slightly old-fashioned. My grandmother calls me "T-Girl" because when I was five that was what I told her I liked being called. At the time she laughed because it was not the logical shortening for my name. Other Thembelas were called Thembi or Thembsie, certainly not T-Girl. At first she said it sounded like I was being called a "tea-girl," and this to her made it all the more strange. I don't remember anymore where I picked up the notion, but it has stuck with Granny. Grandfather never uses it, only his family name and, since he is father's father, my family name too. Everybody calls him Mfene, except my grandmother who calls him by his given name.

Eventually Makhulu and I are inside the house alone. She always has some kind of treat waiting for me. I sit in the kitchen while she brings out whatever favourite of mine she has made that weekend, or has kept for me from a meal during the week. I always eat all of it even though my parents insisted I finish lunch before I left home to go visiting. I have always had a healthy appetite.

Today as we sit around that kitchen table, Makhulu brings out *amafetshu*—fatcakes—and ginger beer. Everybody knows I love *amafetshu* better than anything else in the world. I used to annoy my mother because I would insist on buying them even from the aunties who sold them on the street unprotected from the dust and dirt. My mother used to say they were unhygienic and would make me sick. Makhulu's *mafetshu*, though, are always the best, better even than my mother's. My mother laughs when I say this because she insists that she makes the best *mafetshu* in all of Cape Town.

As Makhulu and I sit together I notice she is not as happy as she usually is. I ask if she is sick. She says no, it is only that she is worried about her friend's misfortune. I wait for her to either explain or not, because I am a child and must not pry. This is not to say I am not eager to hear what has happened to her friend. But I stop myself short of asking which friend, because I really want to know. Children may not ask grown-up people these things. If she sees fit to tell me, she will. If she doesn't, then it is a matter between adults and I am not to be privy to that information. I can't wait to be grown up enough so that I can be told anything I want to know.

Makhulu looks very unhappy now. She is talking about what it was like back home. This always amazes me, because even though Makhulu has lived here for decades she still refers to Libode as home too. Libode is in the Eastern Cape somewhere. I haven't been there since I was a baby, so I don't remember it.

When makhulu Mampinga comes into the kitchen, I begin to wonder whether it is she who has had something bad happen to her. Soon the house has three more grandmothers visiting. Although Sunday afternoons are visiting time, there are seldom so many of them here all at once. It is clear they have come for a reason. And this is how I manage to hear the story. With so many grown-up people confronting a crisis, it is easy to forget there is a child in the room. It is almost like in the train when my friends and I come from school. The mothers and aunties in the train speak grown-up talk with us right there in the carriage. Sometimes we imagine they are so charged up that they entirely forget we are there and we children try to keep really quiet. In my excitement today, I miss the first part of the exchange between the grey women and only come to my senses when makhulu Mampinga is already talking.

"In no time at all they had found a place to live. I was devastated. This meant that I had to start afresh looking for chars. At this stage, as you know, I am no longer a spring chicken. But it is a woman's lot," she is saying.

The other grandmothers are speaking now too, and the story is going to take a long time to tell. They are all making sympathetic sounds. Every now and again they make an exclamation. This delaying is the only thing I do not care for in grown-up talk. Children always get right to the juicy bits, but adults savour every word, especially old grown-ups. I hide my irritation because none of this is my business in any case, but I sometimes have special privileges at Makhulu and Tatomkhulu's place. Eventually makhulu Mampinga continues her story.

"They had at least been kind to me. The madam used to deduct from my pay for many years. I knew that I could get that money when they left to go to Johannesburg. This fact alone was my consolation. It is not that I did not want to see them go. Only that it is much more difficult at my age…you know, to start looking again. And *kule mali inqabe kangaka*—especially with money being so scarce." She took a break here, and for a moment I thought I saw tears in her eyes.

It is makhulu Nokuzola who takes up now from where makhulu Mampinga has left off. I realise this is to allow makhulu Mampinga to pull herself together again before she resumes.

"Look at my own case. I have been looking for a job myself for several months now. One madam told me to stop looking and let my children support me. A sad thing that is, I'm telling you. 'Thelma, let your children work for you now,' she said. Imagine! Just like that, telling somebody she is too old to work." (I only now realise that "Thelma" is makhulu Nokuzola's work name.)

It is my grandmother's turn to sympathise now, and she begins, *"Ei!* This old age is a curse against us in this place now. When I was a little girl, old age meant wisdom. But *you* wouldn't know about that." She is looking at me. It strikes me that Makhulu does not mind that I am here. Addressing herself to me, she continues, "You are from this here township, a city girl. You don't know the old life."

Makhulu Mampinga has pulled herself together enough to be able to continue her story now. She has no more tears in her eyes.

"Anyway, *bafazi*, let me continue with this thing. My madam told me she would have the money ready and a few things for me to take home. This morning I was sitting in the train trying to imagine how much money I would be getting. I could just imagine, all those years, my nice madam had been putting away little by little. I did not worry that she never told me where she was putting it away," makhulu Mampinga says. But she is once again interrupted.

"Ewe kaloku. Yes, indeed, that is why the white people have

so much money. They know of many ways to save their money," makhulu Nokuzola offers.

I notice that the other two grandmothers have not said much. Occasionally they agree or offer a sympathetic sound, but not much else escapes their lips. Not to be outdone, makhulu Mampinga continues her story. It must be very difficult to tell a story under these circumstances, I think to myself. But then, they are all friends and like interrupting each other. It is I, the outsider, who am bothered by their way of going about it.

Makhulu Mampinga says, "Today, however, I was going to reap the benefits of their secret money-making scheme. This money would be more than the money from our *mgalelo* group at Christmas. I thought to myself, I will only use a little of it to celebrate. The rest I will take and deposit at the Post Office as soon as the following day came. Some other chars on the train were teasing me, 'Are you sure *abelungu bakho*—your employers—are going away? Why, then, are you so happy?' *Hayi wethu,* I told them, I am in a good mood, that's all. Today feels like Christmas for me. The train crawled all the way."

"When you are late the train is very slow, my dear. It's the same when you have to wait for it. It takes forever." That was makhulu Thobeka—Esther, as she was known when she did her chars.

"When the train finally arrived at Kenilworth station, I was beside myself with joy. I was going to see all my money. Curiosity had also got the better of me, because I wondered what present my bosses also had in store for me. They always gave me nice gifts at Christmas. Sometimes they gave me the young master's toys for my boys when they were still young. Sometimes books and guns. The wind pushed me up the slope that day because I had no worry. I was wearing the nice lime-green dress madam gave to me last Christmas. It had been her favourite dress years ago, she told me. It was good quality, I could tell. Yes, this dress was quality. We wore the same size as the madam.

"When I got to the house it was very quiet, so I decided they were out. My key was in my purse, so letting myself in would not be a problem. Inside, I could still hear nothing. They must have packed the kitchen first, I remember thinking to myself. As I went through the house, however, I found myself encountered by empty rooms. The house had nothing but dust, with only the wind whistling as it went through the corridors. Empty! I walked in and out of every room, thinking there must be a mistake. Then I thought that the madam had left something for me in one of the rooms. Perhaps in the bathroom. Of course! It must be in one of the cupboards in the kitchen, in one of the hiding places for master Jimmy's sweets and things that had been kept by only the madam and myself. They had left without saying goodbye, but maybe something came up. It didn't matter, really, as long as the money was there. Maybe they left it with my present for the years of service. Now that I thought about it, I could have had much worse bosses."

There are exclamations all around as the grandmothers begin preempting what makhulu Mampinga is about to say. But she gets it out soon enough.

"I looked and looked. I knew every corner of that house, went over each room five times. Eventually with the heat rising from the pit of my stomach into my face, my heart about to start turning as if it were not attached to my body, I sat down. Flat in the middle of the kitchen floor," she says, and then remains quiet for a few moments. I notice there are tears running down her face. "I should have known. A clever woman would have asked for her money there and then when the promise was made. Now my money was gone. Gone. I must have thought about this for an hour before I finally got up, let the key drop to the floor and walked out. It made no sense for me to bother closing the door behind me. It was unimportant. It was I who had been robbed. Eight years, gone. Maybe I would have been better to have mean bosses like you, my friends. At least there are no surprises then."

I also want to cry because everybody in Makhulu's kitchen has become silent. To keep from feeling uncomfortable, I look outside the window. The clouds are starting to gather. Thank goodness it is Cape Town, I think. It will rain, but at least there will be no thunder.

Makhulu Nokuzola says, *"Hayi wethu!* There never was any money. It was a way to justify under-paying you all these years. And you kept saying you had such nice bosses."

I watch as the women sit in my grandmother's kitchen sharing a friend's pain. But I am still shocked. All I can do is shake my head. Then I think to myself, how can I make my escape? I would rather wait until I am big to listen to old people's stories.

Makhulu Charlene and Aunt Thobeka promise to keep an ear open. They both know makhulu Mampinga is old and that it will be hard finding a position for her. People want young blood. She has spent half of her life cleaning other people's houses three times a week. It is now her time to retire and grow old. But she needs the money. Her friends are here to tell her that they care that nobody wants an old woman working for them.

'Injalo ke bafazi! That's the story, then, women. My husband's pension will have to do for now. It is time now for me to be old too," was how makhulu Mampinga's story ends.

"How can you say you will live on your husband's pension? What about your own?" Makhulu asked. But Makhulu has not worked at a pensionable job for a long time. I do not even remember when that might have been. It was around the time she bought a sewing machine and started making dresses and other things. Earlier, she used to work as a seamstress at a factory in Goodwood. Now she has her own "factory" right here in her home, she often says.

It is still hard for me to keep quiet in light of what I have just heard, so I choose to leave the kitchen. I take my last *fetshu* and what is left of my ginger beer and walk towards the *stoep* where the grandfathers are still laughing together. Perhaps they will cheer me up.

Tatomkhulu is telling a story about the tricks they once played on one another as boys. I laugh with them, noting that both my grandparents seem to enjoy reliving the past. I know they like the city too, though. Otherwise they would have moved back to the rural areas like some of their friends did. But they prefer to spend their last days here. When asked about this, Makhulu often says, *'Mh! Uthi mandiyokwenza ntoni mna ezilalini?* Huh? What do you want me to go and do in those places? I have nothing there any more. My friends are all here. So are my children."

Tatomkhulu echoes him.

Their words surprise me, because they both like to reminisce so much about their youth and how things were back then. But maybe all they want is to remember, not go back. Still, they call that place home. But they call kwaLanga home too. I think one is the home of their youth and the other the home of their old age. Grandfather Tatomkhulu is from Bizana and Grandmother Makhulu from Libode, so maybe it is a good thing they came to Cape Town, because otherwise they may never have met. Maybe that is why they don't want to go back: they would have to go back to different places. This is what I say to my grandfather as I join the two old men on the stoep; there is no sun anymore, but they show no sign of moving. My suggestion is met with roaring laughter.

"Hayi ningabantwana bedolophu nyani nina. You indeed are a child brought up in town. We could not have spoken to our own grandparents of such matters," is Tatomkhulu's response.

He makes a joke of it, but I realise my comment was indeed inappropriate. It was alright to think it, but not to say it aloud. As nice as he is about some things, my grandfather is a stickler for tradition. He is as conservative in that way as can be. All these years in Cape Town have left no imprint on him in that regard. This was a matter I should have raised with Makhulu, because she is less strict about such things. Last week I even told her that my sister has a boyfriend. I could never mention boys to Tatomkhulu. He would pretend to laugh it off, but then he would be sure to change the subject.

So, I think, now I will have to keep quiet for a little while. But soon they are interrogating me again about what I want to be when I grow up. I tell them I want to be a vet, which is what I told them last week.

Tatomkhul' uNgwevu challenges this. "But I thought last week you said you wanted to be a doctor? Who will heal *us* if you are so busy healing animals?"

My Tatomkhulu teases, *"Hei!* You know, Ngwevu, these children know of all sorts of things. But the times are on their side. Now they can be anything they put their minds to."

Both grandfathers break into laughter again, and it is with regret I realise I must be starting home. It may not rain for another hour or so, but it is getting late and I do not want my parents to worry. My mother worries even though she knows where I am. Maybe she thinks something will happen to me in the taxi or something. People always make a fuss about taxis, but I have not heard of many accidents in which a minibus taxi was involved. And I know of a lot of accidents. I walk back to the kitchen to bid all grandmothers farewell. Then I say goodbye to my grandfathers. This has been the strangest visit I can ever remember having with my grandparents. Maybe next week things will be back to normal.

A Dark Place

By Andrew McKenna
(Australia)

You died in a dark place
On a sunless day
Rain dripping from gossamer clouds
Crying tears as red as camellia flowers in midwinter snow
My heart bleeds

—Yong-bae's writing box

Her father was the son of farmers from the Village of the Blue Crane, and he knew the hard work of the barley and rice fields and the tobacco they had to cultivate for the Japanese. What Yong-bae remembered most about him were his hands. Soft and delicate, they were not like a man's hands at all, more like leaves that fluttered in a breeze, leaves that protected her for their season and then were gone.

As a boy he had learned to play the *choktae*, the bamboo flute, for the harvest festivals, and as he grew older music became more important to him than helping in the fields. And he was sickly, so while his brothers went out to work he was able to stay at home and practice. He discovered the uncomplicated sounds of the flute. He learned to concentrate his attention at the surface of his skin, to breathe in through every pore of his body, to feel the vibrations of sound in his marrow, to taste the sound in his mouth, to hear it with his hands. He learned to be carried by it and surrender to it, to reach the spirit world through it. He knew it was the song of his soul.

By the time Yong-bae was born her father had long since left the Village of the Blue Crane and gone to live in Seoul where he played the flute and the *t'aep yŏngso*, the Korean oboe, for the masked dance dramas that were popular there. He had left his farming roots behind, but he never forgot where he came from and would often tell her stories of the country. Once, she went back with him to the Village of the Blue Crane for a harvest festival, but the vastness of the countryside frightened her. The field workers' faces were like tree bark, and the way they bent double as they worked made her tired. She couldn't wait to get back to the city. Even her father, guest of honour among the yokel musicians, seemed to reveal a side she had never seen before—a raw, uncompromising hardness, like rocks under water in a stream.

"Agriculture is the foundation of all under Heaven," he told her in the train, but she cried all the way back to Seoul.

She began spending her evenings at the theatre while he rehearsed, watching the actors come and go, a small girl staring at them as they memorised their lines and ran through their paces on the stage, laughing or arguing as they worked. She loved watching the musicians in their beautiful red robes, hearing their small gongs and drums and stringed instruments, the smell of sawdust and paint and makeup and nervousness heated under bright lights, and she swelled with pride when her father played the oboe.

She was so entranced by the performances that the stage manager finally agreed to give her a role backstage even though she was not yet ten. She helped the main actor dress, and passed white cloths to the women dancers.

One day she heard her father performing on the *choktae* in his garden and she wept because she believed she had heard the voice of the dead. She was drawn to the beauty of the music which held at its heart a deep sadness. Here she thought was a chance to explore her own grief, the grief of knowing that all things, all life, must end. She could feel her own death a little in each beautiful note.

She begged her father to teach her to play. He said no. Her mother also asked him, just the basics, but he refused. But her mother was persistent and asked one of her uncles to teach Yong-bae. After a few months her father realised she was talented and, grudgingly at first, took her on as his own student. His lessons were strict. He would never wait if she floundered, and he would teach a piece only once and expect her to play it.

"Always use your ears," he said. And, "Your attitude is more important than cleverness with your fingers." Or, "A single tone can provide enlightenment."

He believed that a musician had to work on an inner strength to become a master, that it was an instrument of introspection and self-knowledge, that music was for the soul and the spirit. From her own experience would come insight.

"To play the flute," he told her, "you have to learn to control your breath through your abdomen, and that is the cornerstone of all meditation. Master this and you master yourself."

He spoke of perfection, of a single breath as a meditation, of "our shore" and "the other shore" being linked by a delicate thread of sound. They were fine sentiments, and his face showed a calm passivity that might have been contentment. But in his heart he had begun to harbour poisonous thoughts.

Japanese soldiers had beaten two of his nephews to death in the Village of the Blue Crane for smoking at a time when the Japanese government was carefully guarding its tobacco monopoly. Their father's heart was broken, and he had thrown himself into the sea. At home Yong-bae's father spoke bitterly about the Japanese, often so loudly that Yong-bae's mother had to tell him to be quiet, for the walls had ears.

More and more often he was disappointed and tired. He was sick in his soul, and it could be heard in his music. Gradually it ceased to heal him. They only found out much later that he had been passed over as leader of the orchestra in favor of a Japanese musician.

One night a delegation of Japanese officers visited the theatre, because its reputation had spread. Only ten minutes into the first scene, where Yong-bae's father was meant to play a haunting section as the ghost appeared, he put down his oboe and stood up. There was a moment of confusion as the musicians were suddenly thrown off and the actors looked uneasily at each other.

Yong-bae's father walked to the front of the stage and cleared his throat.

"There are foreigners in our midst," he said, "Until they leave this land I will play no music for the theatre. All good Koreans should demand they leave. They are not welcome here. They are parasites on the backs of our nation. I curse them and their ancestors."

The performance broke in disarray. The audience began shouting and fled. Alarmed voices rose backstage as the musicians and actors stampeded for the wings. Yong-bae's father stood at the front of the stage watching the mayhem he had created, and she stood watching him, proud and frightened at once. Police whistles shrilled and soldiers poured into the theatre. They beat Yong-bae's father with the butts of their rifles and dragged him away. She saw his face bloodied, as red as his musician's robes. Someone took her arm, and she was suddenly outside in the night.

Her father never came home. The theatre was closed for six months. When it reopened, a Japanese musician had replaced him.

To draw rations under occupation you had to recite an epic poem. When Yong-bae's mother next went to draw their rations she could not do it. Instead, she broke down and sobbed and accused the government men of killing her husband. They laughed and threw her out.

Over the winter they were forced to eat scraps from the market, tree bark and roots out of the garden. The winter was hard, and they were very hungry. In the spring they were forced to take a ship across the sea. There were squid boats trolling under floodlights during the crossing. A cold rain fell, and Yong-bae vomited from seasickness. But when they landed she thought how beautiful Japan looked. The blossoms were out and the clouds had parted on an enormous sky, and the country was green, filled with rice paddies and neat vegetable gardens.

They were taken to Tokyo. Except for soldiers everywhere, it was a beautiful country. The rice paddies rippled under the sun, and tiny villages dotted the countryside. They were barracked in the women's quarters at Asakusa and set to work.

Her mother befriended a Buddhist man who was forced to work

with them. He was regarded as the lowest of the low—a Japanese man forced to work with Korean women slaves. This was because he would not fight in the Pacific War. He would not kill for the emperor. He would not even kill an insect. So the army made him work in the factory. He told Yong-bae's mother that the Japanese would have to pay for what they had brought upon the people of the Pacific, that there was a law of retribution.

Because her hands were small Yong-bae's job was to insert fuses into shell casings. Other girls and small boys did the same work. When war broke out with America air raid sirens often interrupted them. They had a shelter under the factory, but Yong-bae's mother said it was not much use because if the factory was hit they could dig to the centre of the earth but no shelter would be deep enough to spare them. Yong-bae had nightmares.

One night in Asakusa the sirens woke them. An explosion came very close and threw Yong-bae out of bed. People were rushing around screaming, and she was separated from her mother in the dark. She could smell fire. She ran into the street as the anti-aircraft guns opened up. There were many explosions, so many that her eardrums seemed to be stretched tight inside her head. A great whistling filled the night as bombs rained down. The Americans were dropping incendiaries, and much of Tokyo was built of rice paper and wood. She saw people blown apart. A huge wind started to blow as the fires sucked up oxygen. She heard her mother calling through the roar, and they ran to where wardens were directing people. They entered a cellar and sat shoulder to shoulder with other terrified people while above them Tokyo burned. Other people suffocated in the shelters that suffered direct hits, but Yong-bae and her mother were just far enough from the firestorm to survive.

They emerged into a charred ruin, full of smoke and craters. Corpses lay in blackened piles. Yong-bae thought this must be hell. They spent some hungry days, wandering away from the centre of town where there were still houses, and finally they were evacuated to a place called Hakone in the mountains. Yong-bae thought it beautiful, with hot mineral water bubbling out of the ground. There were even boiling waterfalls and steam rising through the ferns. All around were lovely mountains, and the forests were full of trees turning copper and scarlet as winter approached. She was set to work on a farm minding chickens and goats, and that was her happiest time during the war.

From the farm she was sent to Nagasaki to live with other girls. And then it was eleven o'clock one morning in August. They had no news of what had already happened in Hiroshima. She was alone in her room when she heard a plane in the sky, very high up. She pulled her chair to the window and looked out. She couldn't see the plane, but she did see a silver box floating slowly down on a parachute. The city was very quiet. She could not hear the shouts of workmen and streetcars rolling past, birds singing, the policeman's whistle. A duck landed on the lake, sending out ripples as it flapped its wings. And above, just that silver parachute falling, with no sign of the aeroplane.

Her mistress came into the room and shouted at her, thinking Yong-bae was about to climb out the window and run away. She slapped Yong-bae's face, and she fell to the floor.

"What are you doing!" the woman yelled. "I will send you away."

"A parachute is falling," Yong-bae said, and pointed to the window.

The woman glared at her, then pulled over a chair and climbed up to look out. Yog-bae's face was stinging. She hated the woman. She hated everything about Nagasaki. She saw a bedspring that had fallen to the floor and reached out for it, prepared to stab her mistress, even if it meant she herself would be killed.

Then the room was full of the brightest light. No sound, but it was as if the sun had fallen to earth. A blinding blue-white light that made her dizzy with its intensity, so bright she could almost see through the walls. She pressed her hands to her eyes and saw the bones of her hands even with her eyes closed. She even thought she could see her brain behind them. The woman screamed, and there was a great rush of wind, and somehow Yong-bae lost the use of her senses. When they returned she was on the other side of the room, pieces of broken glass covering her face and in her mouth.

Her mistress was lying nearby. Where she had been looking out the window her face and neck and chest were stripped raw like a side of meat. There were strips of paper lying all around her, and Yong-bae wondered what they were. Then she realised they were the woman's skin.

For many days she did not know what had happened. The girls wandered outside and were afraid of what they saw. Soot was falling everywhere. Nagasaki was a blackened wasteland. They did not know about radiation. Within a few hours the police ordered them into town to help carry out the dead.

The worst part was where electric and telephone wires had got twisted around people's legs and they could not pull themselves free. They died like that, begging for water. The river and the pools in the gardens were choked with dead. Yet Yong-bae felt no pity for them. She saw entire families and children incinerated, their bodies twisted and swollen by the great heat. She saw tree branches piled together and wondered what they were until she realised the white bark was bones. But she did not feel pity. In the midst of the incineration she rejoiced, though she herself felt like a ghost.

Many Japanese committed suicide, as did some of the girls she lived with, some of whom were students. Yong-bae stayed alive because she wanted to find her mother and because she wanted to see Japan brought to its knees.

She stayed on for several weeks after the bombing. There was little else she could do. Groups of workers arrived to dig through the rubble. Amazingly, despite the terrible heat of the blast, in a few weeks the vines and flowers returned, exploded into life as if they had just been waiting for the chance, or even as if the bomb had stimulated their growth. She saw dandelions as tall as a horse, grass pushing through walls, morning glories pulling down ruined houses.

There was no transport out of Nagasaki until the Americans arrived. Some of the injured and sick—and there were a great many— were sent to Tokyo when the war was over. Then the roads were flooded with GIs honking the horns of their jeeps and acting in ill-mannered ways. The American authorities would not let her travel. She had to stay in Japan until the spring of 1946 when they finally allowed her a berth on a ship back to Korea. She had not been able to find her mother.

Back in Korea she found herself an outsider. She didn't know who she was or where she should go. Her nights were plagued with nightmares. She wanted to reclaim her family home and get news of her mother. She walked the streets of Seoul and found her old neighbourhood in rubble. The people there talked ill of her and her family. They said her family had deserted them; that it was her fault what had happened. She heard so much of this kind of talk that she began to believe it.

She stood in the street and considered throwing herself in front of a bus. Two little boys were playing nearby, climbing up onto a fence to tear flowers from a camellia bush and then jumping down onto the footpath to trample them, hooting with laughter. What was her life worth? Her family was gone, her country in ruins. In effect, her life was over. Snuffing out what was left of it would be of as little consequence as what those boys were doing to the camellia blossoms. She turned toward the traffic and waited for her moment to arrive. She felt absolutely calm.

Mr. Gurupadam's Affair

By Joanna Shireen
(India)

Mr. Gurupadam was scanning the City section of *The Washington Post* when something warm pressed against his upper arm and a whisp of reddish-brown hair fanned across his nose.

The train had only gone as far as Metro Station, but he had already nodded off twice, lulled by the drone of wheels in the endless tunnels. His spotted tie hung open on his neck. He was extremely tired, even though his boss had told him he could leave earlier than usual. Piles of thick green files and sheaves of paper covered with tiny numbers swam across the backs of his eyelids, and the voices of endless meetings still buzzed in his ears. He longed for a hot shower and his wife's cinnamon-flavored tea with milk. When the train doors slid open on another throng of commuters, he wished he were working anywhere but DC. This was what he wished everyday, and the secret longing for a quiet town where there were no huge rumbling trains stuffed with sweaty, garrulous people gave him a sense of self-important misery.

He folded his copy of the *Washington Post* and glanced cautiously at the young woman who had sat down next to him, then quickly looked away again. His was not a strong heart, a doctor had told him more than ten years ago. Both his father and grandfather died of heart disease, at forty-six and fifty-two, respectively. Mr. Gurupadam had not researched the details, but his mother once told him the condition could be inherited. He had been a sickly child. His mother had nursed him through one infection after another. His entire youth had been a misery of cold hands and feet pressed between warm blankets, his sweaty forehead being wiped continuously with the end of a soft saree, with whispered discussions around the wooden cot on which he lay. While other boys waited for girls at dark street corners and talked about forbidden things, Mr. Gurupadam was moved in and out of crowded hospitals smelling of phenol and had thousands of pills and syrups forced into him and his buttocks jabbed incessantly with syringes. Throughout it all, thick hard-bound accounting textbooks, their pages stained by spilled cough medicine and phlegm, followed him everywhere. He had read and read, until his burning eyes closed in sleep.

Then came his Big Moment: One day when he came home from college he found his mother shivering beside the alcove where she kept a framed picture of the Goddess Laxmi illuminated by two small brass bowls of burning oil. She was holding an opened envelope. Tears were running down the sides of her nose. The envelope contained a letter of confirmation for a job as an accountant. "You are going to America!" she gasped. "Away from this country which is killing you!" Without telling him, she had sent his resumé to several different overseas corporations.

Mr. Gurupadam remembered going to his room and holding up a small hand mirror to his face, chest and arms. At twenty-eight he looked like an emaciated boy who seemed to have stopped growing in his mid-teens. His shoulders were bunched close around his neck as though he were still straining to grow. The peppery beard that spotted his thin jaw was the butt of jokes amongst his few friends, and his thin arms ached if he carried so much as a kilogram of rice home from the store. His relatives said there was a curse on the family and that his going to America was just asking for trouble. But his mother ignored them.

For weeks after the letter arrived Mr. Gurupadam walked around in a daze. There were affairs to be taken care of before he left India, and he dealt with all of them as doggedly as he had submitted to those long hospital stays. His mother presided over everything, standing in lines at various government offices, writing letters, taking passport photographs of him, buying him new clothes. At the airport she cried on his shoulder and he touched her feet, and then he was off.

Within a few months of his arrival in America, she was dead. Mr. Gurupadam had felt the news of her death like the blow of a hammer. The telegram arrived at his work address. He seemed to shrivel up inside as he read it and for a long time sat very still in the little cubicle assigned to him, scratching at his shoes. But when he pushed his chair back and picked up his briefcase to catch the train home, a limp calmness came over him and had remained ever since.

The Wedding: He was shocked when his mother's sister wrote to say she had arranged a marriage for him. It was not in Mr. Gurupadam's nature to rebel against the wishes of his elders, but he felt that this time he must speak up. Girls were to him as impossible a dream as good health. And even though, as his mother had predicted, his condition seemed to improve in America, it seemed to come too late for him to think of marrying. He shied away from office parties, took the long way to the lunchroom if he saw a woman coming down the corridor and arrived late to meetings so he could sit in the chair farthest away from the females in his department.

"Aunty," he had written in a timid hand to his mother's sister. "I do not wish to marry." But it was a lost cause. His aunt spent ninety rupees to fax him the girl's photograph along with some predictions a local priest had written out for him. His aunt called him once from a public telephone and through the incessant buzz on the line pleaded and begged and yelled at him. The girl had made up her mind, she said. It would be good for him to have someone to cook and clean house.

Finally Mr. Gurupadam gave in. He flew to India and, before he knew it, the wedding was accomplished. His memory of it was a blur of crying women, grinning men and flashing cameras. Rice was sprinkled on the couple for good luck and fertility. As he smeared his bride's forehead with red paste, it struck him that the girl was not at all beautiful. But then it also struck him that it didn't matter.

Back in America his co-workers pointed out that the new Mrs. Gurupadam had a patient smile and big eyes, and some of them joked that he couldn't ask for more than that. But what endeared her to Mr. Gurupadam was her lack of interest in his body. In the first weeks after the wedding she had half turned to him at night, then, sensing his abhorence, she turned away again and went to sleep. Scarcely once a month did Mr. Gurupadam turn towards her himself. It wasn't until five years had passed that a son was born to them, and after that neither of them turned towards the other in bed again.

After the boy's birth Mr. Gurupadam found he could not bear the infant's crying and timidly suggested he sleep in a separate room. His wife immediately agreed. After that his affection for her began to grow and they settled down like any other family. She was a quiet woman. She cleaned house and tended to the boy, and he went to work and handed her his paycheck every other week. Sometimes he found her glancing at him furtively while he ate his dinner or watched the ten late news, and he thought he saw a sadness in her eyes much like what he had seen in his mother's during the long years she had sat at his bedside while he suffered through his fevers.

Why all this should be coming back to him now, just as he was about to raise his eyes to look at the young woman who had just sat down beside him on the Metro, he could not fathom. But when he did look at her a shiver ran through his thin body. She was young, very fair, with pink cheeks and lips. Light brown freckles were sprinkled across her nose and cheeks. Her hair was cropped short to emphasize a slender white neck. She was wearing a short red tanktop whose neckline plunged all the way to her small navel. Beneath an expanse of smooth flesh at her midriff, her thighs, encased in a pair of short shorts kept pressing together and drawing apart with each jerk of the train.

"Hi," she said. "Where are you heading?"

He hesitated, unsure how to pronounce the word. "AL-exandria"? Or was it "Al-EX-andria"? Or maybe "Alex-AN-dria"? Twice he opened his mouth to speak, but the word would not form itself.

The girl widened her eyes, shrugged and turned away again.

"Alex-AN-dria," he finally burst out, afraid she might think he could not speak English. He cleared his throat then and picked up the newspaper. But the tiny print made no sense, so he looked out the window at the rushing darkness of the underground.

The train slowed to a stop and several people got on. It was very crowded now. The young woman pressed a bit closer to make way for a family of three with a baby in a stroller. Mr. Gurupadam looked down at his legs where the girl's bare thigh was resting lightly. He held his breath until he thought his lungs would burst, then exhaled slowly so the other passengers wouldn't notice.

When the train started moving again he tried to think of something to say to the girl, but all he could think of were the endless rows of numbers on his computer screen. He could not believe something like this could be happening to him. The years had sucked out of him everything but a sense of the necessity to work and save for the Dreaded Illness that he knew must befall him sooner or later. But the terrible urgings of the teenage boy he had never been seemed to be exploding from every part of his being, more powerful and twice as painful for its happening now instead of at its appointed time. He was trembling beneath his polyester shirt, and a heat, not rising slowly but swift and searing, was rushing through him so violently that he thought the heart attack he believed was inevitable was about to claim him.

"It's so hot in here," the girl said, her soft voice like a balm on the fire he was feeling even as she fueled it.

"Yes," he found heard himself reply in a low, steady voice, "very stuffy."

She smiled, and he saw dimples dancing on her cheeks. From this close, they looked like two deep, constantly moving whirlpools. He felt an urge to put his finger into one of them and see how deep it would go.

"You must be from India," she said.

"I am."

"What an interesting country. I'm studying about the confluence of cultures in school, and we have a whole chapter on India."

"Oh, yes?"

"Is it true that the Portuguese and the French and the Arabs all invaded your country?"

Mr. Gurupadam searched his schoolboy memory for the details of India's history but could barely recall the dank classroom or hard backless wooden benches on which he had sat year after year. 'Yes. That's true.'

"Interesting," the girl said, stressing the first syllable so that the others escaped her red lips in a slurred rush.

"In the monsoons it rains every day, sometimes all day," he added. The rational part of his brain seemed to have broken up into separate parts that were working independently and were each sending him contradictory messages. He thought of his entire past life, and suddenly it seemed but a single day and of no consequence. He felt as though he had just been born and thrust shivering and naked into an enormous, dazzling world full of color and light. "I am from Belgaum," he said. "We have big monsoons there."

The train had emerged from the tunnel. The girl was looking out the window at the trees and the buildings and cars that seemed to be rushing to meet it. 'Where did you say you get off?' she asked absently.

It had been a long time, in another life, but he was sure he had heard that tone of voice before. When he was at college he had a good-looking friend who attracted a lot of girls. They would stop him on the street and ask the time just to strike up a conversation, and their voices always carried a hint of...this same thing. He clutched his copy of the *Post* and wondered how he should respond. Should he suggest coffee? A drink? Was she old enough to drink? Or should he just get off the train with her.

"King Street," he said in a higher pitch this time, almost a squeak.

"Oh," she said with a shrug. "I get off at National Airport."

Mr. Gurupadam felt a pain in a part of him that he hadn't known existed. The young woman must be a tourist. In his mind's eye, where he had never before been wont to see such images, or any images at all, he saw a tiny airplane, no more than a dot in the sky, disappearing into the clouds. He also saw himself on the ground, looking up, up.

"You must tell me something more about your culture for my term paper," the girl said with a giggle. "You don't want me to get an F!"

"Well, Belgaum is a small town in Southern India," Mr. Gurupadam began, stressing each syllable carefully so she could remember it later. As he spoke, every detail about his native town came back to him more clearly even than when he had lived there—the lowing of the cows in the field across the road, the smell of monsoon rains on the cakes of manure his mother laid out for drying, the evening cries of bare-footed boys playing *rabadi* while he sat watching from the verandah, too weak to join them.

For a while the girl sat quietly listening, her small hands pressed together on her lap, her pink-tipped nails curled around them. Her lips were parted dreamily as though inviting more of his reminiscences. Then the train pulled into another stop and her attention was diverted. A homeless man got on. He was blind and had on layers of foul-smelling clothes under a tattered khaki jacket with oversized pockets. From one of these he removed a rusty mouth organ, and as soon as the train began to move again he started to play. The girl's eyes grew wide with pleasure and her slim back straightened. "My grandpa's favorite song. 'The Great Speckled Bird!'"

Mr. Gurupadam nodded, feeling this was a precious confidence. He had no idea what the Great Speckled Bird was.

"My friends think I'm crazy, but I love folk music," she said, gesturing excitedly. "'All music has its roots in the folk tradition, don't you think?"

"I do," Mr. Gurupadam replied earnestly.

The blind man took off his hat and everyone dropped in money, mostly quarters and other small change but a dollar bill here and there. Mr. Gurupadam reached for his wallet and tossed a five dollar bill into the hat. The man moved down the aisle, and his music soon blended with the low drone of the passengers' conversations. Then the girl said, "Look at the river!"

He turned towards the window. The muddy Potomac that he had crossed every day for the last five years undulated beneath the bridge, slapping a dirty froth against the bottoms of the barges and motor boats making their ways up and downstream.

"The rich get to travel in sailboats, but we have to commute by Metro," he said in an attempt at humor.

The girl's expression remained serious. "Look at the sun!" she said, pointing to the big orange ball hovering over the water like a giant penny about to be dropped into a slot machine. It moved lazily along with the train, slashing the river with shimmering reds and oranges. It seemed to him that no sunset had ever been so exquisite. But when he looked back at her she seemed to have lost interest and was bent over his copy of the *Post*. The burnished light seemed to be caught in her hair.

Mr. Gurupadam began to remember other long-forgotten pleasures: running like the wind down a new macadam road in Belgaum; eating hot *upma* and *sambar* while sitting cross-legged on the assiduously swept floor of his home after a month of the clammy rice-and-curd hospital diet; walking to the store by himself to buy a packet of bright pink sweets for a rupee and then walking back slowly without opening the packet, talatalizing himself with the anticipated pleasure.

Suddenly he felt very tired, though just a moment earlier he had felt fresh as a newborn. As the sun shone its dying light directly into his eyes, he had to fight off an urge to cry.

He turned towards the girl and said softly, almost directly into her ear, "It's beautiful."

He rode for a while in silence, happy just to be there. Then the train began wheezing and suddenly came to a stop. Mr. Gurupadam decided to take this opportunity to ask where she was from, but just then a voice on the public address announced, "Next stop: National Airport" and Mr. Gurupadam was struck dumb, just as he had been when he got the telegram announcing his mother's death. Then, no sooner had he heard the announcement than the train arrived at the station. The girl stood up and handed him back his copy of the *Post*. "My stop. See you!"

He stood up with her and took hold of her wrist. "So soon?"

She gave him a look that was more puzzlement than offense. "This is where I get off."

He let go of her wrist and, still holding his newspaper, she jumped through the car doors just as they were about to close. He watched as a young man with a beard and wearing a smart brown jacket put his arm around her and together they walked towards the escalator. Just before they stepped onto it the girl reached behind and deftly tossed the newspaper into a trash bin.

Mr. Gurupadam could not quite take it in that she was gone. He thought of the damage her presence might have done his heart and, placing his hand on his chest, felt carefully for the tender beating of that organ. At first, he could barely feel it, but then it began to pound with a pronounced thut-umph thump, thut-upmh thump. He looked at his wristwatch. Only thirty minutes had passed since he had boarded the train. He closed his eyes. For the first time in many years his mind was not cluttered with anxious thoughts of work or bad health. With his eyes still closed he placed his hand gently on the cushion of the seat the young woman had occupied and traced his fingers in the still warm impression her body had made there. Even the touch of that warm plastic roused in him an aching desire. He withdrew his hand, frightened by the merciless hunger he felt. In this state he let pass the next two Metro stations, including his own, and it was only when the train reached Huntington that he realized his mistake.

He took out his cell phone and dialed his home number to tell his wife he would be delayed. But there was no answer, and he decided not to leave a message. He wanted to surprise her, and knew she would be very surprised indeed. "How different I feel!" he thought as he tapped his toes impatiently for the return train to arrive. The wind flapped his shirt open at the throat. He pushed his hands deep into his pants pockets, leaned against a pillar and began whistling. He took out a pocket comb his wife had given him a long time ago and began pulling it through his thinning gray hair, peering into the glass of a lighted billboard to make sure the strands were all in place.

"Maybe I should dye it," he thought as he stepped into the train that would take him back to his own station. It was all he could do not to keep gazing at his reflection in the window lest everyone else in the car should wonder about him. He thought suddenly of his son, now sixteen. Was this how the boy felt at his first high school dance? A fierce jealousy came over him for all the things the boy had enjoyed that Mr. Gurupadam had not even known existed when he was a youth. But as he stepped off the train his jealousy gave way again to a sense of excited expectation.

The house was dark and empty, but the phone was ringing. He rushed to pick up the handset in the dining room, assuming illogically it would be the girl on the train who was calling. "Hi," he heard a male voice say even before he had a chance to say hello. "Did you get home safe?"

Mr. Gurupadam swallowed hard.

"Ramani?" the voice spoke again, this time hesitantly. Mr. Gurupadam pressed the receiver back in its cradle. He sat down on the living room sofa, feeling suddenly weak and helpless, just as he used to as a child sick with fever.

A few minutes later he heard a tinkle of keys, the front door was opened and there was a whiff of strange perfume. Humming to herself, his wife passed through the small foyer and stood for a moment under the high cathedral windows in the moonlight, not aware of his presence. With a start he saw that she looked almost pretty. Her hair was pulled up into a wide loop and fastened with a silver pin on top of her head. Strands of loose hair clung to her cheeks. Even in the subdued light he could see there was a red flush on her cheeks. Then she turned and saw him, and they stared back at each other in shock and silence.

The World Bank Has A Lot To Learn
(But Not from Where They Think)

By Dana De Zoysa
(Sri Lanka)

It's hard to find anything more visually exotic than a Mumbai streetcorner. Any corner. But seek the Market Economy there? A World Bank & Heritage Foundation Inc. Officially Approved Market Economy? The darling of capitalists and bankers who contemplate the marketplace from their aeries in Manhattan and Zürich? An Officially Approved Market Economy in Mumbai, a city where it's commonplace to see a truck passing with four women standing in the tailgate, about as remote from the World Bank as you can get, their saris fluttering blue/red/gold/green in the exhaust like a rose garden downwind from a coal mine, all of them carrying shovels with which to fill in potholes? An Officially Approved Market Economy (with or without trucks and women with shovels and potholes) that is replicated pretty much all over the world in one form or another, dozens, nay, hundreds of market economies, all different and all composed of people and customs that do not appear on the radars of consultants, advisors, financial analysts, politicians and potentates, despite the fact that such economies are more numerous, more vital, more spirited and infinitely more interesting than the World Bank Officially Approved Market Economy? A *real-econ,* in other words.

Yes, in Mumbai. The *real-econ* market economy is there and, what's more, on a single street corner. In fact, the one nearest my apartment on Best Marg, just down from the Apollo Bund in the Nariman Point part of the city. No Officially Approved entity this:

It's the Market Economy of the Real World Bank.

As a sort of visual canapé, there's a stunning twosome of black ladies from Mali in their brilliant canary-and-tangerine tent-shaped *boubous*, each of which must consume three yards of fabric and the attentions of Lord knows how many village dyers macerating and boiling and leaching for days the seeds and roots and wild flowers that go into the brilliant colors garbing these women, their piled-high hair wrapped in crimson and blue turbans—perfect color-counterpoints to their round-tongued Sahel accents like water running over round stones.

Lesson One to the World Bank: Forget global, look local.

Or, haggling with a stallholder over the price of an unguent, the two Muslim women of the stern Shi'a sect in cloaky black, only their eyes showing, the garb that gives anti-Muslim feminists fits as they selectively nonrecall that not so long ago most Catholic nuns were dressed this way too (and in the contemplative cloistered orders still are). But then, as though sent before our eyes to contradict the ignorances about Islam that non-Muslims love to nourish, we see the Granny-Goose wear of some Borah Muslims, a sect even more doctrinally conservative than Shi'as, yet the most liberal of all Muslims in letting their women choose what they wear. Their dress is the Asian version of the fussily floral, heavily-embroidered coordinated pastels of the 19th-century outfits encountered today only in Laura Ashley shops or forced on daughters whose parents follow some backwater Utah Christian sect but still shop at places like Wal-Mart where, taking one look at these girls in their starched white Anabaptist square collars, you think you have just blundered into *Little House on the Prairie*. So, whose future is the more horizoned, the Borahs or the girls in a Utah Wal-Mart?

Lessons for the World Bank: (a) The image of Islam as a monocratic culture is a lie concocted by publicists in religion's name, not for the betterment of believers but for sacramental lucre, as clear a promo for fast-faith mass-market consumer theology as any you can find; (b) It's hard to fault the dress codes of Islam when the people most likely to do the faulting are mandating similarly strict moral codes of their own back home. When the only difference is the garb, hypocrisy is a transnational coin.

Next we see men faking neurological disorders for the benefit of the tourist trade, who to a man appear to suffer from what might be called *oculus simplissimus touristicosis,* "able to see only tourists," the symptoms of which are an unwillingness to solicit from locals but an unerring eye for tourists, the disorder being manifested by piteous mewling and brandishing of a hand that resembles less a withering atrophy than an impression of a barroom raconteur casting the shadow of a quacking duck with his hands.

Lesson: Potemkin villages for the benefit of visitors are a little more ubiquitous than you think.

In truth, Mumbai has an every-second-counts dissociative inability to separate the act from the play-act, the fact from the nonfact. There is no marketing term for Colaba's ultimate version of reality TV, but by whatever name, by being years behind the Harvard Business School, is in fact years ahead of it.

Or observe the stunningly beautiful threesome of black girls in dreadlocks that you'd swear must be just off the plane from Trinidad, still reeking erotically of ganja and the burnt-grease perfume of dreadlock stabilizers. But then in their first three words you realize they are from Liverpool, because they sound like the Beatles back in Mary Quant days when everybody shopped for bell-bottoms in Chelsea. In the Colaba Causeway Market Economy, what is real can be faked false and what is false can be faked real, just ask the wizened gent selling padded bras.

Lesson: Anderson-style accounting is not a recent development.

Then a couple of spraycan-clad viscose Indian teens, their contours soft as an eyebrow, lovely umber-tan skin and full rich noses with the slight outward curve, voices like honey chattering about Indo-Pop movie hits and heartthrob heroes, the twittery gigglishness of which demonstrates that teentalk here, as everywhere, is a lingo of the loins (left out of discourse in the presence of parents) in which the marvelous curlicues of girl gossip convert desire into the miracles of the lipstick tube and the oversize portrait of the filmthrob hero on the bedroom wall. One of the girls wears a tee-shirt with huge lettering across the front: "I'm the girl your mother warned you about."

Clearly she is far from the section of Mumbai where passersby know her mother. Is this dance around the cosmetics counters really so distant from the half-naked dance around the fire of Surya, the Sun God, Hinduism's seed-capital god, who you can actually feel directly overhead fructifying this era as lovingly he did the Vedic, though those unmoved by matters godly will go no further than conceding it's a bit warmish today? Thus, as was true of those fertility fire dances of old, today, right here on a street corner under the midday Mumbai sun, girls' liptack dreammate lingo, whether Liverpudlian or Mumbaikar, is about boys.

Lessons: (a) Sex sells; (b) Cutesy sex sells better; (c) Youth markets go for the direct approach.

Are you beginning to wonder about the tumultuously associative frothiness of all this? The strung-on sentences five times the length of prim declaratives deemed proper by college prep courses and business-writing classes? The associative flights of ideas and images strung together with commas like beads on a necklace that could land me in a real pickle if I went on like this on an elongated couch in the office of some fellow who has a picture of Freud on the wall?

Lesson: The worst ad hype comes from those who decry it.

Because this is what it's really like to be on a streetcorner in Mumbai, 10:00 a.m. till 8:00 p.m. 24/7, and no breaks for lunch. That fellow Freud could have unblinkered himself a good bit over here. For one, he'd have to redefine insanity, because the entire Colaba Causeway is textbook insanity, just take a look. Why settle for schizophrenia in just a few errant personalities, when you can have 360 degrees of it on a Mumbai street corner simply by turning full circle from where you stand?

Lesson: Reality TV is not new, and in the hands of what Hollywood calls writers, it isn't very well-scripted, either.

Thus far everything said here has been as insignificant in terms of the real world as a schoolroom window filled with those wild colors and inventive shapes that mark a kindergarten water-color lesson.

Let's note something *really* illustrative, like the banana *walla* on the corner of the Causeway and Best Marg. (Disclosure: I buy bananas there. Full disclosure: I know him by name.) *"Walla"* is a jack-of-all-words that usually applies to someone who provides an object or service that otherwise would be of no great importance except that it is considered a minimum daily requirement. Examples: bananas, or endless cups of tea, or the street-stall *iddli* vendors whose mushy fermented rice-flour pancakes look innocent enough until you reach the chillies in the center and the volcano goes off and you need another street *walla* to sell you some cooling curd (high-butterfat yogurt).

Lesson: *Real-econ* markets develop best by first selling the sizzle, then the steak, then the digestive aids.

"Of no great importance" because these folk—India's hundreds of millions of *walla* persons—do not turn up in the *sanctum sanctorum* of the World Bank and its preachy compatriots in their fair-trade temples. It can be legitimately said that we could live without economists (didn't we for thousands of years?) on the grounds that as geniuses of hindsight they rate up there with sports analysts. After all, the banana-*walla* world has managed to survive without economic analysis long before Ph.D.s came along.

Lesson: Because the banana-*walla* world survives without the anointing of the World Bank, and in fact much predates it, streetside GNP is a bigger contributor to social security than the mega-loans World Bank economists crow about.

You can live without the econocuria at the World Bank, but try living without those *wallas.* How could you possibly survive in the Colaba district without their myriad unlicensed stalls, without the pushcart vendors pouring *chai* (sweet milk tea), vending fresh fruits, vegetables, carbohygrease deep-fat- fried nibbles (LDL was around centuries before McDonalds), current newspapers and magazines pulled off stacks on the ground (you'd be ill-read indeed if you expected the India Postal Service to deliver the current issue of an obviously pilferable-for-resale magazine to your door) and useful mechanical implements like screwdrivers, facial tissues, soaps (one brand, four colors), and—if you're local enough—gossip enough to last through the whole day and a dozen neighbors. The banana-*walla* on the corner of Best Marg and Colaba Causeway provides us no-cost delimited-product sales-volume research on a flat piece of cardboard trimmed down from a refrigerator delivery. The bananas are uniformly overripe (tastier that way: refrigeration technology suppresses lingual, glottal, and olfactory stimuli; somebody should do an MBA case study on this). Their skins are streaked with browns and blacks, making for an artistic color scheme which, if you squint your eyes just a little, makes you think Abstract Expressionist started here and is priced cheaper than the taxi fare to a pricey up-Mumbai gallery.

Lesson: If you're in the market for art, the best art is what you see.

This *walla*'s section of "his" sidewalk occupies about twenty square feet of space and twenty seconds of eye time. There's a trigger word in that phrase which has enormous implications for one's stately progress along any street—or thought system—in India. That word is "sidewalk."

Consider the implications inherent in that slender bi-directional piece of concrete Westerners are accustomed to considering "their" (meaning everybody's) right of pedestrian free passage, a space to be kept clean and unencumbered at all times by duly-appointed and paid civic authorities. The cops might bend the rules for two kids with a lemonade stand on a hot Sunday, but try setting up a permanent banana-*walla* stall on a piece of cardboard under the shade of a traffic light in Manhattan and see how far you get. Have you any idea of the number of trees that were sacrificed to the file-cabinet chapels of municipal cathedrals to regulate the urban sidewalk? What would result, in the textbook Libertarian manner, if none of those trees were felled, no code published, and instead there existed the perfect free-market theory of every vendor for themselves? MBA types might rush to their spreadsheets over questions like this, but any Bombay *walla* will tell you in an instant. Very soon there would come into being a natural market mechanism for properly greasing the palm of the proper self-appointed authority—either the local policeman or thug, whoever gets to you first—for looking the other way while you exercise "your" right to "your" twenty square feet in exclusivity, or said policeman/thug (*sama-sama* but for garb) will sell his right to bust you to the next covetous, wealthier *walla* who comes along.

Lesson: Where there's freedom there are thugs, but some wear ties.

The regulated market may be a conceptual foe to, but is in fact an inevitable spawn of, the ideal-case free-market economy. So if an Officially Approved World Bank market economy is impossible in the case of the Colaba Causeway, what happens if you apply the idea of an externally regulated market economy (temporarily overlooking the oxymoron) to the City of Mumbai sidewalk codes? Well, you'd get every street in India, that's what.

Sidewalks in Mumbai, as in most of ex-Brit Asia, are called "five-foot ways," after a British colonial ordinance that allotted a five-foot strip on either side of a thoroughfare for personal passage. Five whole feet? Why, that's an armspan! Enough to accommodate an entire regiment marching abreast with beating drums. Do dream on, code-bearing ideologues, and since you're so naive, make it an economic wet dream and come visit Mumbai. The Brits never gave due thought to the appeal of so much unallocated space to a people who owned no space at all. Title to property deeded onto paper is something for birthright aristocrats and the politically connected. The central cause of Asian poverty isn't absence of a work ethic, it's the inability to borrow money for a business license, house or education because there is no property to put up for collateral. With no title deed you're an encroacher, and please name me the bank that will loan to someone who has nothing to confiscate. That *walla* has brothers, sisters, uncles, aunts, parents, second- and third-cousins running like windrows down both sides of his five-foot property line. Do you foolishly expect him to pay back an impersonal bank, when he is filially obliged to funnel it to family instead? Better to keep it in the family. Not only will you not run afoul of the loan officer, but the taxman neither. Does this in any way quench the entrepreneurial embers? Cast thine eyes about. Compared with what the World Bank proffers, the Mumbai self regulated economy is like a freshman art student's first effort with cast paper hanging next to a Jackson Pollock.

Lesson: If you think that a vibrant, colorful, profit-making, life-style-enhancing goods-and-services economy, far more exciting than anything a supermarket ever offered, cannot develop out of circumstances as woesome as a merciless sidewalk, spend five minutes on a Colaba streetcorner.

Which is not to say that such an endeavor has no social safety net. And, like most social safety nets, this one is grounded on taxes. Those earning their living on twenty square feet of a five-foot way have taxes too—corrupt cops, local politicos who mulct off "party donations," and *gondas*—goons—who act as enforcers for both. It takes a trained eye to spot this system in actual operation. The first thing to look for is silence and a downcast eye as the *walla* dispenses, rather than takes in, hard cash from his money pouch.

Lessons: (a) Corruption is not much intimidated by a legal system motivated by payoffs, (not to mention the fact that a civil suit filed in India today will reach a verdict in approximately 350 years); (b) Substitute "lawyer's fees" in other parts of the world for "350 years" and draw your own conclusions.

One result, unsurprisingly: beggars. Here the World Bank free-market comes into tough sledding. Think not how the beggars got there, for we know India has had them for millennia and this is not the place for an antireligious screed. Rather, think of their organizational stability today, the implications of why, with millions of beggars in Mumbai, there's no tooth-and-claw competition from newcomers for that lucrative-looking curb-corner or the doorway conveniently near an ATM machine. Why aren't such prime locations mobbed with extended palms?

Live here long enough and you see the same waif whining, "No money, you give money, milk only, I show you, you come buy, I hungry." She hits me up every week, and by now we're old pals. But why just her and no others? Mumbai certainly lacks not for waifs. Why does this girl in the ragged blue flounce-dress begging for milk always lead her catch of bleeding-heart tourists to the exact same nearby shop to buy the package? (Heat and sanitation being what they are in Asia, most milk is sold in powdered form.) Why, at the major intersections at whose every red light women pounce on you with their babies and entreaties, why are these always the same women (though the practiced eye sees the babies frequently change moms)? Where's the market mechanisms of competitive price adjustment and entrepreneurial elbowing?

They don't exist. Going freelance as a beggar is suicide by *gonda*. Ever watch those Discovery Channel shows about Chicago in the 1920s? When pols and cops and thugs were both taking whatever they could and the city was an economic sinkhole? Welcome to Mumbai, with its flappers and Gatsbys of today wearing the costumes of Bollywood bimblets and stock market manipulators. The beggars are organized into mafias and, in fact, structurally they are rather like those in old Chicago. The little girl, when her pearl of great price can finally be sold, will end up in a brothel. But for now she gets a rupee for every hundred she receives in kickbacks from the powdered milk shop and gives it over to her mother who gives it over to the *gonda* controlling her corner. For which the mother and the little girl enjoy nights of undisturbed sleep on a newspaper shadowed from the street-lamp by the branches of a date palm.

Look even closer and it is always the same milk box the little girl buys. The milk was emptied of its powder long ago. Today it is filled with the plastic peanuts used to pack crates. No use taking a chance on a box being damaged during this endless round of resales. Lord knows how many substances they went through before arriving at the same heft and feel of powdered milk.

Lesson: Independent contracting everywhere is more heavily predated upon at the shop-floor level than at the management level.

There's a mafia-market system going on right in front of my eyes as I write this. I observe it hardly fifty feet from my Best Marg and Colaba Causeway banana-*walla* spy station. It's run by a taxi driver who hangs out at Stand #4, keeping an eye on his turf, a local brothel named "Comfort Inn." (Lesson: High art in the sleaze world is the single-entendre.) His counterparts, be they pimps or lottery vendors, are all over Mumbai. Ever wonder why you get turned down for a trip to the airport—usually the most lucrative fare in the city because of the high likelihood of a generous tip from foreigners departing

India who can easily be wheedled into parting with their soon-to-be-worthless rupees? That's no bonanza to these fellows. A two-hour trip is two hours away from their minuscule but lucrative empire.

Lessons: (a) Oh, into such gilt cages do they themselves fly; (b) If you found it phrased this way in management textbooks our schools would produce much more interesting managers.

But, alas, we drift from the history and lore of the five-foot walkway. True to the image of iron filings lining themselves up to join the poles of a magnet, the moment the British paved over the mudholes and tree roots and laid the first five-foot walkway out of sawn timbers, sidewalk *wallas* lined themselves up to stake claim to every unencumbered square foot. The only concession demanded by the rent-paying shops about to be obscured behind the piled-high clutter of unrestrained *walla*dom, and begrudged even then, was that the *wallas* yield just enough customer access so as to not cut off access to their premises. Hence today's five-foot way is three feet occupied by stall *wallas* and two for people to pass. Any individual desiring serious progress goes out into the street to fight for right of passage with taxis and bicycles and buses and the fellows pushing petrol-filled barrels and/or fifteen-foot lengths of bamboo on barrows little changed from those carved into Assyrian facades and Theban hieroglyphs. If you think Microsoft versus Oracle is something, go head-to-head for right of way with a barrow pusher and a Mumbai double-decker bus.

Lesson: The end-consumer is always the first fleeced and last served.

According to World Bank economists, the fundamental principle of the market economy is that everything has a price and that price fluctuates according to supply and demand. The World Bank has not spent much time checking out the enforcers, hangers-on, and parasites who enforce the unwritten laws of the Colaba Causeway. It is an utterly inverse economy to the one approved by University of Chicago theorists in their cute bow ties and the Heritage Foundation op-ed writers with their poorly concealed brass knuckles. Instead of prices seeking their lowest common denominator based on supply and demand, Mumbai sidewalk *wallas* set the highest price they think they can get away with. It takes but moments for that price to become known up and down the street. Every other *walla* promptly raises his prices accordingly, under the *real-econ* pricing principle, "If So-and-So Can Get that Much, I'll Ask More." (Quintuple that and you have tourist prices.)

Lessons: (a) It would be awfully nice if globalization advocates would more closely examine the globe they are globalizing; (b) They'll get diarrhea and sniffles if they try, so they won't.

Mumbai is so big, and so great are the infrastructural problems of doing even simple things such as distributing fruit from warehouse to street-hawker stall and corner market, that if you deduct from what you pay for the tangerine backward to the person who grows it, the one who really suffers from the Colaba's *real-econ* is the farmer out in the country. He must accept a pittance for his labor in comparison with the costs of placing it in your hand. He accepts it because if he doesn't someone else will.

Lesson: No matter what economy you devise, its most voluble adherents arrange matters so that the little guy is always the one who gets screwed.

Hence our banana-*walla* is one of hundreds of similar *wallas* necklacing the entire Colaba Causeway, all but closing off the sidewalk for the pedestrian progress originally intended. The likelihood that individual *wallas* will occupy these same pieces of concrete, or that any single *walla* will likely be seen here five or ten years from now, tells you everything you need to know about custom law rather than writ law assuming the regulatory role in Indian cities. These seemingly simple sidewalk empires of today are creatures of time and chance, peopled by both the corrupt and their pawns who are each caught in nets cast by tradition and proclivity and religion and mayhap and luck, upon which they cast nets of their own, twenty square feet at a time, across the Mumbai walks, finding themselves soon entangled with corrupt tax collectors and urban administrators, none of whom bother with formalities like pieces of paper or a sense of propriety. Gills gaping for survival, victim to victimizer to victimhood bequeathed as from mother to child and spouse to spouse, each bound to duty and deed which in due passage of generational nostalgia becomes its own history, the sourcebook of a civilization that, call it caste or call it economy, is but a name for what most people would call hell. Here Dante could be found, except there's no Purgatory and certainly no Paradise. All because of one enormous shift in the mechanism of profit: You are not what you own, you are who you pay to get it. The end justifies the end, and the means justify the means, and that's about the end of things in the theory department. Termites, too, eat the life out of wood and digest it into dust.

So, what does almost every Mumbaikar do when contemplating his dust of the day gone by? Go to a Bollywood film, of course! Where everything is lovely (thanks to special effects and offshore shooting locations) and the birds sing and the voice-overs perfectly timed. A scent of something, yes, but sigh, there also we cannot escape being ruched into a marketer's idea of our place in the great scheme of things. In any given half-hour the heroine will be embraced four to seven times, carry a water jar on her head two to four times, shyly smolder glances at the hero at least three times, go subserviently down on her knee any number of times, indulge in costumey fairytale dancing while somehow singing in perfect pitch without needing to catch her breath, pout, flutter her eyelashes and hide behind the nearest available tall, firm, vertical pillar when the hero nears her. He in turn has been made giddy by the magic wand of her symbol-studded flattery. All this is so obvious that to wrest conclusions from it would litter jetsam on the ubiquity trail.

So instead we must look to reality for our entertainment, on the street corner of Colaba Causeway and Best Marg. There shall we forget the vast stretches of irretrievable theory negated by ordinary streetcorner activity, forget that the original pales before the replica, forget the present and future argument, forget how life reveals meanings and harmonies about which intellect hasn't a clue, and consider the leaps in mood and style, the breadth and design of five minutes spent navigating the sidewalk sea-change of Colaba and Best Marg, metaphor for the fear of insolvency, fear of the unknown, fear translated into images of monsters in local religious shrines, monsters of the long ago, monsters today. Live the *verismo* of every twenty square feet as a mini-colonial empire, corrupt cops on the take and sleazos on the make, today's spice trade of banana and plastic cups of sweet tea, soap in four colors, unguents and cremes and perfumes guaranteed to turn any spare hour into new progeny, the broken-eyed kids who advertise their bodies for sale by coming up alongside you and holding your wrist, the caste of beggars identified by monkeys or parrots chained to their wrists (and please don't be an oaf and enquire who is chained to whom); the incense *wallas* who must mark everything up fifty percent just to recover the costs of their free ads wafting everywhichway, only to vanish by the time their frangipani reaches the narcissus and jasmine of the scent-*walla* ten paces away.

Lesson: Sell the schleps popcorn before you let them see the movie.

Forget that the ugly, gutty, petty side of life can never be outsmarted by the false amity of statistics that honeys the pages of World Bank reports. No, net-cast for the truth instead. Net-cast here on this corner. Where one stray glance picks up the local itinerant knife-grinder, no walkway-bound he, a twentysomething fellow who has rigged his grinding stone between the handlebars of his bicycle to which he has mounted a second sprocket and chain, so that he sharpens by pedaling furiously while leaning the blade onto the stone. The most efficient system imaginable, he even gets his daily exercise. Plus, the sparks fly away from him off the front of the bike so there's no danger of hurting his eyes (protective glasses, they what, *lah*?) He is the most ambulatory, though probably not the freest, man in the district. You know, you just *know*, he has to pay off somebody.

Lesson: The market mechanism encourages as much cynicism as any other system, only it's more sanctimonious about it.

Pause another glance at a street stall offering tamarind accompanying square white *iddlis* of rice flour with raisins, slathered with a thick white sauce of coconut mashed in its own milk and mixed with cashew bits. Surely this is what the gods must have eaten before they decided to become humans, a move they probably have regretted ever since. For gods, as everyone knows, are obliged to live twenty-five thousand years in the being state they elect to become after their twenty-five thousand years as a god. Boy, what a pissy thing to come down from heaven after opting for humanhood only to discover you've opted for a Mumbai street corner.

Lesson: Affix your name to the least possible commitment.

So, away from the gods, too, those dream-releases humans wish but cannot be on this Mumbai streetcorner, away to the Hindu *sadhu* (Godman) herbalist sitting lotus-position in his saffron loincloth like a Buddha without a tree, loops of red holy *rudrushka* beads hanging loosely around his neck, with a vast array of his medicaments before him. Bits of broken bird wing, chips from a dozen or so tree barks, seeds, powders from brilliant-yellow tamarind to deep red paprika, dried leaves in shallow baskets, hedgehog quills, and several dozen icky-goos in dubious phials.

Lesson: For all its technological smugness, allopathy is neither the first nor the best in the snake-oil trade.

At the end of his day he carefully re-lids all the unguent jars, re-baskets the bark and roots and powders, wraps the bird feathers and frog skins in a spindle of cloth, neatly layers his entire pharma-cokinetic shopfront into a pillowcase, rises like Gandhi from a fast, deposits a coin and a prayer in the Shiva temple collection box before which he had been sitting, and simply…vanishes. Swallowed up, just one more exoticism on a street full of them, two miles long, in a city of them, sixty miles long and forty broad.

The market research is over. Nothing has changed on the corner of Best Marg and Colaba Causeway. Except everything. Nothing and everything are pretty much the same in India, so cyclical is the idea of history and so cruel the passage of a life which will only redux itself endlessly. A few bananas sold, a few newspapers and popular magazines have disappeared under tea-and-tiffin-time arms into the cafes where, having been read, they will disappear again into the toilet rooms.

Lesson: Recycling need not be profitable to be economically useful, provided it adopts socially useful forms.

Fifty years ago and fifty years hence not a jot of this will have changed. The individual bodies will be gone but the activities will remain, carried out then as now, done the same way because in India this is how things are done. The machinations of the World Bank are but a conceit: Because we do it this way everybody should do it this way. Up against Colaba, the WB hasn't a chance.

Final Lesson: A real market economy has little to do with markets and even less with economics.

Buscando Un Inca

Por Luis Nieto
(Peru)

Laura Cristóbal, cinco centurias de remordimiento en las valijas, desembarcó en el Cusco dispuesta a encontrar la redención en la utopía, pero al comienzo todo fueron penitencias, pruebas desagradables que hubieran colmado la paciencia de un santo.

Las decepciones empezaron cuando manifestó en la agencia de viajes su deseo de visitar un ayllu y la miraron como a bicho antediluviano: comunidad campesina dirá!. Cuando quedó claro que no había malentendidos, la llevaron a unas comunidades que no se diferenciaban mucho de cualquier pueblito de la sierra madrileña, salvo quizás por la hosquedad de sus habitantes, que a punto estuvieron de arrojarle piedras por fotografiarlos...sin querer soltar una propina.

Más peligrosa resultó su experiencia con un promotor del turismo místico, un antropólogo cusqueño émulo de don Juan (el de Castaneda) que se ofreció gentilmente a abrirle los meandros del alma andina. Había que trepar para ello al Huanacaure, el apu donde según la leyenda Manco Capac enterró la barreta de oro. Una vez en la cumbre, tras embeberse con la belleza de esa mágica ciudad que se extendía a los pies, ingirieron una pócima de San Pedro. Este horrible brebaje, sin embargo, no sólo no ayudó a Laura a comprender más claramente la tripartición del espacio simbólico andino en qollana, payan y cayao, como le había prometido el antropólogo, sino que incluso le hizo perder las elementales nociones de arriba y abajo, de hanan y hurin.

Otro de sus sueños, escuchar de boca de un runa lo menos una de las quince versiones del mito de Inkarri, no lo pudo satisfacer ni Aladino, el chofer de la combi en la que hacía todos los recorridos y que en un descuido del guía—un petimetre que la miraba babeando y que insistía en invitarla a bailar—le dijo que conocía a la persona indicada. La condujo a presencia de un vejete arrugado y sin dientes que mascullaba el castellano a duras penas, pero que en lugar de hablarle del retorno del Inca le empezó a contar de un oso que raptaba doncellas. Laura, que para plantígrados tenía suficiente con el del escudo de su villa, no quiso ni escuchar el final de la historia.

La gota que rebasó el vaso fue su desafortunada incursión en el mundo mágico andino. El anuncio de la radio la llevó a uno de los hoteluchos cercanos al mercado en busca del Gran Maestro Kallawaya, pero lo que hubo en lugar de una iniciación en los antiguos secretos de ese pueblo altiplánico fue el más descarado y menos mágico de los intentos de meter mano a la gringa. Con los frenos vaciados por efectos del alcohol, el gran maestro se empecinó en desnudarla para pasarle un cuy negro por el cuerpo. Tuvo que salir a relucir el mal genio de Aladino para que el borrachín dejase las manos quietas, pero igual a Laura Cristóbal le quedó la impresión de que los peruanos eran un hato de zoofílicos: las doncellas se enredaban con osos y los hombres se excitaban frotando con unas ratas peludas a sus mujeres.

Curada de sus inclinaciones antropológicas, de su afán de encontrarse cara a cara con la historia, decidió volver al redil para terminar de conocer el Cusco como una más de la manada de turistas, cámara fotográfica en bandolera y un enjambre de vendedores de chucherías siguiéndola a todas partes. Compró también varios juegos de las postales de Chambi y aprovechaba las pausas del día para volcar en pocas líneas la decepción que se estaba llevando. El encuentro que cambió su suerte tuvo lugar justamente mientras garabateaba una postal—la de la familia jugando al sapo—en el "Varayoc". Le habían advertido repetidas veces sobre los bricheros, esos cusqueños que viven de engatuzar gringas, y como tal catalogó inmediatamente al tipo—cabello largo, sombrero Túpac Amaru, chaleco de Taquile y camisa de bayeta—que se dirigía a ella desde la mesa del lado. Española?, insistió el gigolo al no recibir respuesta. ¿Brichero?, decidió cortar ella por lo sano. No creas que me molestaría admitirlo si lo fuera—respondió él de lo más fresco, sentándose a la mesa de ella—pero no, no soy brichero, soy un inca, seguramente uno de los últimos incas. Y yo la tataranieta de Pizarro, mucho gusto, le extendió Laura la mano. No estás tan lejos de la verdad, aceptó él el saludo y pasó a lo de los sueños. Yo te he hecho el amor anoche. Busca en tu memoria. Tú estabas en un sitio elevado—al principio te pareció que era una fortaleza incaica, pero luego resultó ser el torreón de un castillo—y un águila describía círculos encima tuyo. No era águila, era un cóndor, yo era ese cóndor. Te estaba rondando, te estaba amansando para hacerte el amor. Dale con la zoofilia, pensó Laura, suficientemente espantada ya con el solo hecho de que un extraño le leyera la mente. Estaba segura, doblemente segura porque efectivamente acababa de hacer memoria, de que no había hablado con nadie sobre su extraño sueño, menos sobre el estado de excitación—la entrepierna mojadita—en que había despertado.

La llegada de tus antepasados fue anunciada por un presagio de signo inverso: durante la fiesta del sol un cóndor fue atacado por varios halcones hasta que el mallki, el ave sagrada, se desplomó agonizante en medio de la gran plaza del Cusco. Yo he cobrado revancha, revancha simbólica. De otro modo no hubiera podido acercarme a ti, no en igualdad de condiciones, sino siempre como vencido a vencedor.

El mate de coca había sido reemplazado por un par de pisco sours. Laura estaba cautiva del encanto, de la magia de avizorar un nuevo mundo: los primeros seres de la creación fueron los munay, vivían en medio del caos, sólo para amarse. Luego fueron creados los llamkaq, pero como todo era trabajo tampoco había felicidad. La tercera edad fue la de los yachay, de los sabios, de los que combinaban amor y trabajo. Tú eres una yachay, fría, puro intelecto. Yo soy un munay, vivo para el amor.

Esa noche Laura durmió inquieta, soñó de nuevo con cóndores que revoloteaban encima de ella sin acabar de decidirse a descender y atacarla. ¿Gonzalo?, se preguntó incrédula al abrir los ojos, recordando al enigmático personaje de la víspera. La había impresionado y la perturbaba, tenía que admitirlo, pero igual decidió no pensar más en él. Atrás había quedado el momento de tender puentes y en sus últimos días en Cusco cualquier acompañante, hasta su fiel Aladino, sólo sería una carga, una verdadera joda. Por eso, ni bien tuvo un par de tostadas y un café en el estómago, partió, siguiendo su primer impulso, a Sacsayhuamán.

Su humor no podía ser mejor. Trepaba las empinadas callejuelas con soltura, como si toda su vida hubiera vivido entre riscos. Volaba casi o, por lo menos, sentía que volaba, que se liberaba poco a poco de tensiones, depresiones, temores, en general de ataduras. Alzaba la vista al cielo, de un azul profundo, y no encontraba una sola nube. Días así, pensó.... Días así son los propicios para entrar en relación con el ukupacha.

Frenó en seco y buscó a su alrededor: a un lado, sentado al borde del camino, estaba Gonzalo, con el sombrero negro en la mano. Era él quien había hablado y, sonriendo, seguía hablándole. ¿Co, co, cómo...?, trastabilló Laura en las palabras. No te preocupes cómo. Vamos, tenemos muchas cosas para hacer, la apuró.

Dejaron Sacsayhuamán a la izquierda y enfilaron hacia Quenco. El ukupacha, empezó a explicarle Gonzalo, es el mundo de adentro, el mundo interior, donde viven los dioses. El kaypacha es el mundo exterior, el de encima, el actual, donde habitamos los humanos. El hanaqpacha es el mundo superior, de promisión y abundancia, al que se llega, tras penoso viaje, una vez muertos. En esta cueva, Illapata—habían llegado en efecto a una cueva—entraremos en relación con el kaypacha. Gonzalo sacó un envoltorio de la bolsa que tenía colgada al hombro y, como aclaró, empezó a hacer un despacho. Laura contenía la respiración para no perderse detalle, preguntaba por cada cosa, por cada semillita, cada lanita, cada hoja que Gonzalo, susurrando extraños conjuros en quechua, cogía en sus manos.

No puedo andar pregonando que soy un inca, le explicó una vez acabado el despacho, mientras se dirigían, en un volkswagen destartalado surgido de la nada, a la laguna de Huacarpay, treinta kilómetros al sur de la ciudad, pero eso sí, puedo proclamar que soy salq'a, brujo. Mi maestro fue el altomisayoq Benito Kana, de Huasao, el único que conversaba no sólo con el Pitusiray y el Huanacaure, sino con el mismísimo apu Ausangate. Don Benito me eligió, me dejó su mesa.

La historia, un poco confusa pero excitante, perturbadora, continuó a orillas de la laguna, entre las totoras, donde, tras enterrar el despacho para entrar en relación con el ukupacha, el mundo subterráneo, empezaron a besarse, a revolcarse, a enredarse en las prendas de las que querían deshacerse, Laura, olvidadas las suspicacias, diciendo ahora comprendo por qué dices que eres munay y él acariciando sus senos, Laura jugueteando con esa rebelde caballera negra, delineando esos rasgos angulosos, y él hablando, con su voz inquietante como el ulular del viento, de la fiesta de la nieve, de los pabluchas que ascienden a la cumbre del nevado y luego traen el hielo hasta el Corpus del Cusco para ordenarse sacerdotes andinos en las narices de los curas, en la catedral misma, Laura gimiendo de placer, diciendo quiero ser una munay y él incrédulo de tener a mujer tan provocativa y bella en sus brazos, Laura emocionada hasta las lágrimas de haber encontrado un inca y él pensando maldición mi imperio por ella....

In Search of an Inca
(Buscando un Inca)

By Luis Nieto
(Peru)
Translated by Diane Johnson

Laura Cristóbal—five centuries of remorse in her suitcases—disembarked in Cuzco, Peru, prepared to find redemption in utopia. But, right from the start, it was all penance, disagreeable tests that would have overwhelmed the patience of a saint.

The disappointments began at the travel agency when she stated her desire to visit an *ayllu* and they looked at here like an antediluvian insect: "You mean a peasant community?" When it became clear there was no misunderstanding, they took her to some villages that were not much different from any village in the mountains near Madrid, with the possible exception of the sullenness of the inhabitants who, at being photographed, were prepared to hurl rocks and thus unwittingly blow a nice tip.

Her experience with an anthropologist from Cuzco turned out to be more dangerous. He graciously offered to open the meanderings of the Andean soul to her. In order to do so, they had to climb up to the sacred hilltop of Huanacaure where, according to legend, Manco Capac buried his golden staff. Once at the top, after becoming engrossed in the beauty of the magical city spread at their feet, they ingested a potion from San Pedro. This horrible drink not only did not help Laura to understand the tripartite division of Andean symbolic space into *collana, payan* and *cayao* more clearly, as the anthropologist had promised, but actually made her lose her basic notions of up and down, of *hanan* and *hurin*.

Not even Aladino, the chauffeur of the mini-bus in which she made all her trips, could satisfy her other dream: to hear at least one of the fifteen versions of the myth of Inkarri from the mouth of a real *runa*. The careless guide—a fop who drooled at the very sight of her and who insisted on asking her to dance—told her he knew where just such a guide could be found and took her to a wrinkled old codger with no teeth who was barely able to mumble some rudimentary Spanish. Instead of speaking of the return of the Inca, he started to tell her the story of a bear that kidnapped maidens. Laura, who had already had enough of plantigrades from the coat of arms of her native city, refused to listen to the rest of the story.

The straw that broke the camel's back was her unfortunate incursion into the world of Andean magic. The ad on the radio directed her to one of the fleabag hotels near the market in search of Kallawaya, the Great Teacher. But, instead of an initiation into the ancient secrets of the highland people, she discovered a most impudent and unmagical attempt to paw her *gringa* flesh. Her inhibitions gone thanks to the effects of some alcohol, the great teacher insisted on undressing her and then passing a black guinea pig all over her body. Aladino managed keep the drunkard's hands off her, but all the same, there remained for Laura the impression that Peruvians were a herd of zoophilists: maidens who became entangled with bears who in turn became excited by rubbing women with hairy rats.

Cured of her anthropological inclinations—of her zeal to meet history face to face—she decided to return to the fold and came to know Cuzco like just any other tourist, brandishing her camera while a swarm of trinket-sellers followed here everywhere. She also bought several sets of postcards by the Peruvian photographer Chambi and managed to convey in a few lines the illusion that she was getting along just fine. The encounter that finally turned things around for her occurred as she was scribbling away on one of these—the one with the family playing the toad game—in the Café Varayoc.

She had been warned repeatedly about *bricheros*, those Cusqueans who live just to seduce *gringas*, and that was how she immediately pegged the guy who had just addressed her from the next table—

long hair, Tupac Amaru hat, vest from the Lago Titicaca island of Taquile and shaggy wool shirt.

"Are you Spanish?" he persisted after receiving no answer.

"Are you a *brichero*?" she replied, deciding to cut to the chase.

"Don't think I would hesitate to admit it if I were," he responded brashly, sitting down at her table. "But, no, I'm not a *brichero*. I'm an Inca, surely one of the last."

"And I'm the great-great granddaughter of Pizarro. Nice to meet you," she said, offering her hand.

"You're not far from the truth," he said, accepting the greeting at face value and passing on to her dreams. "I made love to you last night. Search your memory. You were at a high altitude—at first it seemed an Inca fortress to you, but it turned out to be the tower of a castle—and an eagle flew in circles above. No, it wasn't an eagle, it was a condor. And I was that condor. I was circling you. I was preparing you for my lovemaking."

Give up the zoophilism, Laura thought, already frightened by the fact that a stranger was reading her mind. She was sure—doubly sure because she just now remembered the dream—that she hadn't told anybody about it, not to mention the state of wet excitement in which she had awakened.

"Your ancestors' arrival was heralded by a bad omen: during the Sun festival a condor was attacked by several falcons until the *mallki*, the sacred bird, fell dead in the middle of Cuzco's main plaza. I was gathering revenge, symbolic revenge. There was no other way I could have approached you, not certainly as an equal, but only as conquered or conqueror."

Their coca tea was replaced by a pair of *pisco* sours. Laura was now captive to the spell, to the magic of seeing a new world unfold.

"The first beings of creation were the *munay*; they lived in the middle of chaos, loving only each other. Then the *llank'aq* were created, but since everything required hard work, there wasn't much happiness. The third age was that of the *yachay*, the sages, those who combined love and work. You are a *yachay*, cold, pure intellect. I am a *munay*; I live for love."

Laura slept uneasily that night. She dreamed again of condors that fluttered above without having yet decided to descend and attack her. "Gonzalo?" she thought incredulously as she opened her eyes, remembering that strange evening. He had impressed and perturbed her, she had to admit, but all the same she decided not to think about him anymore. The moment for building bridges had passed. In her last days in Cuzco, any companion, even her faithful Aladino, would only be a burden and a nuisance. For that reason, with no better than a couple of pieces of toast and some coffee on her stomach, she set out, following her first impulse, for Sacsayhuam.

Her mood couldn't have been better. She climbed the steep alleys with ease as if she had lived all her life among mountain crags. Raising her eyes to the profoundly blue sky, she felt capable of flying, felt liberated little by little of all tension, depression, fear—of physical bonds in general. Days like this, she thought.... Days like this are propitious for entering into relation with the *ukupacha*."

She stopped and looked around: Gonzalo was sitting at the side of the road, his black hat in his hand. Smiling, he continued, "Don't worry how. Come on, we have a lot to do."

They left Sacsayhuam and headed toward Quenco. "The *ukupacha*," Gonzalo explained, "is the world within, the inner world where the gods live. The *kaypacha* is the exterior world, the actual—the one we inhabit. The *hanaqpacha* is the higher world of promise and abundance, where one arrives after a painful journey following death. In this cave, *Illapata*"—they had in fact arrived at a cave—"we will enter into relation with the *kaypacha*."

Gonzalo removed a bundle from the bag hanging from his shoulder and, explaining as he worked, began to prepare a shrine. Laura held her breath so as not to miss any detail, asking about each tiny seed, each little piece of wool, each coca leaf that Gonzalo, whispering strange incantations in Quechua, collected in his hands.

When the shrine was finished he said, "You can't go around divulging that I'm an Inca," as he steered a ramshackle Volkswagen toward Lake Huacarpay, thirty kilometers to the south of the city. "But, yes, I can tell you that I am a *layqa*, a sorcerer. My teacher was the *altumisayuq* Benito Kana of Huasao, the only person who conversed not only with the Pitusiray and the Huanacaure, but also with the mountain god Ausangate itself. Don Benito chose me. He bequeathed me his office."

The story—confusing but exciting, even perturbing—continued all the way to the shores of the lake, and then into the rushes where, burying the shrine for the purpose of entering into relation with *uku-pacha*, the subterranean world, they began kissing, rolling over and over on the ground, entangling themselves in the physical accidents from which they were attempting to break loose: Laura, her suspicions put aside, "I understand why you say that you are *munay*." He, caressing her breasts as she toys with that rebellious head of black hair, tracing his angular features. His voice like the ululation of the wind at the Snow Festival, like the voices of the devotees who climb to the top of the highest peak and bring back ice to Cuzco's Feast of Corpus Christi, where they ordain Andean priests under the very noses of the curates in the cathedral. Laura moaning with pleasure: "I want to be a *munay*!" He, unable to believe he has a woman so provocative and so beautiful in his arms. She, moved to tears at having finally found her Inca. He thinking, Damn my empire for her...!

The Queen Of Tobacco

By Beatrice Lamwaka
(Uganda)

I lifted my head off the pillow. Mosquitoes shamelessly buzzed near my left ear. I had already spent a long time in bed without feeling sleepy. I thought of the fifty years I had spent on this earth, but all that came to mind were the ten sons I bore, who had neglected me for their wives and children…my sons and the long hours I had spent in the garden. They say god created everyone for a purpose. But, what was the purpose of an old woman who couldn't afford tobacco for ten shillings? All she could do was beg and beg. Could god create a no-good just to beg and beg until her last hour? These questions filled my mind. Oh how I wish Lutukamoi hadn't gone hunting and…that elephant had not killed him. What an old woman can wish for.

The urge for *taa*, ground tobacco, was back again. I felt nauseous, and for once I was envious of Alim, who always looked at me with bewilderment every time I told her I needed to smoke. I knew it would be a long night, like it always was when I failed to get a spoonful of tobacco.

It was probably ten o'clock. The compound was quiet, only Atuku's baby, Otim, was yelling every time his mother gave him a slap for disturbing her.

I stretched my hand out to grab the old tin where I kept tobacco. I knew it was empty, but I checked all the same. Somehow something could have happened. The gods could have decided to show their presence.

"Don't I always pour water for them before I drink, even food I give them," I told myself aloud.

But it was as if the empty tin contained all the disappointment I had gathered throughout my life, so I threw it across the hut, hitting the water pot noisily.

At first I had hated the idea of sleeping alone in my hut, but now I cherished the privacy.

Lazily I dragged myself out of the rugs I called my bed to check if the fire I had used to cook the evening meal was still burning. I used my finger to explore the ashes. It was still hot, I could get a live coal, I told myself.

The pawpaw leaves I had smoked earlier had not helped my craving for tobacco. Instead, they had increased it mercilessly.

Without thinking, I tore off a piece of my bed sheet, rolled it like a cigarette and was about to light it when I realised what a shameful thing I was doing. With nothing left to do, I went back to bed.

I lay there like a watchdog for a long time with nothing to occupy my sluggish mind. Then suddenly there was the sweet smell of tobacco entering my nostrils.

Excited, I threw off my blanket and followed the smell into Akwero's deserted hut, built away from the compound. I did not care to question who this late-night smoker might be. I was too determined to have my share.

As I neared the door of the hut I cleared my throat to announce my presence. Dead silence was the only response to my intrusion.

"Odi!" I said.

"Mama, come in," a strange voice answered.

I bent down a little to avoid my head striking the grass roof.

When my foot was inside I took a quick glance to see who my saviour could be. But what I saw made my whole body shrink with fear: men of various sizes dressed in dark clothes with rifles slung on their backs. And on the floor lay *pangas* and axes.

"Mama, what do you want?" the man near the door asked.

I gained some confidence when he called me Mama. But how else should he address a fifty-old-woman dying for a smoke? I lowered my voice as best I could and said, "My sons, tobacco," and exhaled heavily.

My answer produced laughter, but they laughed silently as if trained to laugh so as not to be heard. I joined in the laughter, only mine was the laugh of a coward trying to calm herself.

"Okello! Give her some," a voice near me said.

Okello thrust his hand into his pocket and pulled out a black bag tied together with string.

"Give her all of it," the voice said.

"Mama, let me help you," a voice in the middle of the hut said. He took the bag from Okello and poured some dried, pounded to-bacco into his hand. With his other hand he took a piece of paper from the man who was giving orders, then carefully rolled a cigarette and put into my hand the thing I had been aching for.

"Thank you," I said.

A man near the fire picked up some burning wood. I put the cigarette in my mouth and lit it. I saw now that all the men were smoking. We formed a smoking class, myself included. Finally I had the thing that had been keeping me awake all night. We all seemed united, united by this bond. We inhaled and exhaled as if we had rehearsed this all our lives and today was the big day to show off our talents. I was the happiest of all. The Queen of Tobacco. I didn't care what happened next, as long as I had got the thing that could make me sleep. I didn't even care if they killed me. But why would they? They had called me "Mama." Who would kill his mother? I told myself, and began to smoke with more confidence.

When the cigarette was finished I thanked them and said it was time for me to leave, the rest of the tobacco still clutched in my hands.

"Not yet," the leader said. "Mama, you should know that a visi-tor does not leave immediately after eating her food."

"My son, you have spoken right," I replied.

They all nodded in unison. I took this opportunity to count them. They were nine in number. Nine against one. There was dan-ger in lingering, I told myself. I had to outwit them.

"My sons, daybreak is soon," I said.

"Didn't you know that when you came here?" a voice said.

I decided not to look at any of them squarely.

"Don't be rude to Mama," another said.

I was determined not to confront this one either.

"Mama, we have come to take the cows you have. We know you will go now and give the alarm, and we do not want that."

The cows he was speaking of belonged to my co-wife, Atima. I did not care if they took them, because they were her great source of pride.

"I will not give the alarm," I said.

"You think we are stupid?"

How could I explain to them that Atima had never given me a moment's peace ever since her daughter had married? Or how Atima had called me a witch when one of her children fell sick? How could I tell them this, I kept thinking.

"Tell us what we should do with you?"

"Let me go into my hut, and you can lock me up there."

"Are there no other people there?"

"I sleep alone."

"Time is running out, we must do it fast."

"Maybe we should just lock up her mouth with a padlock."

"That's a good idea."

"Please don't hurt me," I begged, going on my knees.

"We shall make you quiet for the rest of the night," their leader said.

I begged them to let me go, but nobody took any notice of my plea. I had become a ghost to them. One said I was an old woman who meant no harm. The others didn't agree with him and said I had a tongue and soon they would be caught. Is that what they wanted?

I thought this was a good opportunity for me to slip out of the hut. But as soon I started inching toward the door a coarse hand grabbed me.

"See what she is capable of?"

They all turned to stare at me.

"Okay, now watch," he said.

Grabbing me by the hair, he pulled me down. I felt my bones object noisily. My mouth was now flat against the rough floor that had not been compacted with cow dung in quite a long time. With the force of a possessed animal he ground my mouth against it, back and forth. I didn't resist, afraid I would only cause myself more pain. I thought I was going to die and closed my eyes as if to say goodbye to the world. I didn't even think to scream. I could feel the ground was wet either with my saliva or my blood. When he suddenly let me go, I let out a yell like a hyena.

"Silence!"

"We will shoot you!"

My head felt heavy and numb. My face was burning as if pepper had been rubbed on it.

"Now we can take her home, just to be sure she doesn't breathe a word to anyone."

A handful of them followed my unsteady steps toward my hut. When they were sure I would be alone there, they left without saying another word.

I realised I still had the bag of tobacco clutched in my hands. I knew I was safe now, so I put the bag in the pot, and it was only then that I realised I was shaking from hair to toes. I let my exhausted flesh sink onto the bed. I do not know how long I lay there, but I kept thinking about what had just happened to me and shook all the more.

When I opened my eyes I saw that my lips were badly swollen and I knew it was dawn. Atima's scream startled me. Then I heard footsteps and the voices of Okello, Lanyero, Ojok, Arac, Aber. I opened my mouth to call Arac, but I couldn't move my upper lip and, looking down, it was so grotesquely big that I had no trouble seeing it.

I heard Ojok calling my name and then his heavy step approaching my door. I sat still as a dummy waiting for the shocked expression on his face and his demand to know what had happened. How would I be able to tell him? How could I tell them I had seen the men who took the cattle, or that I had shared a cigarete with them?

VS Naipaul: A Life In Full

By Raymond Ramcharitar
(Trinidad & Tobago)

In a review of VS Naipaul's latest novel, *Half a Life*, in the London *Guardian* a few weeks ago, one-time Naipaul protégé Paul Theroux concluded sardonically: "Without Naipaul's name on it, *Half a Life* would be turned down in a flash. With his name on it, of course, its trajectory is certain: great reviews, poor sales, and a literary prize."

Well, even a stopped clock is right twice a day, and Theroux must be decomposing atom by atom in the horror of his prophecy right about now, and he'll have plenty of company. With the award of the Nobel Prize for Literature, Sir Vidiadhar Surajprasad Naipaul will now have received every literary award of importance open to him, from the Booker to the WH Smith Award.

The Nobel has been long seen as his Waterloo, given the conservatism of the judges in favour of political correctness and Naipaul's lifelong refusal to be politically correct. Not to mention that with the award to Dario Fo a few years ago (no one was more surprised than Fo himself was, the reports went), the prize lost some of its élan for some people.

But whether this signals a change in Nobel selection politics or is just a spike in the graph, this year's choice is one of the better ones the Academy has made for several years, and one of the more controversial. There is hardly a corn on the feet of the denizens of the brave new world of globalist political correctness that Naipaul hasn't stomped on: the feminists, the post-colonialists, the Afrocentrists, the Islamicists, the entire sub-continent of India, most of the Caribbean, and intellectuals of virtually every stripe and proclivity who do not relish having their theories blemished by mere fact. All have formed an extraordinary consensus in their hatred of him.

But several things make the Naipaul award particularly appropriate. As an observer of global consciousness, his prescience, and its precise translation into prose, is astounding. In his Islamic travel books, Naipaul presented the Islamic world as backward and isolationist, a view which earned him the disdain of critics like (Palestinian-American) Edward Said—until the September 11th attacks made those sentiments seem prophetic. His views on Africa ("Africa has no future.") have been bitterly criticised, but not refuted. And the same can be said for his views on the West Indies—"unfinished societies" where "power was recognized, but dignity was allowed to no one."

As a writer of prose fiction, his mastery of and departure from the conventional novel might not have been entirely original, but they are certainly among the most successful attempts of the century to force the traditional nineteenth-century novel to evolve. This is something Joyce supposedly had the final word on with *Ulysses* and which only a few other artists—Nabokov with *Pale Fire*, and Milan Kundera with his entire oeuvre—have seriously attempted to continue.

After the early picaresque works beginning with *Miguel Street*, Naipaul mastered the conventional novel form (linear narrative, stock characters, and the requisite social-political theme) with *A House for Mr Biswas*, and thereafter produced *The Mimic Men, Guerillas, A Bend in the River* and a few other autobio-historical fiction narratives like *In a Free State, The Loss of Eldorado* and the travel works. But it wasn't until 1987 that he produced his most enduring masterpiece—*The Enigma of Arrival* which, apart from containing some of the most beautiful prose in English, blends pastoral fantasy, autobiography, essay and social critique into a form that is, and is not, a novel. With its experimental narrative sequence *A Way in the World*, his next work, is an enigmatic book whose secrets are perhaps not for this age. And now with *Half a Life*, Naipaul has returned to the world of the conventional novel in triumph—or perhaps just in exhaustion.

But more fascinating than any particular artistic achievement is the place Naipaul holds in the intellectual world. He occupies several mutually exclusive positions: He has preeminence in the literary sphere, but he has denounced most contemporary literary activity as tripe; he's a former colonial who has trashed his place of birth because it is the home of stupidity, theft and a region where nothing original is created; he's an emigrant who has denounced his adoptive British home, calling Prime Minister Tony Blair a cultural vandal. And as an artist he has always held his position to be one of dedication to the uncompromising truth—a Utopia if there ever was one in its literal meaning. These qualities—self-imposed exile, permanent dissatisfaction with the world's idea of itself and impatience with those unable to keep up—perfectly illustrate the post-modern condition: living in a state of permanent uncertainty, a disdain for atavism and an unquenchable urge for the future. Hence the crux of what it is to be Naipaul: The boundaries between Sir Vidia and his art are permeable and infinitely elastic.

In each of the novels there is the resurgence of autobiographical themes, what Caryl Phillips, reviewing *Letters to a Father and Son* in the *New York Review of Books* last year, called a "self-aggrandizing, and frankly embarrassing narrative into the literary conscience of the West."

But Naipaul may be just as hard on himself as he is on everyone else, and might even have a sense of humour about it—a very dark one, let it be said. His celebrated admission that he was a "great prostitute man" to the *New Yorker* 's Stephen Schiff in 1995 raised the matter of his poor treatment of his long-suffering wife, Pat. His unwillingness to pick up a check at restaurants (and many other petulant revelations) were revealed in Theroux's stinky tell-all last year. Naipaul is well-known for being a demon about money and reducing unprepared interviewers to tears, as he did a certain Trinidadian journalist who has since happily recovered.

Which brings us to Trinidad itself. Most bookstores here carry his books, and I believe the poor Carnival-loving youth are even coerced to read them for exams. How much of those books they (and their teachers) actually understand is another matter. How much of Naipaul any Trinidadian understands is an open question. The decadent classes, at least, know his work; but it's fashionable if not de rigeur, for black intellectuals to revile him. As for Indians, well, who knows if the average Indian businessman even owns a book that contains anything other than receipts.

Naipaul's lack of popularity in his homeland is not without cause. Throughout his career he has made harsh statements about Trinidad—"harsh" being a way of saying "the truth we don't want to hear." His most incisive work about the islands remains *The Middle Passage*. Written in the 1960s, Naipaul talks about Trinidadian "second rate newspapers," a cinema-going audience capable of responding only to a narrative that is projected onto a screen, television advertisements that feature either very light brown or white actors, and—most damningly—his statement that "the only convention the West Indian knows is his involvement with the white world." That he's still right forty years later has certainly not made him the darling of Trinidadians who talk the talk but walk the walk of racial subservience. But Naipual's criticisms are by no means unique. Many have been echoed with considerably more virulence by Derek Walcott in his autobiographical *Another Life* and in his essays "What the Twilight Says" and "The Muse of History," published back in the 1970s.

The award of the Nobel Prize at least may cause more Trinidadians, as well as people all over the world, to look again at the first Trinidadian (and we're claiming him, dammit) to win the planet's most prestigious literary honour.

Ali's Pictures

By Veronica Khokhlova
(Ukraine)

But where we live
we speak only of death and think
of somewhere else
     —Karen Alkalay-Gut

Ali falls asleep immediately after a long day of trying to be what she cannot be. She tries to be a newspaper reporter; but she doesn't really want to be one. She just needs to make some money over the summer to stop being dependent on her parents. She's exhausted from running all over campus, observing things she could have turned into wonderful photographs. Instead, she has to write about them, journalistically, and with a slight accent. Ali can't help the accent, even when she writes.

She feels she uses too many words when she writes about a biology professor's wife who, on the day a tornado hit town, was sucking gasoline out of her car through a tube connected to a plastic milk bottle and then ran upstairs with that gas to feed the generator that helped nurture the unique bacteria that were her husband's decade-long work.

Way too many words she uses. Pictures would say it so much better. But the newspaper has enough photographers already.

Ali falls asleep on her bed by the window, and I try to lie quiet on the mattress we have laid on the floor next to the bed. Suddenly sirens go off nearby. While the noise rages I lie thinking about Haifa and how one night, in order to fall asleep, instead of sheep I used to count the sounds of distant ambulances.

I can't sleep listening to such a bedlam, but I can't bear to see Ali awakened. So I leave the house to conduct an impromptu investigation. Driving around the neighborhood, I smell burnt rubber. The street parallel to ours is blocked, awash in the blinding lights of police cars and fire trucks. I can only get to the fire on foot, so I go back to the house and talk one of our sleepless housemates into leaving his computer for a while to keep me company.

One building is already a wreck. We sit on some steps across the street, watching the police and firefighters, smoking and talking about life's unpredictabilities. Even a small college town has plenty of surprises in store. The night is warm, someone has just become homeless, and one journalist who would have loved to cover the story is, hopefully, asleep.

The next morning I wake up at seven to drive Ali to class. If I don't give her a ride she has to take a bus and so get an hour less of sleep. I ask whether the noise woke her last night, but she says she didn't hear a thing. I'm glad and don't bother telling her that she slept through a good story.

Even now, two years later, it cheers me to think she slept well that night—as if she had been my daughter instead of just my friend.

Somebody's Daughter, Somebody's Son

Two years later, Ali is dead. Nine other people have been killed with her. I wonder if she knew any of them. I doubt it. I know how much she liked to take solo walks in the crowded parts of every city she visited. This time the city happened to be Tel Aviv.

Ali: a Jewish girl, not an Arab boy. A redhead.

Her father used to be my father's best school friend back in Russia. Ali's real name was Alexandra.

My father emigrated to the United States in 1975 when he was twenty-three, without a cent in his pocket, leaving nothing worthwhile behind but his memories and a few relatives who pretended they were not Jewish. In the States he met my American-born mother.

Ali's father caught my own father's spirit of adventure soon afterwards and managed to persuade his wife and her parents to move to Israel with him.

It wasn't just an itch to see the world that lured them out of the Soviet Union during one of its most stagnant, stifling periods. Once, when I was eleven I was sitting on the couch with my father watching television, a feature on a Holocaust survivor whose memoir had just been published. At one point I asked him what "anti-Semitism" meant. He turned toward me, took off his silver-rimmed glasses and carefully wiped them on his T-shirt. Then he put them back on, got up and lit a cigarette.

"You don't know what anti-Semitism is?"

I shook my head.

"You're serious?"

After an awkward pause, he said, "Here is yet another reason why I was right to emigrate!" Then he went looking for my mother to tell her how smart he was to be raising his kids in the United States, and how lucky she was as an American not to have to live in Russia, and how blessed—blessedly ignorant—his daughter was as well.

Ali grew up in Tel Aviv but visited us every year, always in the summer. We used to spend time in Israel, too, during winter break. But most of my mother's Israeli relatives lived in and near Haifa, and we never had quite enough time to get down to Tel Aviv to visit Ali's family. My memories of Israel are full of my aunts' and cousins' food, which I was always full of when I was there.

From her visits with my family Ali learned that a typical American Jewish family was comprised of a few hundred grandparents, cousins, in-laws, uncles, aunts, nieces and nephews, some of whom were lawyers, some hippies selling stuff at flea markets down South, a few shrinks, a few Communists and one or two who somehow happened to be Italian and Catholic. Many seemed to be spending their lives commuting to and from each other's suburban homes to spread gossip, celebrate wedding anniversaries, birthdays, all the Jewish holidays as well as Christmas and to watch Stanley Cup games.

Ali was used to our medley of a family and fit in almost perfectly. Only a few of my relatives treated her as a foreigner, though discretely, with studied good manners and subdued interest, calling her exclusively by her full, non-Arabic, name—Alexandra.

"Ali" was the name given her by her parents' Arab friends who had studied in the Soviet Union, spoke Russian fluently and seemed too preoccupied with scientific theories to be bothered by someone's being Jewish. But, for my father, Ali was always Sasha, and sometimes when he was in an especially sentimental mood, he called her Shurka. Both diminutives were Russian and both were used for females as well as males, he once explained to me. He pronounced either name with a nostalgic smile and with a funny accent that he managed to otherwise conceal.

My father played chess with Ali ever since she was eight years old, something that made me jealous, whether it was because he was paying so much attention to her or because of the time that she was devoting to him instead of to me. Often they switched to Russian, which no one in our extended family understood. But despite my jealousies, I loved listening to them, as if they were total strangers miraculously transported to our house, like unicorns that would vanish if I so much as said a single word in English.

Ali's family always seemed overwhelmingly small to me. Her parents and maternal grandparents lived in Israel, and her only aunt was married to a Russian in Minsk. The aunt had chosen to stay in the Soviet Union, not inclined to emulate her brother's act of abandoning the glorious motherland. Twenty years later she regretted her decision and in every letter to her Israeli splinter of the family complained that her salary had shrunk to $15 a month and that she was starving. She visited Israel once, as a guest and potential immigrant, but quickly moved back to Belarus, unable to stand the Israeli heat, the constant fear of terrorism and the very alien Hebrew language.

During our own family trips to Israel we eventually learned not to worry much about suicide bombers and other threats that made that country seem like an erupting volcano if all you knew about it was what you read in the newspapers or saw on TV. The situation there was hardest for my mother to bear. She sometimes called her cousins in Haifa in the wee hours to ask if they had survived the explosion she had just seen reported on television. They would angrily interrupt her panic-stricken tears with, "Yes, Bella, we are fine! For God's sake, it's two a.m.! What explosion? Where? It's across the country from us!"

My Israeli relatives' typical answer to even the most carefully worded question about Palestinians was a condescending, "Arabs? Ah, they work for us."

Ali's parents often had Palestinian friends for dinner.

I remember how, during one of our rare visits to Tel Aviv, at a dinner party a handsome young civil engineer named Wasfi, whose English was as fluent as his Russian, confessed to my mother that his brother had two wives. At first my mother was horrified, but her curiosity prevailed and Wasfi explained that his brother's first wife was only sixteen when they married, and by the time their first child was born he could see that she was a lousy cook and preferred reading and watching TV to being a conventional housewife. After they had three unwashed and underfed toddlers running around the house, he finally decided he couldn't take it any longer.

His second wife was in her mid-thirties. As soon as she entered her husband's household the rooms began to shine, the garden bloomed and the younger wife and her children began to gain weight.

At that point my mother swallowed uneasily and said, "But, why couldn't he just hire a cleaning woman and a babysitter?"

"Well, of course, he could have. But he preferred a second wife," Wasfi said, smiling in my direction so flirtatiously it nearly made my mother choke.

One night as we were sitting around the TV, watching the news of yet another bombing in Israel, my father muttered with disgust: "It's all your Arab friends, Sasha."

Ali turned toward him, as did we all, even my mother. We all knew he shouldn't have said it, but it seemed wrong to argue with him at that moment: There were six dead, including the suicide bomber, fifty more wounded. No one we knew, thank God, but horrible anyway. There was the usual footage of people in shock, tears and blood running down their faces, other people in uniforms helping them into ambulances—there was an entire fleet of ambulances and fire trucks. Ali got up from the couch and on her way out of the room turned and said something in Russian to my father.

"They're all the same, Sasha, when it comes to dealing with us!" he called after her in English, laughed bitterly and covered his face with his big hands.

A Redhead and a Red Cat

Ali once told me how she had learned the English phrase "to dodge bullets."

During her first year in college her next-door neighbors were David, a tall angular guy, and his red cat. David was a harmless graduate student in medieval history who suffered from an obvious crush on Ali. In his inflamed mind the coincidence of Ali's hair being the same color as his cat's fur had a huge, almost supernatural significance. The cat's name was Benny.

Benny liked to follow David everywhere, and there was always the danger that a car would run him over. David said he had invented a system for keeping Benny from leaving the backyard. He would walk slowly to the back door of a neighboring building, Benny following close behind. Then he would dive through a doorway that led into a mailroom and eventually out onto the street. The cat remained behind, paralyzed with confusion.

"I call it 'dodging Benny,'" he explained to Ali. "D-o-d-g-i-n-g. We use this word when we talk about bullets flying over a battlefield, for instance."

When I think about Ali I try to avoid remembering this story, even though I like it. Used to like it, I mean. Just as I used to like David and Benny, though now I don't think I'd care to see either of them again. No more red cats and no Russian for me, please. And no Israel, or Palestine.

Ali is still dodging bullets, up there. Maybe she manages to take a picture of me once in a while when she's not too busy.

Sunset In The Hills

By Rumjhum Biswas
(India)

The old woman knelt before the medley of images in the little prayer room. Some were made of brass, some of clay. There was even a papier-mâché lingam. Her gray wisps of hair were still wet. How she managed to bathe at the unearthly hour of three-thirty a.m. was a feat her daughters and later her daughters-in-law had given up marveling at. The mist outside was heavy. Some of it crept inside the house like long tendrils of ether. She finished her prayers quickly with a feeling of guilt. All these years, even when her house had been full—with her children, her husband's myriad needy relatives and the servants—and the part in her hair had been proudly branded with vermilion, she had never cut short her twice-daily ritual in her little prayer room. She got up, holding her knee and wincing at the pain in her joint. Her grandson was coming all the way to Shillong from Calcutta just to see her, with his wife and her little great-grandson.

She hurried to the vegetarian kitchen, one of two kitchens in the rambling wooden house, where even garlic and onions were banned. The other was the original, larger kitchen, set a little away from the main house but connected to it by a narrow bridge-like corridor. That was where the rest of the family's food used to be cooked. Now there was little use for it. There were only the three of them left, herself and the youngest two of her children—a daughter, grown into a thirty-four-year-old spinster who preferred the vegetarian meals cooked by her mother, and a twenty-eight-year-old scatter-brain who preferred the company of the Hill people to ordinary Bengali boys his own age.

Every time she thought of those Hill people she sighed—an old, tired sigh that seemed to escape from deep inside her. It wasn't like this in the old days. Back then there was no hatred between the Hill people and her own. The Hill people's customs were shockingly matriarchal and liberal, but they hadn't resented the bookish Bengalis and their *babu* ways. They hadn't begrudged them their government posts nor the slopes where their homes sprang up like so many red-capped mushrooms. Even Kabi Guru Rabindranath Thakur had drawn inspiration for his poetry here! The climate was colder then. Peaches, apricots, plums and pears spread their fragrant blossoms far and hung their fruit low. There was no smoke then either, save for the wood-fed cooking fires curling up from chimneys.

But all that had changed. Just like her house. Once bustling with people and merry with the laughter of children, her home now bore a tired, battered look. The old woman smiled sadly to herself as she cut vegetables, resting her right knee against the *bonthi's* wooden board while her hands deftly worked against its sharp metal blade. As her mind went back to the past, the voices and laughter of the people she had known and loved wafted in from all corners of the house—friends, relatives with children of their own. Now they were all either dead or had moved away. Gone from this picturesque little hill town to the cities, scattered all over India. Gone for the promise of a better life, and gone because politics, distrust and hatred had replaced the easy camaraderie between two peoples that her generation had known. Large cauldrons of shining copper and brass were used for cooking then. She remembered the two mild-mannered Nepali boys who used to lift the heavy vessels, serve the food and keep her kitchen clean. A friend once remarked that having a meal at her house was like eating at a wedding; there were so many dishes and so many people to share them with!

Her sons had often encouraged her to come live with them in Calcutta, Guwahati, even Delhi. But she always refused. At first she gave her unmarried daughter as the excuse, but afterwards she stopped bothering with excuses at all. "It's no use," she told them. "I can't leave this place. This is my home. This is the house that your father built for us. This town is as much my home as it is the Hill people's. They can't take it away from me. And I don't think they will. We have lived side by side for so long.... No, let me be. This is where I belong."

She started kneading into balls the boiled and mashed green bananas. Her grandson, granddaughter-in-law and little great-grandson (oh, thank you, Lord, for letting me live long enough!) would be here with her today. The image of her grandson as a baby rose up before her: chubby, sloe-eyed and always smiling. His own little one was sure to look like him. She had only seen her granddaughter-in-law once, at the wedding. A pretty girl, but shorthaired. City bred. Would she like this old place and its old people?

"How time flies," she thought. The sun was high up in the sky. The mist had vanished. Plump clouds were gathering for another burst of feathery rain. She had finished making the *koftas*, and the *payesh* was cooling on the table. They would be here any minute. It was just a three-hour drive from Guwahati.

The sound of a car crunching to a halt outside her house interrupted her thoughts. She hurried out. There they were! The little one all rosy and dimpled (just as she had pictured him) looking around in round-eyed wonder. His mother, uncomfortable in a sari, was settling her face into the right expression for the occasion. Her grandson, getting on the plump side now—his wife must be a good cook, she thought approvingly—was running down the cobbled path and up the white stairs, past the creeping lipstick vines and black-eyed Susans, to catch her up in his arms.

"*Dida! Dida!*" he cried, twirling her round and round.

"Put me down, you naughty boy," she said, laughing. "I've made your favorite *koftas*," said the old woman, taking the child into her arms. But he immediately started to bawl.

"He's a little tired and dazed," his mother apologized. "Everything's so new to him."

They went inside the house. The boy's mother busied herself with the child, coaxing him to suck at his water bottle, adjusting his clothes. But the boy's father was gazing around the house with pleasure, his eyes glowing with memories—memories she shared with him.

"*Dida*, it looks the same. Only quieter and sort of empty."

"They've all left for the cities," the old woman replied. But her grandson was too occupied with the past to catch the sorrow in her voice. He was running about the house now, recalling the years gone by, excitedly pointing out familiar objects to his wife. Each piece of furniture and knickknack had its own story. For the old woman the memories were rushing in. She sank down into a chair and let them wash over her, greeting them like old friends. Her house was full of people again, just like in the old days. Laughing, squabbling, teasing, complaining.

"*Dida*, these *koftas* are the best in the world!" Her grandson still talked with his mouth full, she noted fondly.

"Leave some for me, you hog!" from his wife who was feeling quite at home now.

"Mumm, mumm," murmured the child, clutching his empty milk bottle. He didn't mind sitting on his great-grandmother's lap. He had decided it was an experienced lap, though a bit bony. The old woman watched them finish the meal. She watched the young wife clear away the table.

"Now you too must eat, *Dida*." Her granddaughter-in-law's voice was like a soft caress.

The baby had fallen asleep in her arms. She felt she could hold him all day. But, concerned that their *Dida* hadn't eaten, the boy's mother took him and laid him down on the old woman's cot. Then they all sat around her in her vegetarian kitchen, chattering away while she herself ate. Her knees bunched under her chin, her thin, almost translucent hand mixing the rice and *dal* on the bell-metal plate on the floor, she ate with great relish. Her happiness flavored the simple meal with the rich aromas and spices of those long-gone days.

They continued to chatter while the old woman lay down on her cot, next to her great-grandson. The baby smelt of powder and milk. He felt soft and warm, just like her children, nephews and nieces before they all grew up. "How time flies," she sighed.

The sun was beginning to dip low. The valley was awash in red, gold and mauve. Gray smoke wafted lazily above the pine trees. The birds had begun to descend noisily on their nests.

"*Dida?*" Softly, afraid to intrude on her thoughts, her grandson touched her hair. "*Dida*, we have to go now."

She looked up at him, his face surrounded by the first shadows of the evening. She felt her house was beginning to grow empty again. She wanted to say, "Stay awhile. Just for a few days." But the words remained in her heart unspoken. It had been very hard for her when they had first left. But she had learned to live with their absence. They still loved her. This she knew. But they also had their own lives to live. And the cities were where prosperity and security waited.

"Yes, *Dadubhai.*" She kissed them both on their foreheads. But when the little one caught hold of her finger, she found it hard to stop a tear from falling.

The old woman stood waiting at the gate while the car strained up the steep narrow path leading to the main road. She waved and smiled her wrinkled smile, squinting in the gloaming to still see their faces. Her granddaughter-in-law was quietly wiping her own eyes. Her grandson's face was set in that men-don't-cry grimace she remembered so well. The car jerked forward. The sun slipped out of the sky, pulling down the light with it. And then she couldn't see them anymore.

An Issue Of Blood

By Mita Ghose
(India)

"Mamma...?"

"Come, *Bugloo shona*...chweetie pie.... Come, *Buglai*.... Come, come, darling...."

Drawn by the sound of voices, he pauses in the doorway, a miniature Tintin haloed in gold by the early morning light. My baby. Beautiful as an angel, but all too human. Rocking on his feet, poised to turn away from the threshold at the first hint of turmoil. Sound instincts in one so young.

"For pity's sake! Don't call him by those sickening names. This is one very bright kid, in case you haven't noticed, not some retard."

"I'll call my son what I damn well please."

"Yours? Really? Since when? Since some slut decided to dump her 'mistake' on a garbage heap and give you the only chance you'll probably ever have of playing mother?"

That beautiful baritone knows exactly how to cut. As finely as a surgeon's scalpel. In thin slivers, so you don't even notice when you begin to bleed. And yet, this is a voice made for seduction, for insidiously destroying all defences. I should know. It's a voice that stirs up memories, some deceptively sweet, others putrefying silently in the dark recesses of my mind. Swallow. Breathe. Count ten. The time is now. A sunny Sunday morning. Like the one before it. Safely predictable. Predictably unsafe.

"Lovely! Blame the woman as usual, the universal scapegoat. You, of course, have nothing to do with it."

"I'm not the one, damn you, who bleeds torrents at the very suggestion of sex. Actually, I'm bloody relieved he's not your biological brat. Don't have to worry wondering whether he's going to turn out like his drooling idiot of a Dadu!"

It must be an irresistible temptation for him to delve deeply into wounds he has already opened so many times. My brat. Yet, he loves this child. By default? Drooling idiot...my father...bound to me in sickness, health, love and conflict, together always, till marriage we did part. Marriage, I mean, to the man I had tried so hard to resist. Terrifying, because he was so alien to my sphere of experience.... Picture-perfect...so beautiful to look at, so charming, so influential, so wealthy. So persuasive. So everything I was not. And obsessed, unbelievably, with me. Why, God, didn't I ask myself why? What had stilled my instincts and numbed my brain, preventing me from questioning his reasons for hankering after little me, a social nonentity, a complete misfit in his world? Without the recognition then that my name calls up today, a notoriety that makes him hate me and try to conceal the grudging respect he can't help feeling. Why didn't I ask myself what it was that drove him towards me, this man who could have had any woman? Would it have helped even to have asked, when even now I can't find an answer that makes any sense?

Could it have been an Eliza Doolittle fetish, I often wonder, the excitement of social slumming? Surely a novelty for this man, cloistered within the insularity of his class. Or was it the fascination of homing in on a difficult target, a prey in flight, the thrill of the chase, that inspired him who had always been himself the object of pursuit? A man whose seductive marksmanship was Olympic class, who never knew the meaning of the word failure. Points I might have pondered back then. Pointless now to ponder. And yet I cannot help turning them over in my mind.... If only I had known, had recognised the true nature of the secret compulsions that masquerade as love.

Too late for us now, locked as we are in immortal matrimony, mortal combat. Me versus him. Both irrevocably committed to the common goal of keeping the skeleton hidden in the closet, as secret as a cache of contraband ivory. One odd couple among many such, but unique, nonetheless, in the details of our private anger and hidden grief.

The same feelings that burn my insides obscure my vision and blur the sharpness of his beautiful profile. Panic overwhelms me because I know I cannot afford that response. I. Will. Not. Lose. Control. Imagine the mayhem, if I do. The blood, even. My private nightmare. His as well.

"Eliminate stress from your life," says Dr. Bose, M.O., F.R.C.O.G., D.Sc., A.B.C.D.X.Y.Z. (Edinburgh? London? Timbuctoo?). Why not cut off my head? Take out my heart too, along with my uterus and ovaries. Neuter me clean. No malfunctioning womb at all to curse or worry into fruitfulness. "You probably don't have much to do with yourself," the doctor says.

"No, I don't."

"Too much time on your hands for brooding and worrying about the state of the world, hmmm? Have you tried yoga? Meditation? You need to be out and about. Vigorous physical activity. A brisk walk in the morning to start with, hmmm?"

I have walked mile after mile, you patronising overqualified know-it-all, from the crack of dawn till God knows when, trying to drain my body of its energy and exorcise my demons. Day after day. And lain awake at night exhausted, speechless, empty, so devoid of feeling that I couldn't even bring myself to shed a tear. Not if someone had wrung me out like a rag. And yet, the blood still oozes forth, drop by relentless drop.

"You just aren't motivated enough for exercise, are you? Now, if you were overweight.... I'm prescribing iron tablets again. They should take care of the anaemia.... You're an intelligent woman, aren't you? What stops you from taking better care of yourself? Meanwhile, these tests.... Get them done at Glamorgan Medical Centre, please. Nowhere else. We're not going for a biopsy right away. We'll see how it goes, shall we? A little spotting isn't such a big deal, hmmm?"

A little spotting. Haemorrhage after haemorrhage. All that blood wasted. Not even a respectable miscarriage to stem the flood of silent accusation: sterile, sterile, sterile. Not even an immaculate conception. Just to prove a point.

My little one's tentative steps propel him towards me, and he anchors his fingers into the folds of my negligée. Unsettled by the crosscurrents of rage and despair? Seeking safety, hope? From me? That's a laugh. All he's doing is trying to master the art of balance, or get a hug. Can I, the ersatz mother, even tell which it is? I place my hands gently on the silken down of his fragile skull. A strange sensation surges through me: reassurance that here is a creature more helpless than I. Can this be the source of the courage that gives me the nerve to strike back?

"That drooling idiot," I hear myself say with biting precision, "gave me love. Recognise the word? No. It doesn't feature in your vocabulary. He's the man you went out of your way to cultivate when you set your sights on me. And then treated with contempt once you had what you wanted. Now that he's ill, unable to defend himself, you insult him day in and day out. Bravo! If that isn't just like a gentleman, a true product of your class. Didn't your expensive public school teach you that Alzheimer's isn't a hereditary disease? Or did it leave you as ignorant as your high-and-mighty parents who never felt the need to educate themselves about what lay beyond their long noses?"

What use are words that can hurt me as much as the person they're intended for? And yet I engage in these futile exchanges that can only increase the animosity between us. Back and forth they go, the wounding words, across the jagged line that divides us. But the image such dialogue conjures up—the sagging puppet in a wheelchair…my father, the centre of my little world, the parent who played a dual rôle in the absence of the other parent long dead and gone. Tough and tender, with laughs to spare for the world's absurdities until they caught up with him. All that frustration and sadness contained beyond the bursting point. Now he inexorably self-destructs, a sharp decline followed by a plateau, then another decline. Further and further from reality, sliding into dementia, drooling, dribbling, soiling himself, shedding all recognizable signs of what goes into making a human being human. Oblivious, thank God, to his own indignity. But look, Baba, no tears. No wobble in my voice. Dignity is all, as you taught me so well but can no longer practise yourself.

"Really?" retorts my husband. "Not hereditary? How, then, do you explain yourself? Weird as can be—scribbling those pieces of gloom and doom, shut off from the world, locked up in your precious self. You're a pain, you know—a royal embarrassment. And look at your sister. Everybody who's anybody in this city knows she's successfully running not only her own life but a thriving business as well."

"Off again on a tangent! As if you didn't know what the whole world knows: The firm is Mehta's. And the money. And the brains behind it. When was my sister ever anything other than window dressing? Mehta's little toy?"

"You're eaten up with envy," he shouts back. "Sticks in your craw, doesn't it, that someone without your looks or education could do better than you? Someone without your trump card—a husband to hoist her, at one shot, several rungs up the social ladder. Someone with the guts to achieve what she has without her rightful share of anything—including love from Daddy dearest who never noticed her because he was so besotted with his first-born, the spitting bloody image of his dear departed wife. What did that father of yours ever do for your sister before he started gibbering and soiling his pants? Yet look where she is! And look at you, his pet!"

"You never could abide my relationship with Baba because your own parents never shared anything with you except their wealth and privilege. And you talk about envy. You pretend you don't understand why Baba's pension was never enough to send Lichu abroad for college. And would it have been worth it even if he could? For someone whose scholastic aptitude was less than nil? As for your great regard for her, I wonder where that stems from. Merely, I suspect, from the fact that we're so different. 'My enemy's enemy....' Oh, I agree she's way ahead of me. She could teach me a few tricks about selling myself. But then, my readers don't have to be wined, dined or serviced before they buy my novels. Lichu only knows how to promote one thing, but she does it par excellence. How the world loves her! And, boy, does she love the world back! Well, good for her. That was always her forte. Even when she was still in her teens—modelling 'special' lingerie, if you please!"

"Shut up!"

"She's a stupendous success. Especially now that she's turned exclusive…available no longer to all and sundry but only to the heads of multinationals. Prostitution, they called it in the good old days."

His smile is insidiously sweet. If I hadn't known its true meaning I might even have smiled back—the usual response of anyone who didn't know him as well as I did.

"Spare me your nun's story," he says. "You can't bear it that Lichu is bright and smart and sexy. That she's jolly good company. And obviously great in bed, or men who could afford any woman they wanted wouldn't be chasing after her. Not a great beauty, but a real woman. Not a fraud like you—all the curves and contours of a corpse!"

Back to square one, where it hurts most.

"That shouldn't surprise you of all people, should it, considering what a *man* you are."

Nothing like hitting below the belt. The thrill of being right on target. So gratifying. But it never lasts long and doesn't come cheap. The pain is blinding. And then…the taste of blood in my mouth. Did he break my cheekbone this time? I can feel the flesh swelling up. It will turn blue in a couple of hours, shading off into yellow by cocktail time. Thank God we're not going out this evening. Why does he do it? Why do I goad him into doing it?

"*Buglai Baba, aaja…aaja, beta….*" Malini, dark and desiccated, in widow's white, appears in the doorway. How long has she been standing there? It's the ayah's job to eavesdrop and clear the field for battle. Her gaze, before she lowers it, is inquisitive, watchful. Was there a glint of malice too? Does it please her to know that beneath the varnish of affluence gutter instincts still prevail?

"Go on, Bugs," he says, smiling his dazzling smile. "Mashi's calling you. Time for chow. Smart boy, go on now."

My baby turns towards him and grins delightedly. "Ba-ba?" How they betray you, the ones you love the most!

"I'll feed him, Malini," I manage, keeping the hurt and resentment out of my voice. "You go have your tea. Come, *Bugloo shona.*"

Tiny fingers wrap themselves tight around my finger. My son.

Still mine. I stand up, careful to hold myself erect, the way drunks compensate by becoming over-precise in movement and speech. The child teeters precariously, then rights himself, astonished by his newfound agility. He gazes up at me as though to say, "Did you see that?"

I smile for his sake, though my cheek is throbbing. Uncertain at first, his mouth responds with a wide grin. Two teeth on top, two on the bottom, not quite aligned. My insides melt. How brutal it can be, the expression of love. As devastating as a cruel word that cuts the ground from beneath your feet. Is this beautiful child just another emotional trap in the making? Please, God, not him too.

He spent almost a year in an orphanage, a golden child, standing out from the others but just as devoid of an identity and just as unwanted. What does such a life do to a child? Then manna from heaven: a set of parents, no longer young, but desperate for a child to serve as a buffer between them. And an elegant home, clothes and toys, as much food as he can eat and waste, lawns to crawl over, cars to ride in, holidays on sand and snow and cruise liners, more friends than he could know what to do with.

And, of course, his parents' endless bickering. Followed by sudden lulls. A short reprieve earned by a lightning-swift blow, a swollen jaw, a bruised eyelid, a cut lip. No fractures so far, but the fridge is always stocked with ice cubes and the medicine cabinet with salves, lotions and painkillers. The dressing-table drawers spill over with make-up sticks in different shades to match summer and winter complexions. Estée Lauder, Christian Dior, Shiseido. And the tears, meanwhile, kept on hold. Life must go on. No matter how lonesome one is this night and every night. What does life in such a house do to a child?

Why can't this man find someone else? I often think. Someone bright and sexy. He says I've made him unfit for any woman, his rage disguising the tears no real man can shed. I've destroyed him with my frozen-fish stare, my cutting words, my frigid limbs, my teeth-gritting endurance. And all that blood, discharged, one would think, in a fury of resistance.

Divorce? How dare I even suggest it after the damage I've done?

I am his private tragedy and doormat. His victim and his nemesis. His partner in misery.

But why can't I let go? Because I'll lose my trophy husband, my identity as the wife of the great man? Because alimony in this country amounts to a pittance? Better to think about it later on, after *Bugloo* has grown up. After I stop "spotting."

"My trophy wife," he murmurs at the next do we attend, his voice soft as velvet, his arm clinching my waist. High on the success of a new business venture, he is smiling his gorgeous smile. Trophy wife and showpiece husband. Made for each other. My new book is out. A bestseller. Success breeds success breeds wonder breeds reluctant respect. Money is one thing, but recognition you haven't had to pay for in cash or in kind is something else altogether. If you have one, you pine for the other.

"I'm terrified she'll go and win the Nobel Prize. Asian writers seem to be the 'in' thing these days." The perfect blend of off-hand affection and disdain for the absurdity of the idea. Polite laughter follows. "Don't laugh, my friends! She's very good. But when she's bad, she's horrid…. And I don't just mean the prose." More laughter. The whole world laughs with you if you're wealthy enough to queer its pitch how you choose.

"Hi, there! How was Sardinia? You S.O.B., you never told us where you were off to! Adventure sport again? Scared we'd turn up at the wrong time?"

"How's the tyke? Teething with a vengeance, I heard. My twins are going through the same misery. Nina's at the end of her tether."

The stream of words flows past as if at a great distance. The only certainty is his arm like a clamp around my middle. Holding and suffocating me. What if I pry it loose? Will I be swept away? What if I scream HELP?"

Did I actually scream? Why are they staring at me? Is it pity or is it admiration of lucky Mrs. So-and-so in her salmon-pink *paithani* shot with gold, her cabochon ruby earrings from Yangon chosen by her charming, devoted husband who never strays despite the not-so-subtle overtures from other women and his wife's inability to conceive? The treachery of fate. *Naseeb.* God knows what stock that adopted child of theirs springs from. What a tragedy for a man who deserves half a dozen legitimate heirs of his own.

My child's face swims up to me through the haze, his eyes bright with trust and intelligence, his mouth aquiver with uncertainty verging on hope. Look, Mamma, no hands. I concentrate on my mouth, my best feature, he once said, and the memory of that compliment perversely triggers feelings of tenderness and even arousal, breaking through the wall I have built up over the years to protect myself. Amazing, how my body can still betray me. My muscles relax despite the vise around my middle. My lips curve upwards. My dimples deepen, though my cheeks feel dry and fragile as paper. I smile, and the world smiles back at the famous Ranjan Sen's wife. I give in. I surrender. And just then feel a spurt of blood issue forth. Just a little spotting.… Nothing unusual.

I Could Take You to a Place

By James Jay Egan
(USA)

Paul descended into Woodenbridge village from the west as the rain began letting up. His glasses were beaded with rainwater, hair matted, raincoat dripping and shoes heavy with water. He walked down the road along the river into the vale.

He crossed the Aughrim River on the stone bridge and, alone, scrambled down the bank on the downstream side, inside the thick green undergrowth of raspberries and false raspberries and woodvines like wild grapes but with smaller leaves. The river lay hidden beneath a canopy of box elders and green ash.

Below, the stone bridge had two semicircular runs. The near run was shallow and pebbly. At and below the bridge foundation between the two runs was a shoal of pebbles. The far run was deep, dark and swift. In the morning he had caught his only trout there, casting far up under the bridge, a German brown, on a number-twenty black ant with light hackles. He remembered the trout and smiled to himself. He knew he would write a postcard to his grandfather tomorrow: Caught a tiny, silver trout. 7". On the fly. In the Old World. No. 20 jointed black ant. Water cool, not cold. Rivers read the same. Overfished. No mosquitoes. Send love. Tell Grandma. Studies not interfering with education. J. Paul.

Paul stepped in the shallow water over the gray and blue-green pebbles to the shoal. Standing there, he lit a cigarette with a damp match, and the smoke was heavy and thick in the wet air. The smoke did not disperse in the hidden spot below the bridge. He sat with his back to the bridge footing and took apart his reel and rod, separating the rod into five pieces. He wrapped the reel in a sock and lay it in his canvas pack. The rod he wrapped in a woman's sock. He took out his antique aluminum pocket book of flies. He replaced the black ant alongside the other terrestrials and selected the other flies he had used during the day, the streamers, nymphs and dries. He blew on each one to dry them and stiffen the hackles and replaced them carefully in their respective places.

He sat still while a car drove over the bridge above him. He put the cigarette butt with the other butts from the day in a plastic bag in his front shirt pocket.

He had fished in the morning upstream from this bridge, having caught the very small German brown trout in the deep run below the bridge. He had fished upstream to the village of Aughrim and then in the afternoon walked the road between the hedgerows and through the pastureland from Aughrim back to Woodenbridge.

After resting there awhile and smoking again, he got up and joined the road over the bridge. He left the bridge and started up to the front of the Woodenbridge Hotel, a white, wealthy-looking Victorian place having that mansion-on-a-hill quality.

The bar menu stood posted outside the door. He read the items and prices. He leaned back and took off his pack, set it on the walkway, then took off his raincoat. He shook the jacket free of the rain. He folded the raincoat and put it, wet, inside his pack. Then he took off his glasses and dried them clean with his dry handkerchief from his shirt pocket. The front of his thighs and lower part of his pants were soaked and his shoes were muddy, but he grabbed his pack and went in.

The hotel's reception chamber was a rich reddish room with dark wood trim. A man stood behind the desk. Paul guessed he'd been eyeing him from the time he had scrambled up from the place below the bridge.

"Sir," the man said with a straight-faced English accent. "May I help you?" He looked at Paul through his glasses.

Paul asked for the bar. The Englishman walked him through curtained French doors into another red room, darker yet, and empty.

"Will you be needing a room?" The man stood hunched and leaned forward.

"No. I'm just going to eat. I'll start out with a pint of Guinness." Paul sat down at the bar.

"I'll fetch a menu," the man said after he'd poured half the pint.

"I know what I want," Paul said. He asked for the seafood chowder.

When the chowder came he finished it quickly. The gentleman had been back and forth through the glass doors joining the reception room with the bar. Paul drank another pint. His legs were tired, but began to feel loose and light. He got up, setting a five pound note on the bar. The hotel man watched him, then took the note and said thank you, ringing up the check.

"What river is this out here?" Paul asked, pointing.

"Ah, the Aughrim."

"No, the other one that spills into the Aughrim and runs over there."

"Oh, yes, the Avoca River."

"What's the next village up that way?"

"Avoca Village is three miles up river."

Paul picked up his pack and walked out of the bar room, through the glass doors to the reception room. It was raining outside again. The hotel man followed him and stood behind the front desk while Paul put on his raincoat.

"What's the time?" Paul asked.

"The time?" the man said. "Yes, almost six."

Paul nodded and walked out. Outside in the rain he turned left, away from the stone bridge over the Aughrim River, leaving the vale and Woodenbridge Hotel behind him.

The rain was light but he was wet again quickly. He walked toward Avoca Village on the road that followed the Avoca River. He heard a car coming up behind him, turned around and put his thumb out. The car didn't stop. He looked at the three people inside as they drove by.

He walked while drying his glasses. The sky was gray and low, and the Wicklows were light and dark greens. White sheep and brown cows grazed on the sides of the hills, and hedges divided the grass, clover and alfalfa fields. Dark green conifer forests of tall spruces and balsams stood far up on the rounded summits.

Another car came along. Paul turned, walking backwards, and put out his arm. The car had two women in it. The women didn't stop, and he turned back up the road.

The hedge along the narrow road was high and well-trimmed. He noticed dark, waxy-leafed holly, light green raspberries and five-leaved wood-vine. Sometimes he could see over the hedge down into the valley, across a pasture, to the river. The riverbed and water were discolored with rust from the mining operations upstream. The Aughrim River had been clear and clean. This river was a reddish-brown. It looked like it had been a good trout river. The river looked classically fishable, with open banks, some pools and a lot of shallow riffles.

He heard another car coming up behind him, and looked over his shoulder. A man sat in the driver's seat. Paul turned around fully and walked backwards, putting his arm and thumb out far. The car drove by, and Paul looked at the driver. Ahead he saw the brake lights come on. The car came to a stop thirty yards up and he jogged up to it and opened the door on the left side.

"Thanks," he said, climbing in.

"Sure. Where you going?" The man spoke American.

"Don't know." He took off his glasses to dry them again, looked over, smiled, and said, "The next village?"

The man next to him looked straight ahead, nodded and shifted. He was tall and cramped inside the car, over forty and graying. He had glasses, too. He was an American driving in Ireland.

"Where you from?" the man asked.

"Milwaukee. The good land. Been there?"

"Sure," the man nodded. And then said, "Need somewhere to stay?"

"No." Paul looked out his window, the one on the left, at the hedge.

They rode in silence, Paul looking at the beads of rain dancing by on his window, then looking through them at the hedge. Then he looked straight ahead, and up at the clouds.

They drove over a lip, passed a ruined church and then started down into a valley. A sign on the left read "Abhoca—Avoca." They passed a farm house, a craftshop, an estate and then a housing project. They drove down to and alongside the river, then turned sharply onto a skewed bridge. Because of the high stone walls of the bridge, Paul couldn't see the river below.

"Want a beer?" the man asked as they passed over the bridge and into town.

"No, thanks."

"I'll buy," the man said, almost stopping, pointing to his right at Nagle's Pub.

"Sure."

They parked alongside the road and Paul took his pack, and they crossed the street and went into Nagle's. The place was part pub, part restaurant and hotel, situated along the river. Inside it was bright and quiet, with half a dozen silent Irishmen scattered through the room. The American pointed to a table by the window, and Paul went over and sat down in his raincoat. The man nodded to a few chaps beside the fireplace, shook the hand of a fellow at the bar, and talked with the barmen while they poured and settled a pint of Guinness and poured a lager.

The American came over with the pints.

"Guinness or Bud?" he asked.

"Guinness."

"Good."

Paul watched the Guinness settle in front of him in the Harp glass, with its cream rising to the top. Finally, when it had settled, he drank.

"Thanks for the beer."

The American nodded.

"You're American," Paul said finally, watching his pint.

"American-Irish," the man said. "Irish until they kick me out."

"How long you been here?"

"About twenty-four years. Came over in 'seventy."

"I was born in 'seventy. How old were you then?"

"About nineteen or twenty I suppose."

"Where'd you come from?"

"Chicago."

"Sports fan?"

"No."

They drank off and on. Two short codgers came into the pub and sat at the bar.

"I had a dream," the American said, "a nightmare, that my friends and I were at a party, smoking grass, being cool. And the draft board came to the door, and the police and MPs and Army were behind these old geezers and bitches in suits. And they lined me and my friends up and the Army men started potting us off. I woke up and decided I had to get the hell out of America. I didn't know what I'd do, but I knew I couldn't stay any longer. I wasn't going over there."

Paul didn't say anything. He looked at his pint, then ahead at the bar. The American was looking at the table, then looked behind Paul out the window.

"A week later I got my draft notice, and the next day I was gone to Portugal."

"Ever been back?"

"No."

Paul said, "My old man was over there when I was born. I didn't meet him until I was six months old, and we visited him on leave in Hawaii. They've got photos." He lifted up his glass. He finished the pint, leaving a layer of foam at the bottom.

"Need a place to stay?" the man asked. "My wife runs a bed and breakfast a mile up the road."

"No. Thanks." Paul stood and shouldered his pack. "Thanks for the beer. Take it easy." The man nodded and continued his beer.

Outside the rain had let up. An old lady walked by and Paul asked her about the next town.

A Family Business

By Padma Prasad
(India/USA)

The artist he finally hired was a short young man with a thick beard, long hair and a serious, earnest gaze. His shirt collar was frayed, and he even had a hint of a potbelly that was severely arrested by a worn-out leather belt.

The young man listened intensely as Chen explained the job to him. Just two years out of art school, he was certainly inexperienced but seemed talented enough for Chen, who had become desperate for an illustrator. Chen carefully examined his portfolio and gave him a basic test in technique. The young man, Guru, deftly stroked out a very professional-looking sketch.

"We can stop searching," Chen announced to his family that evening. "The new man will come to work at nine o'clock, not to-morrow but the day after. Wednesday. Tomorrow, he says, is not an auspicious day for him. Which is good, because that, my dear, will give *you* time to get ready."

His daughter regarded him with a sturdy, unblinking gaze, her mind calculating what needed to be done. For a long time the de-sire to prove herself to her father had inspired her. When she first showed him her work, he had dismissed it with a cursory glance. He would not admit as much, but he liked women to be women. This elder daughter, Kim, however, had always defied him both openly and subtly. Finally he had had to acknowledge that she was a ma-jor part of his success. Her long conical fingers were born to draw. Her mathematically precise eyes honed in on the hidden angles and curves of natural objects—leaves, flowers, fruit. When his weavers translated her designs onto fabric, the result was profitable beyond his dreams.

He had invited the sons of his friends to woo her. Kim remained polite but uncooperative. When she saw her father was still not about to give up, she sent her fingers out on strike. It was only when Chen almost lost an important order from Dream-Ins Inc. that he gave up. After that her designs grew even more confident.

The young man—Guru—came to work punctually on Wednesday morning and set up his drafting table, brushes and other materials with a rhythmic but studied care. When Kim first saw him, his shirtsleeves were tightly rolled up, his face purposeful, his fingers already moving like precision instruments.

"This is what you have to do," she said as soon as he noticed her.

She opened a file folder, her eyes on his face. For once, she thought, her father had done something she could approve of. The young man followed her concepts of design and color with almost no explanation. She drew deep, satisfying breaths as Guru's fingers began working, translating each line and shade into a pattern of squares for the weavers. She felt his understanding as something physical and was almost afraid to watch him for too long.

The light fragrance she wore lingered with Guru after she was gone. It was almost as if she remained there beside him, approving. In the morning when he sat down at his table he knew she had been there the night before after he had left—some papers were slightly askew, a brush out of place, sometimes a short brown hair lay on the cover of a folder.

Soon it was time for Chen to give him his first check.

"We are very pleased with your work, Guru," he said, patting him on the back.

"Thank you, Mr. Chen," Guru said, drawing his hand through his hair which moved like a mass of metal wires.

Chen made a face at the gesture. "You don't find this...hairstyle a nuisance?" he said with a false laugh.

The next day Kim stared at Guru in disbelief, too amazed even to look expressionless. His head was shaved and glistening and his beard gone. Not even the trace of a moustache remained. He smiled back and waited. But she merely bent her head over an open file and said, "I see you've altered the color of these flowers, over here."

"I was wondering when you would come by for that piece."

He pulled open the drawer of his desk and took out the original pattern she had left with him, with the color she had specified. She tilted her head over the two different versions, then took a deep breath and said, "Here is today's design."

The paper trembled in her hand. He steadied it with his own and, selecting an appropriate pen, added a tiny squiggle to the top of each geometric petal in her design. "There. Now it is more perfect."

She stared down at the drawing as if he had just vandalized it. "Maybe you should stick to your own work, and let me do mine."

Just then Chen appeared, waving an opened letter, a big smile on his face.

"Guru, Guru, my friend. Look at this. We have received an award: 'The most innovative fabric design of the year,'" he read. "Do you remember the second design Kim gave you? That was the lucky one!"

"It was very beautiful," Guru replied without emotion.

"New hairstyle, Guru? Nice, very nice. They want to interview me for the newspaper. They may even want to talk to you. Both of you. My design team!"

After that, Guru stuck to doing exactly what he was told. If he felt a line was needed or a tint was missing, he ignored the feeling. Soon he grew tired of the work and felt himself ripe for a change. Chen noticed the alteration in his attitude. He said nothing, but when Guru showed no interest in the newspaper article that was subsequently published, Chen decided to talk to him.

"Something is bothering you, Guru. Is everything alright at home, with your family?"

"Why do you ask?"

"Your face has changed. It has a different expression, as if your head is full of serious thoughts."

"It has always been like that. Maybe you just see my face more clearly now because the hair is gone."

"I see. Maybe that's what it is."

A few days later Kim approached Guru's desk. "Please take a look at this. For some reason I'm not able to finish it."

Guru regarded her for what seemed a long time before he turned his attention to the drawing she was holding. Suddenly she moved some papers aside and sat down on his desk.

"So, tell me, do you pray to that Indian animal god?" she asked.

"What animal god?"

"The one with the elephant head. I've seen pictures." Her eyes were darting about his face as if with a mind of their own. "You actually pray to him? Does he answer your prayers?"

"I don't think any god does that. We have to find our own answers."

"What do you use to pray, then? A prayer book? A Bible?"

"I just talk. Sometimes he listens, sometimes he doesn't. What difference is it to you, anyway. May I please get on with my work?" He turned away from her. "If you want to leave the drawing with me, I'll look at it later."

But she refused to move.

"Why did you shave your head?" She was swinging her legs now, the expression on her face frank and intense. He noted with surprise that her eyes were more brown than black and that there was a very dark mole on the left side of her nose, like an ornament. He drew his hand across the fuzz of new hair on his scalp and smiled back at her.

Guru left early that day. But instead of going to his room he walked to a nearby park and sat down on his favorite, shaky bench. Already many of the trees were leafless. The patterns made by their branches soothed him. When the full moon rose he was ready to talk to the moon god. But Kim's pattern was also on his mind. As he contemplated the dark sky he saw that a set of three circles would complete each of her motifs. He sketched them in the dirt with a stick and thought how similar the design was to the ones his mother made to decorate the floors of their house on festival days.

Then he realized he was hungry. Careful not to disturb the equilibrium of the bench, he got to his feet and headed toward the hotdog man who ran a business just outside the park. The man had a fixed routine for each hotdog he sold and became agitated when it was disturbed by an impatient or overbearing customer. Guru's hand raised in greeting was enough for him today to begin his routine. "Today, it's on me."

When Guru protested the man replied, "Free for you, yes. My daughter has finally left her crazy boyfriend. And I'm celebrating."

Guru laughed. He knew how long the hotdog man had prayed for his daughter to find a boyfriend. When she did find one and it turned out to be an abusive relationship she was unable to get out of, the pain seemed to settle like cooking grease into the creases of the hotdog man's face and he began looking at people with blurred, crazy eyes. That was when he started concentrating with manic precision on the halving of each hotdog bun and the perfect grilling of each hotdog before allowing anyone to buy it.

"So you are free at last," Guru said as he accepted a veggie dog and liberally applied some special spicy sauce.

"You bet. We said nothing to her, eh, no whys, no whats when she showed up all roughed up, like you never seen anyone your whole life. There I was thinking, This is my baby, my little baby. She's going back to school and her mother has bought a beautiful necklace with little gold petals for her."

"Gold petals is a good pattern," Guru said.

When he reached his rooms it was close to 9:00 p.m. His brother was waiting for him. His face was stern and serious. "Is this your normal time to get home?"

"I had some work to finish."

"How is it going there?"

"Good, pretty good."

"Have they mentioned a raise?"

"Not yet. But they like my work."

"You haven't come to visit very much since you started working there. Little Boy misses you."

After three sons, now in their mid-teens and early twenties, his wife had had a late pregnancy, and Little Boy, now two years old, was the result.

"I'll come by this weekend."

"Mother is very sick. Uncle Balu called from Madras. I was only just there the beginning of this year. It might be a good idea for you to go see her."

"Now?"

"She's been much worse this week. You don't want to have it on your conscience. And it would do her good to see you. She can see how well you're looking after yourself, and that will put her at peace," he said. "I spoke to my travel-agent friend. There's been a cancellation. I booked it, a night flight for tomorrow."

"Tomorrow? But I have to give some notice."

"Things happen. They'll understand."

Guru spent a restless night and woke with a headache. Not once did he think of defying his brother. When he saw Kim she looked radiant, and her mood affected him deeply. It was like sitting in the park and talking to the moon god. As he began to clear his drafting table, she said, "How long will you be gone?"

"Three, maybe four weeks. My mother will be very happy to see me. I'm the youngest, you know. She worries about me. It's good to have someone worrying about you. You don't get into so much trouble. I'm the youngest.... I already said that. There's almost fifteen years between me and my brother. That's why she worries all the time about me. I'm all by myself, and this is still a new country for me. Every day she prays for my health and prosperity. I don't pray myself that much. I don't have to, because she is praying, you see. When someone else worries about you, it makes things a lot easier." He paused and looked into her dark eyes. "Much more efficient. You can focus completely on the business at hand."

Avoiding his eyes, she said, "Your father, what about him?"

"He died when I was four. I don't remember him. He was quite a hero, though. Everyone still talks about him. He was very strong, like a wrestler. He could eat seven hens at one meal. Really. And he had quite an interesting death. He was a rice farmer. One day, just after the rains, his tractor went into a rut and got stuck in the mud.

He jumped out, set himself behind the stuck wheel and lifted it out of the mud. Really. But the strain was too much for him, and without even realizing it he had a stroke. He drove home and only then collapsed in the front yard. My mother should have done a little more worrying about him. But at the time all she was thinking about was making sure everyone was fed."

Then Guru showed her the new design he had come up with. "You know, this reminds me strongly of the patterns my mother makes in front of the house every morning."

When she responded with a puzzled look, he said, "Marketing."

"Marketing?"

"When the gods go for their morning walk, they will, you know, be lured into the house that looks most attractive."

He started to laugh, and Kim could see that, although his complexion was dark, his gums were pink and almost all his teeth showed when he laughed.

"Your mother believes this?"

"Yes, of course. Even when she is unable to get out of bed, she will make sure somebody does it. Before dawn. That's the best time. Otherwise, it's very bad for the house if you leave the front of it undecorated. Like there's been a death in the family.... I have an idea. When I return I'll bring her patterns with me and you can see what you can do with them."

Guru told her where he had left everything and even wrote a set of instructions on how to proceed in case he did not see her again. Chen was away in Ottawa that week but had called to wish Guru a safe journey.

"I almost forgot," Kim said. "My father told me to give you this month's check before you leave."

"That's very kind of him." As he was leaving he said, "So, you seem very happy today. Is it because I will not be around to interfere with your work for a while?"

She shook her head. "When my father called this morning he said he has decided to open a new office in Ottawa. He wants me to run this office until he is set up there."

"Congratulations," he said. "By the way, you know the design that won the prize? I made some changes in that too."

She nodded. "I know."

"I will return soon."

He put the envelope containing his check into his pocket and left her standing near the window.

When he reached his room his brother was waiting for him with a suitcase full of things for his mother and various other relatives. His brother's wife had also made some snacks for the plane ride. Guru was glad his brother had brought along his little son for the ride to the airport. The boy's curiosity distracted him from brooding too much.

His brother promised to check his rooms every week and water his philodendron. Guru felt feverish and anxious. During the drive to the airport he kept checking to make sure he had his ticket and passport. Only after he was safely inside the plane did he breathe easily, and it was only as the plane was taxiing down the runway that he remembered the check still in his pocket. He had meant to give it to his brother. He opened the envelope and saw there was a note inside as well.

"Do *you* worry about anyone, Guru?" she had written in her delicate hand.

Her Story

By Nora Brandon
(Ireland)

The first thing I want to say is that I take full responsibility for the part I played. I acted deliberately, though obviously not fully aware of the consequences. All I ever wanted—all *we* ever wanted—was to be left alone.

What my husband thinks is hard to tell. He spends his days tending his patch of yams. When he comes home just before the sun dips abruptly below the horizon, he has nothing but supper and sleep on his mind. A far cry from the days when nighttime and love-making were synonymous, when we took for granted that the cool breezes wafting in from the sea after sunset were sent just to cool our ravenous flesh, not merely to make sleep possible so we can face another day of toil. We lived off mangoes and wild banana and the milk of friendly goats that wandered by, as curious and fearless of us as we were of them.

Wouldn't you want something like that to go on forever? To wake up every day without a care in your mind, without ever doubting that the day ahead would be just as wonderful as the one before it? A life entirely without fear? That's what our love was like, though my husband seemed inclined to wonder why we had been granted so much bliss. He never said so outright, but sometimes he would sigh and lie back on our bed of hibiscus leaves and muse, "Isn't it splendid, that this will go on forever. Aren't we blessed."

In retrospect his words seem ominous. A woman learns to pick up on any sign of restlessness in her man. It's built into us. But it was only later I came to see that he actually was half-hoping our paradise would end. "Boredom" I would call it now, though back then the word hadn't been invented (by him, of course).

For me, what we had was much too precious to lose to carelessness. I somehow knew that if we lost our Garden it would mean other catastrophes as well. The great irony is that by trying to ensure our bliss I made certain that it came to an end.

But how could I know that at the time? I was made for bliss, was a creature of Bliss Itself. It—He—assured us that so long as we refrained from eating the fruit of that one tree, an insignificant and, as it turned out, tasteless variety we now feed only to our animals, we had nothing to worry about.

What was the point to that prohibition? A "test," my husband assures me (He still talks to my husband, though He's refused to utter a single word to myself since that day). But a test of what? Is it not perverse to grant two creatures a love like that on condition that they not try to do anything to ensure that it never end? If I had a fear that something somehow might come into our Garden to take our bliss away, am I to be forever blamed for trying to avert it? "Faith," my husband says. I lacked faith. I let the Evil One whisper disobedience in my ear. But no "Evil One" ever whispered anything to me. I was simply following my instincts.

My husband certainly never would have gone against the word of his Creator on his own, not just because he's of a more obedient nature than I am but because our love meant less to him. He was always contented with less, fell into a sated sleep when I was still eager for more. He loved me as far as it was within his capacity but, for him, love was not the all-consuming thing it was for me. He had other pleasures—long walks, cataloging various plants and animals, talking with Him. It's no wonder He still has a soft spot for my husband, while both of them refer to me as the Mother of All Iniquity, a Cesspool of Wickedness...and worse. Between them they've even concocted a story that I was created from one of my husband's ribs. As if I were nothing but a bit of bone and cartilage! And the first thing He did when He showed us the exit to our Garden was to curse me with an issue of blood, which in their eyes marks me as something unclean.

Why did I assume that by eating the forbidden fruit our bliss would be secured forever? My reasoning seems a bit weak now, I admit. It's almost as though I were two women, one before and another after. The mentality of that earlier Eve is as different from who I am today as this slack, weathered flesh is from the lithe, beautiful girl I used to be. When all of creation is conspiring toward your happiness, animals we must now hunt and kill as if they were our natural enemies freely offering their milk and eggs, fruit of every kind literally dropping into our laps, streams so clear and sweet that we felt a kind of intoxication from drinking their waters, when all that is happening you don't imagine any of it can actually end. We knew He was the author of our bliss, but we only knew it because He said so. He didn't hurl lightning bolts from the sky the way He does now or make the earth shake beneath our feet until we cry out for mercy. He walked between us, smiling and answering our questions just as I now try to answer my children's. Who could imagine His taking so seriously that edict against the fruit of a particular tree?

My husband says there was never any doubt in his own mind that He meant what He said. "Why, then," I ask, "did you eat it too?" But he just hangs his head and gets that shamefaced, angry look his first-born assumes when he's done something he ought not have. The truth is, neither of us had any inkling of the savage temper lurking beneath the placid facade of our Creator. He seemed so much the gentle old man—you should have seen him handle a new-born kitten or talk to the sparrows in their own language—neither I nor my husband could imagine what a wrath lurked beneath that benevolent surface. I see the same temper now in my husband and our older son. When he's had too much palm wine and is taking a switch to me over some supposed infraction of his will, an overboiled egg or under-laundered loincloth, he claims to be acting with divine authority. He makes the same claim when he's slapping the boys around.

"You'll kill them," I say, "or turn them into beasts."

"Stay out of it!" he warns, his face flushed with holy rage. If I persist he turns his anger toward me, which is my purpose of course, especially when he's beating Abel who can't take it the way his older brother can. Cain just stands there, chin thrust forward, refusing to cry, matching wills with his father. I believe they actually get some kind of perverse pleasure out of this violence, though no matter how many times he's beaten, the boy still adores that man.

It's the same with my husband and his God. The more pestilence He sends, the longer the drought or more calamitous the mudslide, the greater are the sacrifices my husband offers in response. You could say he offers them in order to appease His anger, but I've noticed something besides fear on his face, a kind of rapture as the smoke from the slaughtered calf—whose meat we can ill afford to lose—rises to the heavens. It's a look of enthrallment I used to see in the Garden when I thought, yes, he does love me after all. When the sacrifice is over and we finally get to eat what's left of the charred flesh, I foolishly expect him to turn toward me with that same look and it will be as it was before. But the mere sight of me reminds him what he's lost, makes his face cloud over with rage and disgust, though he rarely strikes me until later, after he's had a bellyful of wine.

It's not myself, though, it's the children I feel sorry for. They've never known anything but this wretched struggle for existence, have never seen their parents as anything but two people with a desperate grievance against each other. I tell them about the Garden when I've had a bit too much to drink myself. But I can see they no longer believe me. To them it's just a bedtime story, something I make up to help them sleep when the hyenas are screaming too close by, just as I make up little songs in imitation of the birds and draw pictures of animals. Their father says I'm filling their heads with "woman's talk," and in a way he's right because they can't be wasting their days pining for their parents' lost paradise. Life is a cruel business best left to those who accept it as it is, not as it might have been.

Only, when I see little Abel petting his favorite lamb and I recall how not so long ago we would no more think of harming such a creature than we would do violence to each other, I feel so wretched that I think, God help me, of ending it and leaving the three of them to get on with this brutish existence on their own. I've seen many creatures die. Whatever misery they felt in their last agonies, every one of them seemed at peace when the end came. The best thing would be never to have been created at all, to have remained in the oblivion to which we're probably all headed anyway.

When I voice these thoughts to my husband he tells me I'm speaking blasphemy and that I must sacrifice some small animal in expiation for my sin. If I say, "Why should a lamb or dove have to pay for my words?" he tells me if I don't do as he says I'll cause some great calamity to be visited on us. But what greater curse could we attract than that which we already live under?

I'm grateful the boys at least have each other. Despite his temper I know Cain loves his brother, and Abel dotes on Cain. If we haven't managed to gather enough berries for both of them, Abel insists Cain share some of his. When Cain is smarting from his father's whippings, it's only Abel who can soothe his anger and rub healing herbs on his wounds. Cain won't let his mother near him at such times and even calls me names he's heard his father call me. I wonder if you can imagine how that makes a mother feel?

I don't wish to sound ungrateful. We had a love such that future generations, should there be any, will find it hard to believe. My husband is documenting his own version of what happened, insisting that our children commit it to memory. My great hope is that Abel, whom I have taken into my confidence, will pass on to his own descendants his mother's account of how the world ended up in such a wretched state.

And, despite everything, my life is not totally without compensations and even occasional joy. The sunsets are still magnificent, and the birds—especially one yellow bird that likes to hang about when I'm doing wash down at the river—sing almost as sweetly as they did in our Garden. Even my dour and self-absorbed husband sometimes shows signs of the tenderness I once took for granted. And of course I have the children, whom I love every bit as I once loved their father. It's what I live for, my ability to love. To let it die would be to succumb to a kind of living death. We were, after all, made for love, and I will not let anything or Anyone deprive me entirely of my birthright.

Pratima

By Rasik Shah
(Kenya/Canada)

Pratima and her married friend Manju were in the habit of driving to downtown Nairobi about once a week, usually taking Pratima's compact Mercedes—running around in flowing silk or chiffon saris, visiting hairdressers, shopping at the meat and vegetable markets on Market Street, stopping by the flower shop and bakery at the Westlands Shopping Centre. They normally parked at the metered stalls near stores called Dharamshi Lakhamshi & Co. and Shahtex. Street kids would direct her to an empty parking spot in the area, earning a few shillings in tips. There was a lame youth, probably fourteen or fifteen, who hobbled around on crutches collecting silver coins from drivers; his job was to oversee the feeding of the city council parking meters. He knew roughly how long a driver was to be gone, and fed the meter at intervals of every half hour a shilling or two at a time, until the driver returned.

The way Pratima had things organized, there were usually a few extra shillings left in the hands of her overseer by the time she returned to her car. That lame boy (Mrefu, "the tall one") controlled the territory near the Dharamshi Lakhamshi & Co. store. He was reliable, and she felt glad whenever she saw him limp up to her car and greet her with a smile and felt worried whenever he failed to turn up. Never had he failed to account for the money he was entrusted with, although of course he usually got to keep any leftover change. Of course, he was also her protection against the theft of her windshield wipers and hubcaps.

But that day Pratima had parked the car at the big Juma Mosque parking grounds, away from the familiar territory controlled by Mrefu. When she and Manju returned from the African Heritage shop on Kenyatta Avenue, three well-dressed men were standing near her light-blue Merc, apparently having a discussion. As Pratima approached, the one in the middle opened his leather brief case and pulled out a machine-gun. Then the other two also drew guns, pointing them at Manju who was standing near the passenger door.

"Fungua mlango!" shouted the one with the machine-gun.

It took only a second for Pratima to realize this was a carjacking. Conventional wisdom in such cases dictated one ought not to resist but simply do as one was told. She pulled out the car keys from her handbag and handed them to the man with the machine-gun. He snatched them from her, but then pointed the muzzle of his gun toward the back door of the car and shouted, *"Ingia dani!"*

Pratima took a look at the gun and then at the man's face. It was a young, handsome face, with well-chiseled features. She noted the excitement there, his nostrils expanding and contracting in a quick pulsating motion.

"Take the car," she said in Swahili.

"Ingia dani!" the man commanded. This was serious business.

"Haya," Pratima murmured and got into the back seat as the man held the door open and then shut it on her. Meanwhile, the other two men shoved Manju inside on the other side of the car. Then one of them pushed in beside her. The second entered from the other side and sandwiched himself in between Pratima and Manju. The one with the machine-gun was already in the driver's seat, turning the ignition key.

There were people watching all this from about twenty-five yards away. But no-one was shouting for help or even moving. Pratima was struck by their passivity. Surely they could see something was wrong!

The driver reversed and in a deft maneuver jerked the car onto Muindi Mbingu Street. Seated right behind him, Pratima observed the neat hairline at the back of his head. Out of the corner of her eye she saw Manju adjust her sari and then realized her own sari had fallen off her shoulder and that her chest was visibly heaving. She put the sari back on her shoulder and wrapped it across her chest.

They sped through the big Ngara roundabout near the Globe Cinema, and soon the car was on Forthall Road, doing eighty kilometers an hour. All the while the three men conversed in Kikuyu. They passed a traffic cop just after the Pangani shops, but he was busy dealing with a *matatu* vehicle he had stopped. They never stop you when you need them, Pratima said to herself as she sank further into her seat. Meanwhile, the hijackers were discussing their captives, Pratima could tell; she had observed the driver eye her through the rearview mirror. He had caught her watching him and smiled faintly.

Suddenly Pratima realized the reason she could not take her eyes off him was because he reminded her of her son, Nitin. He looked to be about the same age, and his features were somewhat similar: a squarish face with a sharp nose, side whiskers well below the ear. She glanced towards Manju and saw that the two men in the back seat were also watching them. The one next to her was pressing hard against her.

Manju was of the generation that had grown up in the prosperous '70s and '80s, when young women of a new generation had enjoyed a lot of freedom. But Pratima herself had remained remarkably conservative. She was happy with her husband, Jaswant, who owned and operated a furniture-making business. Jaswant drank with the boys on Friday nights and played golf on weekends but had hardly any other vice.

The car was approaching the Muthaiga roundabout. Pratima hoped it would follow the Thika fork, and her heart sank as it turned left toward Kiambu and Karura Forest. There were lots of lonely spots and side roads in Karura Forest. She thought, this could be the last half hour of her life. She thought of her family. Nitin had just turned nineteen and completed his A-levels, ready to go to university in the UK. Sheffield College of Engineering had reserved a place for him for the coming September. Reeta, her daughter, was doing her O-levels and was on the verge of adulthood; what an attractive young woman she would become. Her family had committed itself to the new Kenya. They were all citizens and liked the country. They even socialized with new African friends and business associates. It was a good life. They had not been tempted by the idea of living in the West, though Pratima's brother, Dharam, had migrated to the UK and was always waxing lyrical about his life there. She had visited his new home in the industrial Midlands city of Birmingham. She had not liked the way the immigration officer questioned her when she flew in, nor did she like the condescending way British people treated her.

There was no question that Kenya had been going down. If only the politicians would control their greed.... The telephones didn't work, the water supply was irregular, power cuts were frequent. Everything could be fixed with a little *magendo,* greasing of the palm. And the horror of the new crime wave! Daring robberies occurred all the time, the police themselves were often involved in the crime and were utterly useless in providing protection. Finally, last week she and Jaswant both decided that once the kids had been sent off to university, they would reconsider emigrating.

The car was speeding down a valley, approaching Karura Forest. The men had begun a lively discussion among themselves. One of them was pointing to a dirt road just beyond the bridge at the bottom of the incline. The car slowed down. It was going to turn. Pratima started to tremble and began saying the *jappa* prayer to herself.

"Pull yourself together," she told herself.

She would rather die than be violated. She would not be able to face the shame of it. She would kill herself first. Somewhat calmer as she came to this decision, she turned to take a look at the others in the car. Manju was trembling and had her eyes closed. Of the two, Pratima knew she herself had better reserves of control and strength. On the other hand, Pratima knew an intriguing secret about Manju: Manju had been having a clandestine affair with her African boss. Manju could possibly draw on that knowledge, be able to deal with the lust of these men, talk them out of it, she did not know. The important thing was to keep one's wits.

The car pulled up on a grassy knoll by some evergreen trees. The driver and the other two men stepped out and held a discussion.

The spot was lonely and there was no sign of any one within miles. Then the driver approached Pratima's door and yanked it open.

"Toka inje!" he shouted.

Pratima did not like the look on his face. He did not look handsome any more.

"You, come with me this way," he said in English.

Pratima was surprised at his perfect elocution. One of the other men had already gone behind the trees and then come back. The driver said something to him in Kikuyu, and the man headed for the car. Holding Pratima by her hand, the driver led her towards the trees.

She realized this was her last chance. She was thinking of Nitin, his muscular, youthful body. This man was probably a year or two older than Nitin. Would Nitin ever stoop to do something as heinous as this man was about to do? No, no, she told herself, and suddenly found her voice.

"You are like my son, his age, his height, even his appearance. If you do anything to me it is like doing it to your own mother," she said. The words in Swahili poured out in a torrent.

"Quiet!" he shouted and pulled her further into the bush. They could not be seen now by the others. One of the other men had taken Manju to the other side of the knoll. Pratima caught a glimpse of the third man going back to the car. He was trying to pull the long seat cushion from the back seat.

"You are my son," she said firmly, looking into his eyes. "Tell me what your name is," she said, maintaining eye contact. He blinked. There was hesitation.

"Chris. "

"You are my son forever. If you do something now, I will die and think my son is also dead," she said without knowing what she meant by the words. "Chris, where is your mother?"

He had stopped walking. The man with the seat cushion emerged from behind a tall acacia tree and approached them. He got to within five yards, then dumped the cushion on the grass and turned back towards the car.

"You will have to kill me before I lie on that cushion," she said, then added, "In any case, you have to tell me if your mother is alive. She is not alive, is she? I am your mother now," she said, her voice trembling. "I can love you like a son. I have a husband at home. You are my son," she said. She held his hand tightly. "Hug me as you would hug your mother."

Tears rolled down her cheeks. He saw them and wavered.

"Hug me now, please."

He did not move. She put her arms around his shoulders and drew him to her. He pulled away with a jerk and shouted out to the man who had brought the cushion.

"Kiguru, take that cushion back to the car."

He looked angry. He turned to her and said, "Let us go back to the car." Then he shouted a further order to Kiguru, pointing in the direction where the third man had taken Manju.

By now they had reached the car.

"Give me your purse, and take those bangles and earrings off," he said. Pratima handed him the three pairs of gold bangles from her hands and then unscrewed her pearl earrings.

Manju appeared in the company of the other two men. Her sari was hanging from her shoulders and dragging behind her. She was in tears. Pratima heard the man called Chris issue commands in Kikuyu to the others. Then he said to Pratima, "Just hand over your bag and your jewelery. Tell your friend to do the same. Nothing will be done to you."

Manju went to the car and produced her handbag and gave it to him. Then she took off her bangles and earrings and handed them to him as well. The three men all got into the car and the man called Chris revved up the engine. As he turned and then started took off in the direction of the main road, he turned and waved toward the two women.

Pratima turned to Manju, who broke into tears. "My God, what shall we do now?" she said between sobs.

"How far did they go with you?" Pratima asked.

"He had me on the ground, but the other man turned up while he was still fumbling, and then they packed up, just like that. What did you say to that driver fellow? I think he issued the orders."

The car was gone, they had no money. There could be wild animals in the bush, or more robbers. They started walking back down the dirt road. After a few minutes they saw an old man with a walking stick coming towards them. When he got close Pratima walked up to him.

"Jambo, mzee, saidia sisi," she said, *"ntaka rudhi uku Nairobi."*

The old man nodded sympathetically. He said a few words in Kikuyu and pointed in the direction they were already headed. That seemed to be the way to the main road to Nairobi.

The two women walked another hundred yards, then stopped for a rest on a stone culvert. Soon a bunch of children appeared from the direction where they had left the old man. One of them spoke Swahili and said they were sent by the *mzee* to help them. The children escorted the women to the main road, told them to turn left and wait there for a lift.

In less than ten minutes a car came along going in the direction of Nairobi. The children waved at it to stop. It was a van driven by an Asian man. His family was in the back. The women squeezed into the long back seat where room was made for them. As the driver put the van back into gear, they began to tell their story. Behind them, the children waved goodbye.

The Last Colony
Notes from a Visit to Zimbabwe

By Richard Czujko
(South Africa)

In 1890 a small group of adventurers, the Pioneers, travelled north of the South African border under the patronage of Cecil Rhodes to establish a new British colony. They stopped at a place that became the capital, Salisbury, and the colony itself was subsequently named Rhodesia. A mere ninety years later the Union Jack was lowered for the final time in the capital, renamed Harare, as the last of Britain's African colonies was reborn as the independent state of Zimbabwe. In the intervening period, there had been rebellions, land grabs, European settlement and an impressive amount of development, all culminating in a ruinous guerrilla war.

April 18, 1980 should have marked the beginning of a new era of democracy, but the people of Zimbabwe soon found that the end of foreign colonialism did not mean the end of oppression. The ruling elite of President Mugabe's Zanu-PF party established themselves as the new tyrants. Almost immediately disturbances broke out in the new nation's second largest city, Bulawayo, home of the minority Ndebele (also known as Matabele). Mugabe, himself of the larger Shona tribe, accused elements of the Ndebele guerrillas, his erstwhile allies, of being responsible for the unrest, and in a nationwide broadcast made a chillingly prophetic statement. In impeccable English he declared, "I cannot allow...lawlessness to establish a reign of terror," vowing he had a "clear and unshirkable responsibility to act...in full protection of the people." But it took several years before he finally crushed Ndebele resistance with his North Korean-trained Fifth Brigade, butchering thousands in the process. With the troublesome Ndebele vanquished, Mugabe and his party proceeded to entrench themselves in power.

Later, a new threat emerged, the formation of the Movement for Democratic Change (MDC), an opposition coalition headed by a former trade-union leader, Morgan Tsvangirai. Matters came to a head when Mugabe announced there would be a referendum in early 2000, in which he asked Zimbabweans to give him and his party virtually unlimited powers. He lost that referendum, and this marked a turning point in his reign. His confidence shaken, Mugabe set about exacting revenge. The MDC was declared to be a front organization for the whites, and as a result white farmers and their workers were targeted by Zanu-PF. White farms were invaded by "war veterans," supposedly guerrillas who had participated in the liberation war of twenty years earlier, though many of these so-called veterans were still in their twenties and could not have participated in that conflict. They were in fact mainly recruits from the ranks of the unemployed. Many farmers were driven off their lands and several were murdered, and most of the farms were earmarked for expropriation. The economy of Zimbabwe rapidly worsened, with frequent food and fuel shortages accompanied by rampant inflation. Then, in a hotly disputed presidential election in early 2002, Mugabe was declared the winner. The international community's reaction was to impose limited sanctions on him and his party henchmen. Undeterred, he introduced draconian laws to limit press freedom, and the police were ordered to forcibly break up street protests.

This was the situation in Zimbabwe when I set out to travel there from South Africa by road, my first visit in nearly three years.

As I approached the Beit Bridge border post I felt some trepidation, expecting at least long delays, but I need not have worried. The immigration official was so taken aback at the sight of a real visitor that he promptly stamped my passport and waved me through. There were signs posted warning the unwary to beware of pickpockets, but no tourists other than myself were anywhere in sight.

During the drive along the largely deserted A4 towards Harare, the southern part of the country appeared to be more arid than usual for mid-May, but I recalled that the rainy season had not been a good one. Then I noted more disturbing indicators of what the country was going through: trucks marked "Drought Relief—Priority Vehicle;" a group of about a hundred people queuing for maize meal in the main street of a small town; and graffiti on a road sign declaring "MDC rules"—the majority of the Ndebele, who live in the south, voted for the opposition. The stone and wood carvers still displayed their wares along the roadside, but there were no tourists to buy them.

Another striking example of the divide between the more prosperous north and the poorer south was the prevalence of "scotch carts," conveyances pulled by donkeys in the south, though few to be seen further north. I also noted that the police in the south rattled around in Land Rovers, while their northern counterparts had Mercedes patrol cars. The clear impression was that the ruling elite was deliberately neglecting the south.

Approaching the more verdant countryside closer to Harare, I was struck by the eerily deserted fields. For kilometre after kilometre, the farmland had reverted to bush occupied by roaming cattle and random shacks. Some of the fields still sported shrivelled maize stalks, now dwarfed by weeds, while wood from felled trees lay stacked next to the road. The farm invasions had changed the landscape. White farmers, many of them veterans of the second world war who had colonised vast tracts of land, had been replaced by new colonists—Mugabe's supporters. As the *Economist* of 29 June 2002 put it, "...the land is usually handed out to ruling-party loyalists, rather than skilled farmers."

Former farmhands have also been forced off the land and currently languish in refugee camps, while many of the white farmers have moved to neighbouring states such as Botswana and Mozambique, emulating the Pioneers of 1890. Yet, despite the harsh treatment accorded them, part of their plight was surely self-inflicted. They occupied a special place in the history of the country and were generally well-to-do, with holiday cottages in the lake country or the mountains and their children boarding at private schools. In *Survival*

Course, Chris Cocks describes the farming community as a "dreadful social strata, an archaic colonial hangover." In certain areas, farm owners even refused to socialize with their own white managers. More than one white Zimbabwean told me that, while they sympathised with the plight of the farmers, they felt they—the farmers—had it coming to them.

A bizarre footnote to the journey northward was the occasional appearance of wheelchairs that would appear out of nowhere, their occupants clutching tin cans, careening down the centre of the road, desperate circumstances driving them to duel with road trains, buses and cars in the hope of earning a few dollars. But Harare itself looked normal enough, notwithstanding a report in a local newspaper that the U.S. State Department had warned Americans about deteriorating conditions in the country. The police maintained a visible but low-key presence, with regular roadblocks on main routes. I was stopped once but subjected to only a cursory search. There was no shortage of fuel at the time, though residents assured me this was a temporary blessing and that shortages were bound to reoccur. A persistent story doing the rounds was that Libya was supplying Zimbabwe with fuel in return for land. If true, this would make Libya only the latest in a long line of colonisers. In December 2002, the government ran out of foreign currency to pay for fuel imports and motorists were forced to queue for days to obtain a few litres. A grim joke circulated that the Christmas road-death toll should be the lowest in history.

Meanwhile, President Mugabe himself began following the example of former European colonial powers in becoming involved in the internal affairs of a foreign country. He sent troops to the Congo, ostensibly to assist the government to fight rebel forces but also in hopes of exploiting mineral deposits there. At night I heard transport aircraft thundering overhead, which locals claimed were bringing back casualties in body bags. No private aircraft, apart from civilian airlines, were allowed to operate at night, I was informed, and no one was sure how many Zimbabwean soldiers have died, as the government is very secretive about this.

The poor were rarely to be seen in the capital. Modern Japanese sedans graced the streets; four-wheel-drive vehicles and satellite dishes were commonplace. Most street and traffic lights were operational, and the city was generally clean, the garbage still collected twice a week. I stayed in one of the more affluent suburbs where it was quite safe to walk the streets. But virtually every house had high concrete walls or hedges, a reminder that crime was very much a problem. As one businessman remarked, "At the end of the day people retreat behind their eight-foot walls and watch cable TV." He was referring to well-to-do blacks and whites alike. The poor have no such diversions and are at the mercy of the ruling party's marauding bands of thugs. Ironically, in one of the major suburban shopping malls the black security guards wear British-style police helmets, and even the main square in the capital's centre is laid out in the shape of the Union Jack.

Visitors to Harare soon learn that there are two immediate hazards: dodging rim-bending potholes and avoiding the road where the president's mansion is located. As some South African tourists discovered a few months back, stopping outside the mansion after dark to ask the heavily armed guards for directions can lead to instant arrest. Those tourists were released after a night in jail, but others have reportedly been shot. I found that the officials I encountered in the city conducted themselves in a correct manner, and there was none of the desperate bribing that one hears of in some developing countries. In fact, I had the sense I would probably be arrested if I attempted to bribe an official. Everything seemed normal on the surface, but occasionally the more menacing aspects of life became apparent. A bystander interrupted a conversation I was having with a woodcraft vendor about the lack of tourists thereabout. The bystander declared, "We don't want tourists," after which the vendor promptly clammed up. The bystander was probably a government spy.

Despite the superficial air of prosperity, the underlying mood was sombre. Inflation is a serious problem for poor Zimbabweans, especially for pensioners living on fixed incomes. Foreign currency is unobtainable without the right connections, so there is a thriving black market (euphemistically termed the "parallel market") where an American dollar could fetch upwards of 600 Zimbabwean dollars (the official exchange rate was about 60). Maize meal, sugar and cooking oil were unobtainable during the time of my visit, and it is surely no coincidence that these are staple items for the poor. A European diplomat confided that he obtained his supply of maize from a white farmer who is a long-standing supporter of Mugabe and therefore unaffected by the farm invasions. He told me the European Union was prepared to assist Zimbabwe with drought relief and AIDS programs, but only if such help was done through non-governmental agencies. This is precisely where aid efforts have floundered, despite the rampant spread of HIV/AIDS, with an infection rate estimated at one third of the population, according to the United Methodist Church website ("AIDS Pandemic Hits Hardest in Africa," by Lesley Crosson, 29 October 2002, http://gbgm-umc.org/health/aidsafrica/africahardesthit.cfm. The Zimbabwe government wants total control of any relief that enters the country. Conversations with Zimbabweans were often underlined with a nervous, "So far, we are okay."

There was a backlog at the crematorium in Harare, as gas for the furnace has been virtually unobtainable. The undertakers apologise for the inconvenience and promise that professional standards would be maintained. This is just one of the problems bedevilling everyday life in Zimbabwe, yet both businesses and ordinary citizens calmly go on with their lives as best they can.

As shortages and lack of services have worsened, people have adapted and found ways to overcome them. A network of interdependent contacts has been built up, through businesses, churches and families, and has become vital for survival. A well-prepared household typically includes gas and electric stoves, a generator, gas cylinders and fuel containers in its effort to remain self-sufficient, but this sort of preparation alone is not enough. People also have to know when and how supplies of scarce commodities can be obtained and by what means they are likely to be delivered.

Fuel, or rather the lack of it, provides a prime example of how resourceful people have had to become. The only petrol stations with fuel are those few designated to supply commuter taxis. No other garage has fuel, and, as staff cannot be laid off, excess personnel have in effect become glorified security guards. Harare residents have given up queuing for what have invariably turned out to be phantom deliveries, and petrol is being traded on the black market. I obtained some from a friend who had a business contact, although it was at a rate three or four times higher than the official rate. This still worked out to be about the same as the South African price, since the official fuel price is controlled by the government and is much lower than the black market price.

Numerous Zimbabweans, even some taxi owners, sell their allocations on the black market at a profit, and the streets were incongruously crowded with new German and Japanese cars. But a common sight was a bus or car parked at the side of a road with a plastic or tin container standing next to it. There its driver stoically waited until someone stopped to sell him a few precious litres.

Another entrepreneurial activity that has sprung up during the crisis is supplying banknotes. The banks are critically short of notes and numerous ATMs have closed. So people have appeared who will provide Zimbabwean notes, preferably in exchange for rands or pounds. As the largest denomination of a Zimbabwean note is five hundred dollars, this means that suitcases or satchels are required to carry around any meaningful amount of cash. In desperation the government recently introduced travellers checks as bank notes. The populace has generally been dismissive of this ploy.

I met a retiree who had only been able to withdraw twelve thousand dollars (less than fifty rand) from her bank, and asked her how she coped. "We only eat once or twice a day, and draw money whenever we can," she said. Like so many other people, she adapted to the hardships as best she could. Bank staff tend to be sympathetic. At one branch where the maximum amount for withdrawal was ten thousand Zimbabwean dollars per day, the teller sympathetically confided to me that more notes might be available in a couple days.

The struggle for simple survival has forced Zimbabweans to look beyond their country's borders, not for foreign intervention but for jobs. Families try to send at least one relative to South Africa or overseas to earn hard currency to send back to Zimbabwe to support those left behind. In this way a large number of expatriate Zimbabweans are contributing significantly to the economy.

The housing market remains fairly buoyant as overseas buyers with foreign capital regularly take advantage of bargain prices. I observed one case where a retiree moving to England sold his Harare house to another Zimbabwean already working in the UK.

As a result of the day-to-day struggle, politics has taken a back seat for ordinary Zimbabweans. They certainly do not look for relief from the outside world, and even President Bush's recent African safari did not raise much interest. People were more concerned with the news that the opposition party's mayor of Harare had been suspended from his duties and charged with mismanagement for sacking workers arbitrarily and not providing an adequate water supply. According to one resident I spoke with, the mayor's only crime was that he had been trying to make the city function despite a lack of cooperation from President Mugabe's Zanu PF ruling party.

The independent newspapers disparagingly call the ruling elite "chefs," and the independent *Daily News*, whose reporters are regularly arrested, is the one sold most often at road intersections. Zanu-PF headquarters has been nicknamed the "shake-shake" building, since it resembles a saltshaker. It is situated on a road called Rotten Row.

The elections held at the beginning of 2002 saw blacks and whites queuing together for hours in Harare, where the general assumption was that if you were white you must vote for the opposition MDC. As the majority of urban blacks themselves voted MDC (Harare has an opposition-party mayor), this mutuality of political interests has tended to improve relations between the races.

Another cause for concern during the period of my visit was the government's decision to discontinue the British "O" and "A" level examinations and replace them with a Zimbabwean certificate. Pupils who wished to write the British examinations will probably have to travel to adjoining countries. As one teacher put it, "Mugabe wants a nation of uneducated serfs. This will force a lot of blacks as well as whites to leave the country."

In the midst of the prevailing gloom, a local amateur theatre company was presenting a traditional production of *The King and*

I, with a mainly white cast performing in front of an appreciative, predominantly white audience. The message, intentional or not, was clear: Mugabe, like the King of Siam, should abandon autocratic rule and allow democracy to take root.

The contrast between the promise of post-colonial prosperity and the reality of the repressive regime that actually followed seemed somehow symbolised by a wrecked car that had been left for a month on the pavement just a few feet from the entrance to the imposing glass-and-steel Reserve Bank building. The crooks who had used the car abandoned it after crashing it into a wall. And there it remained on Samora Machel Avenue, no one bothering to remove it.

I had one more adventure before I was out of the country: a night journey by bus to the South African border—not a trip for the faint-hearted. Several times the driver had to take evasive action to avoid oncoming vehicles running without lights, or donkeys taking their rest in the middle of the road. At the border, passengers were required to step through a shallow basin of liquid that was supposed to prevent the spread of foot-and-mouth disease, but it felt that by doing so what I was really doing was inoculating myself against the woes of the troubled nation I was leaving.

Face Value

By Anjana Basu
(India)

Think glamour. Long drop-dead eyelashes batting, the sweep of an eyebrow, a scarlet pout. Think men thinking women's things, the way women think they think. Lipstick, golden cylinders unwinding red crayon tongues to be stroked onto pursed kiss-inviting lips. The neat click shut of gold or mother-of-pearl compact clasps. Then the lips prim together, and she's all ready with a new face. Think allure, the stark red-and-white mask of a geisha, the ultimate graphic design for the faces of all women.

This is the face she was born with: flat-planed, broad, flat-nosed, thin-lipped. The other was the face she had before the world was made: tawny blush sculpting cheekbones out of non-existence, two thin gold lines making sense out of a Donald Duck beak nose and the gilt glitter of eyeshadow to idolize it all. Makeup is the ultimate illusion.

"It's all right to gild the lily," my mother said, making nonsense of naturalist protests. At thirteen, life was frilly petticoats and the cancan of a Park Street restaurant with a windmill and a Parisian flair. Thickly mascara'ed and eyelinered mothers pushing their daughters in and out for a special birthday treat. A pink powder room with frilly-skirted tables and flashing mirrors where the mothers touch up their faces and compare shades of lipstick——all universally Max Factor and unblushingly red. Then the cancan, a froth of more frills and legs, dimly embarrassing to some thirteen-year-old senses, but a foretaste of night life and adult excitement.

All the people who are somebody come here in suits, chiffons and cigarette holders, to sit between the muralled walls and listen to the crooner breathe huskily into the mike and watch the same dancers. This is where the big bad world turns. This is glamour.

Even the crooner has blue eyeshadow on. Pure sapphire, startling against pink skin.

I remember thick buttery cakes set in squares. Bright emerald, turquoise, sapphire and violet. Those cakes were basic, without today's psychedelic swirls of peacock colour. Fingers spreading it on thick, with no sticks muffled in sponge to help.

The more drama around the eyes, the better. Thickly-layered hooded lids with tragedy in the shadows underneath, loves lost in one bristly emerald flutter of the lashes, late nights, desperate gambles in a game of hearts, sad sirenical silences. Curtains hung around the windows of the soul.

They did it with *kajal* in the past, after hours of slow-burning a *mansha* leaf with *ghee* and catching the sooty residue. Great pools of haunted light defined by two sweeps of a finger. Padmini by *diya*-light praying for the defeat of Ala ud din Khilji. Nurjehan. A whole line of kohled, antimonied beauties with *kajal latas* tied to the end of their saris, glimpsed in mirrors and miniature paintings, until the 1920s discovery that *kajal* smudges and looks terribly un-chic when compared to eyeliner. Then all the beauties bobbed and shingled in a desperate attempt to be *firang* about it, while kohl becomes the secret weapon of the Russian Ballet stranded in Paris.

Maharanis tripping in and out of Maxim's with jade cigarette holders long to *there*, clutching jewelled turtle mascots and trying desperately to look like Edna May or any other currently popular swoon queen. Chiffon saris invented to lend a float of formal sophistication to a woven cotton summer. High heels to teeter on and necessitate a clinging clutch at a male escort's arm. Sandals very useful for romance, long spiky heels with a touch of glitter in the right places. Respectable women don't walk in them. Respectable women don't teeter or clutch. Decent flat-footed women glower and think dark thoughts.

"I am fragile. I am a vision you can wear on your arm for a

while. You can walk into a room with me and heads will turn." Chinese women approximated the effect with bound feet, swaying like lilies in the breeze. The greater the sway, the greater the implied, offered, femininity. Enlightenment unbound the feet and found easier ways to sway, but the memory lingered. The slow clink of an anklet couldn't begin to compete with that combination of authoritative heeltaps and swaying form.

Then came lipstick. In Bankimchandra they did it with *paan* juice. The experienced allowable brownish-red. The Raj brought in the gold cylinders and the ultimate red. "Red Hot and Cool," they called it in the saxophone shadows of Indian nightclubs, and they brushed it on for effect. You could tell a woman who'd been around by her brush-whittled lipstick, worn down to the bone.

The faster they were, the faster they flicked out their tubes and lipsticked their mouths in their compact reflections while the men watched in open or discreet admiration, and other women, condemned to laws of decency, dragged their feet en route to the Ladies. Decent women lipsticked their mouths and brushed their hair in powder-room intimacy. These things were as intimate as getting ready for bed, meant only for the eyes of a brother or husband. Decent women didn't lipstick traces of themselves on the crystal.

But they did it openly in the nightclubs or at the racecourse in the world of Anglo-Indians. And the gossip it caused! An Anglo-Indian beauty with a scarlet mouth under the sweep of a cloche—obviously someone's governess. Sir So-and-So's daughter's, you know, he went to Oxford, went very brown sahib, his wife's dead. But then, governesses all had tragic love lives written into the shadows under their eyes. Anyone who looked like that had to have a romantic past lingering somewhere. More so than scrubbed young faces without a blush or a trace of crimson and candid enquiring eyes that didn't ambush you from the shadows.

The red mouth was brazen. The red mouth signalled danger. It said STOP and waved a flag at a bull. It stuck out a mile. "Do you close your eyes when you're kissed?" asked the Revlon ad copy. Shell-shocked women in World War II came round in ambulances and screamed for their lipsticks. "Now I look like myself," they said to their mirrors, blotting out the strain and the pain. While actresses tried everywhere to perfect the kissproof lipstick—more economical and much better-mannered, imagine leaving telltale traces all over the place!

With lipstick went powder, finely sifted through layers and layers of silk. The answer to the faint gleam of sweat on the nose. "I'm going to powder my nose," ladies whispered discreetly to their escorts, covering up more urgent necessities with the platitude. The Ladies Room was originally called the Powder Room and, stocked cannisters of powder, six inches deep and instantly replaceable, topped with a swansdown puff. The silver powder box became an indispensable part of a bride's equipment, side by side with the *paan daan*. Determinedly different ladies imported theirs in porcelain with musical attachments, and ballerinas turned on their toes in tinkling time to the sweeps of the puff. The tiny silver shovels that went with them made them handy compact refillers.

In nightclubs and at the big parties they handed out compacts as favours or prizes for dance competitions. Compacts that today would be described as "important" in the pages of high-fashion magazines. Flashy squares of mother of pearl, discs of gold, tortoise shell with a little line of diamonds let in. They were meant to be held. They signalled significantly every time they were produced, whether in the darkness of boites, or by chandelier light. Sliding out of velvet and leather pouches. Compacts snapping shut in bursts like abrupt applause in darkened auditoriums or theatre foyers.

The sixties saw Liz Taylor in seven layers of eyeshadow sailing down the Nile to sink Richard Burton. The sixties saw Suchitra Sen stranded at the mike of a nightclub, eyes rimmed black and shiny with an eyeliner brush and sad emphasis sitting on the lower lids. Nothing of it was subtle and all of it belonged to the night. Love was adult, forbidden and wrong, without a stray gleam of innocence and highlighted by rouge. And both the wrongness and the scarlet cheeks enhanced the allure and took it three steps out of the bald, bare, everyday world.

Natural was out. Hair was coaxed, teased, bouffant, bee hived and lacquered firmly into place for combat. Madam leaped out of her speeding jeep because her producer-driver forgot himself in mid-gear, and the incident was the talk of Tollywood, but not a single hair of her head was out of place. Women slept sitting up after a trip to the hairdresser's, though all Cleopatra did was flip her wig. Filmstars put their hair in a plait over one shoulder for morning shots and back-combed it bouffant at night, with one lock sticking out so.

Behind the screens and the scenes, the makeup men worked their magic with their square Leichner boxes and their greasepaint, altering, erasing. Artists in the canvas of the flesh. Glamour is an illusion. The stardust gets into your eyes and stays there.

A hairstyle can quicken the pace of a heartbeat. An altered lipline and enhanced smile can transform a life. Not to mention the effects of a changed complexion. "My son wants a fair bride, so if you could just lighten it by a few shades...and then if you changed the shade of your lipstick and drew the lipline a little lower than usual…. And, yes, eyeliner all around...." Bleached skin, plucked eyebrows, a gold-mesh evening bag firmly clutched in a moist palm, gilded toenails sheathed in high-heeled Cleopatra sandals. By the rules of romance, these things alter a life. A mere switch from Red Silk to Cherries-in-the- Snow is apparently all it takes, if you listen to the advertisers, though the rules of life put more emphasis on changes of attitude.

Romantic shadows put in with a strict eye on the beauty rules. "Makeup must never go beyond the chin line, otherwise it shows up terribly." Dark makeup, light makeup, one for day, one for night. "The trick is to put it all on and look perfectly natural in full sunlight." "I wanted to be grown-up," said my aunt, "and whenever I was studying I was stretched out on your great uncle's black leather sofa with the nail enamel we had then—it was called Durogloss—and listening to the Armed Forces Band on the radio."

Makeup is what little girls watch with big, round eyes. The pats and layers of foundation, the blusher and the lipstick. Makeup is what little girls like best to play at, if allowed, dying for their first dressing table, dying to be "booful like my Mummy."

Growing up, practicing sweeps with the mascara wand. Easier than the toothbrush and the black matte cake of the fifties. A swirl, two careful sweeps to each eye. Fifties actresses carried as many as eight layers of mascara on their lashes, ten if they wanted the weight and the eye smoke to be more pronounced. (False eyelashes could be gummed over the real ones, then mascara stroked on, with a wait between each coat as it dried.)

Young girls skipping to the hairdresser's and blinking bravely at the tweezers and the stylist's approach. Being beautiful is painful, though not perhaps as painful as the Chinese lily feet. However, some of them never return to confront the ordeal again. Others keep coming back, regardless of pain, allergy or anything else. Glamour is a neatly cultivated arch above the eye, or a neatly cultivated natural line. And even if Brooke Shields once made the bristly look fashionable, now it's back to the plucked fine line or, if desperate, the fine tattooed line.

And, when you can get the look right, then you're really grown up. Makeup was useful for slipping into "A" movies before the days of U/A. A little penciling, a touch of pink lipstick, and a girl could jump from sixteen to twenty in a matter of minutes. Makeup got you into adult parties where you sipped shandy and pretended you knew it all, when you actually didn't but you'd die if anyone found out.

It was the advantage you had over boys. Knowing their eyes would go to your red lips. Knowing a compact snap said, "Look at me," the way the slither of silk hissed danger. All you had to do was choose the statement you wished to make, in a world where men drowned in pools of eyes fringed by starry lashes, romance lingered like a song on the corners of moonlit terraces for silken ladies draped in the misty soft focus of powder.

Which was why Women's Lib turned violently against it, parading clean scrubbed skin and close-bitten nails. The non-use was the statement. We want you to know us for our bare-faced selves. No frills, no fantasies, no big bat eyes to distract you from the context of your sentence. No red lips to focus your attention elsewhere.

Women make more complex statements with their eyeliner and blush stick. Stroking in confidence. Putting on a dash of generosity. Blotting it out with a sweep of cleanser and starting again on a clean canvas. Springtime under the eyes, seriousness around the mouth.

Shades can do it. Pink mouth, rosy cheeks, a flush radiating to the eyes heightened by pearly liner. A daytime face glancing at sweet sixteen, carefree femininity and innocent sexuality. Brown and orange and tawny to spell sophistication. All the shades they split into fractions of fractions of fractions in the laboratories of Paris and Cheseborough. China Orchid, Copper Peach, Tangerine Sun, Rose Topaz, Wine, Burnt Madeira. Dior, Estee Lauder, St Laurent, stirring vast vats of colour, gelling, conglomerating. Tans for autumn, brights for winter gloom.

Dark eyes emphasised for glance contact on direct confidential days. Yellow and purple eyeshadow for light banter. Gilt lipstick for a touch of conversational dazzle without real substance…. Shades of the rainbow, shades of moods, the titles on a book jacket, a woman's personal credits flashing on the screen of her face….

Milne In Toronto

By Anthony Milne
(Trinidad & Tobago)

2 Jan 04

God, I didn't know it was going to be like this. I didn't know what it was going to be like at all. But not like this: silent, cold and dark as death; in a house in the heart of Toronto; on a street with grotesque black trees with leafless branches ending in twisted witches' fingers.

On Christmas Day I had been alone, just come up from a place where the rains had given way to bright sun and warm jumbie breezes were rushing down the valley from the Caribbean Sea. Real Christmas weather, Mrs Mayyou said, squeezing her cocoa bracelets. There was sorrel and pastels, ginger beer and marinating garlic pork. I forgot to beg a taste before leaving.

Now this, in a self-consciously bilingual city where the dry Presbyterian ethic prevails: beer stores closed, homes silent. Three hundred miles to the east was Catholic francophone Montreal where purveyors of alcohol and Christmas cheer were thriving.

I left Trinidad on Air Canada the day after the official start of winter. We were to arrive at Lester Pearson airport in Toronto in the evening after a direct five-hour flight. We got there after midnight, even with watches turned back an hour, after a baffling three-and-a-half-hour delay on the ground at Piarco. With the delay I had time to hesitate: Did I understand what I was doing? Where I was going?

At first we thought the postponed departure had to do with

cleaning the aircraft's cabin. Then a "technical fault," baffling and unnerving, something to do with the cockpit compass or with the aircraft's main computer. Eventually the French-Canadian captain came up to the departure lounge to confirm the problem was the computer, though the back-up was still functioning. He and his co-pilot had been working intensely on the problem. He had called Air Canada's headquarters in Montreal to find out his options.

It would take a day or two to fly in a part from Winnipeg which would put things right. There was need for a change of crew, and regulations about fuel and weight. The aircraft could be flown to Miami minus baggage or passengers.... And so on.

Half an hour later we were suddenly ordered to board the plane. We would fly direct to Toronto. The captain would explain en route. He did, hours afterwards. I didn't quite make out what he said, except perhaps that the main computer had come alive again.

Vashti, a Trinidad-Canadian I met onboard, had promised to give me a drive downtown, but between Immigration and Customs I lost her. So I made the twenty-minute trip in a taxi driven by a Pakistani immigrant, John, who liked his homeland but needed the job here. Then the children, at school or already working, had assimilated and didn't want to go back. It became a familiar story.

The next few days I spent in shock, slowly getting my bearings in the short, extremely cold days, never higher than ten degrees centigrade even in the bursts of sunshine. There was rain sometimes, but no snow.

I bought my first "tokens" and took the subway, watched the news, glanced at the newspapers. I saw that half the people on the streets and in the shops were immigrants with accents, a high proportion of them Koreans and from other parts of the Far East. Quite unexpected were the vagrants: young people wrapped up against the cold; tattered older people who looked homeless or ill. This in a country that has been described as the most highly developed in the world.

Big in the news was the discovery at a slaughterhouse in Washington state of an animal, barely able to stand as it approached the knife, with mad-cow disease that had allegedly been shipped in from

Canada—province of Alberta. A border war of new import-export regulations threatened.

There were stories of several "landed immigrants," some of them long-time residents of Canada, not able to re-enter the country because they did not have the new permanent-resident cards. The deadline for having these was December 31. Thousands were still being processed.

Meanwhile, the Canadian dollar has been showing a remarkable increase in value. On December 30th it jumped 1.3 percent, increasing to US 77.26 cents, a ten-year high. The Toronto *Globe and Mail* declared in a front-page lead on December 31st that the Canadian dollar could increase in value to US 80 to 82 cents in the months ahead. The principal reasons for the rise of the "looney," as the dollar is called here: the falling value of US currency, rising interest rates in Canada—which pleases bond investors—and rising commodity prices; the Canadian dollar is a leading "commodity currency."

Even more exciting is the prospect of a general election here in April or May, now that the Liberals have a new leader and prime minister in Paul Martin, former finance minister, who replaced Jean Chretien.

The shortest day of the year is past, but the fearful Canadian winter has just begun. Lord, for the Roti Palace on Bathurst Street and Bob the postman from San Fernando!

The High Stool

By Abha Iyengar
(India)

There was so much of it. Cheese, tomatoes, bread, mangoes, rice, butter, eggs. The fridge was overflowing. Bottles and bottles of cold mineral water. The first day I had to stop my eyes from popping. The kitchen was large too, all aluminum and granite and high-polished wood that made your eyes blink in the white light of the sun. The sun filled the kitchen, pouring in through the plate-glass windows. Madam told me I could draw the blinds when it grew too hot and turn on the fan as well while I cut the vegetables. She gave me a high stool to sit on to work. I tried it a few times but finally gave up, preferring to squat on the floor instead to do my cutting and peeling. That's how I did it in my first home in the village, and that was the way I did it in my *chawl* here in the city. I did not think I could ever get used to using a stool.

Madam fixed my salary on the first day, just as she had fixed my working hours. I asked for a sum that seemed to me exorbitant and was surprised when she readily agreed. She even threw in the midday meal. That was good, since my stomach started growling after seeing all the food inside the fridge.

The ceiling fan whirred pleasantly as I sat on the cool kitchen floor doing my chores. For me it was a luxury just to have such a big uncluttered work space all to myself. I think my room in the *chawl* must have been as big as this kitchen, but the space there was always occupied by an entire family. When relatives visited, it became even more cramped and we had to put mats down on the mud floor outside to sleep. Neighbors stopped by to borrow salt or share the latest gossip over a cup of tea. There was always a lot of noise and activity, and only stopped for a few hours between midnight and dawn.

There was a *chullah* in one corner for cooking and a string along the other end to hang clothes on. Black wires dangled dangerously—connections for the light and fan and the black-and-white television that was the focal point for our evening. My children forgot hunger when they watched their favorite shows. They crowded around the television with their friends, jostling for elbow room, the place smelling of their sweat and dirt, their intense faces shining in the glow of the flickering screen.

The walls were lined with pots and pans and prints of Gods and Goddesses. They symbolized our life. We prayed to them for enough food to fill our stomachs. As I sat on my haunches in front of the clay stove, filling it with brown sticks that hardly burned, I would think of the glimmering gas range in Madam's kitchen and its instant flame.

My first week Madam asked me to stay late on Friday for a party she was planning. I was hesitant, since my family expected me home to prepare their own food, but Madam made up my mind by saying she would pay overtime.

I arranged for my eldest daughter, only nine years old, to do the cooking and cleaning for that one day. My husband usually came home late anyway from his job with a construction company. He worked long hours in the hope that they would make him a permanent employee. Even so, he did not like the idea of my staying late at Madam's, but in the end agreed because of the extra money involved.

Immediately on my arrival Friday morning I got busy cooking and preparing the dishes Madam had asked for. I loved to cook, and because she provided me with all the ingredients and gave me a free hand, I came up with delicious and sometimes even exotic fare. Just before the guests were scheduled to arrive she gave me a sari to change into. It was a pretty pink polyester with blue and yellow flowers. She also handed me a sweet-smelling soap and a towel and comb and told me to take a bath in a tub located just off the kitchen, and to make sure to clean up after myself.

Bathed and dressed, when I looked in the bathroom mirror to put my *bindi* back on my forehead, I saw what a difference a real bath could make to my appearance.

"Why, Tara, you look so young and pretty," Madam said when she saw me.

Till then I had scarcely been conscious of my looks. But I was still young-looking at twenty-five and, despite the children I had borne, my figure was trim. All the hard work I did ensured there was not an extra ounce of flesh on me. My skin was brown and smooth, my eyes big, my lips full. My hair was black and well-oiled, combed back into a neat bun. Madam often marveled how my sari never was askew and my *pallav* always in place despite the long hours I worked. I wanted to tell her that in my village one learned the art of keeping one's sari in place, or the men would call out, "Look at that girl. She does not know how to conduct herself in the presence of men. See how her *pallav* is falling. Her mother needs to teach her a few things."

My mother would have died of mortification if she had heard such words.

But life in Madam's world was very different. Madam went about in short skirts and even briefer tops. Her breasts pushed out over the tops of her blouses, and her thighs showed beneath her skirt hems. Her flesh oozed out of whatever clothes she wore, always trying to break out of the restrictions of cloth and thread. It was gooey-pink flesh that often turned to ashy white or blotchy red.

When Madam's husband came home from work, her face paled at the sight of him. He never said anything to me. I knew nothing about him, except that he made lots of money and his family was very comfortable. But Madam seemed to shrink in his presence, except sometimes when she suddenly got angry and her face puffed up and sprouted big red spots and she threw things around. At such times I could not understand her behaviour, but I kept my counsel.

The guests began arriving. The small *diyas* and colored candles

I had helped Madam arrange lent a soft glow to the surroundings. Rose petals floated in shallow earthen vessels placed in strategic corners. Soft music played in the background. Out in the garden, fountains tinkled and paper lanterns created magical patterns of light and shadow. Madam smiled and laughed as she welcomed the guests. Her husband stood beside her, very imposing in a grey suit. Soon the guests had filled the house and the air was thick with tobacco smoke, the scent of expensive perfumes and chattering voices. By the time the last of them left I was exhausted.

Madam came into the kitchen as I was stacking the dirty dishes, having rinsed them preparatory to scrubbing them clean.

"Leave the dishes, Tara," she said, "leave them. Come, sit by me."

Her lipstick had smudged a bit and was leaking from the sides of her mouth. The kohl she wore had spread and darkened the circles under her eyes. She caught hold of my hand and led me into the bedroom. I was reluctant to enter her that room, but since her husband was nowhere to be seen, I soon relaxed. I sat down on the floor, and she put her legs up on the bed. They were fat smooth legs, with red spidery veins at the knees and ankles.

"Please massage my feet, Tara."

I looked at the clock as she plopped onto her stomach, her feet dangling from the side of the bed. I seemed to have no choice, so I began pressing her small feet, soft and yielding as bread dough in my firm hands. I do not know when she fell asleep, but when I heard her begin to snore I decided it was okay to leave.

Suddenly the lights went out. Power cuts were common in the summer months, so I simply waited for the generator to start humming and the lights to come back on. A sudden movement in the dark caught my eye, but before I could react I was thrust against the wall, the wind knocked out of me.

"Don't move."

I recognized the voice of Madam's husband. Without saying another word he lifted my petticoat, at the same time clamping his hand over my mouth.

The lights came back on, but I closed my eyes in terror. His hands held me in a tight grip, my back hard against the wall. I was scarcely able to comprehend what was happening.:

Madam awoke with a start. Her husband moved away from me now. He told Madam to give me some money. "Make sure she reports for work tomorrow," were his parting words as he turned on his heels and left the room.

Madam rose from the bed and told me to wash up. I began bawling, until she hit me hard across the face, her own face breaking out in those red blotches. They even spread to her chest and arms, glaring at me like angry red eyes.

"Quiet, now," she said. "I will pay you for what he has done. Forget about it."

I sank to the floor, my head in my hands.

"I cannot satisfy his hunger," she said in a quieter voice, her face contorting with emotion.

She walked over to her large wardrobe covered with big, shiny mirrors. Then, pulling my hands away from my face, she thrust some money into them, closing her fingers tight on it.

Her driver took me home. As the car glided along the road toward my village, I sunk down into the plush backseats. This, I thought, would be my life from now on.

"Stop here," I said, preferring to get out before reaching the *chawl*.

The car's headlights lit up the road ahead for a moment before disappearing. My daughter opened the door for me, relief flooding into her face. I found my way through the darkness and lay down next to my husband who was fast asleep and had obviously not heard my knocking. I felt like waking him, but did not. I just lay and stared up at the slow ceiling fan, circulating hot air onto my face.

I did not sleep and was up early. My husband was very pleased to have me there to serve him morning tea. He did not notice the dark smudges under my eyes. I told him Madam would pay me the overtime when I reported for work that day, though I had already counted the notes she had given me. Such a large amount would require an explanation and, besides, I had already decided to hide away some of it.

Now I stay late at Madam's quite often. My husband and children don't ask any questions. We have moved to a two-room flat in a better area, with an attached bath and running water. My children are well-dressed and go to proper schools. Many saris hang in my cupboard, all given me by Madam. With the money I earn I have bought my family's unwitting acceptance of the work I do, and Madam has in turn bought my silence.

I sit easily on the high stool in the kitchen and no longer on the floor. Sometimes my *pallav* falls when I serve Madam's party guests, but my indiscretion does not bother me, as it might have in the past.

Ayatollah Khomeini and His Tormentors

By Abbas Zaidi
(Pakistan)

For as long as he was alive, Ayatollah Rohallah Khomeini was the West's perfect Other. Even today he is remembered as a terror-inspiring, anti-West, semi-crazed Islamist, a medieval anachronism somehow come to life at the end of the twentieth century and then demonised, just as his ideal, the Prophet Muhammad, had been in his own day. The Italians even made a pornographic movie portraying the Ayatollah as a sex maniac, the same charge that has been traditionally levelled against the Prophet of Islam and which has appeared even more frequently after the 9/11 attacks. Popular Christian preachers like Jerry Falwell, Pat Robertson and Jerry Vines called the Prophet Muhammad a "terrorist," "paedophile," "devil-possessed" and more, not to mention what right-wing organizations like the Army of God have had to say about Islam and its Prophet.

Like Adolf Hitler, the Ayatollah belonged to the upheavals of the twentieth century, but no one can seriously argue that any crime of the Ayatollah even remotely compares with Hitler's. Yet Hitler has been getting a better press than the Ayatollah. There is hardly a voice in the West that speaks *for* the Ayatollah. Even when *Time* in 1980 declared the Ayatollah "Man of the Year," it had nothing good to say about him and blamed him for "brazenly defying the West."

One thing that *can* be said for the Ayatollah is that he stood up for what he believed in. The untold miseries and countless deaths that the Shah's regime brought upon the Iranian people are well documented. And it was the Americans, preachers of democracy, freedom and human rights, who had the Shah installed by overthrowing the democratically elected Mossadaq government in the 1950s. The Ayatollah wanted to wrest Iran back from American control, but the administration in Washington and American public opinion (largely fashioned by the media) could not accept that possibility. The pattern was not unlike today's, when mainstream America has closed ranks behind its president's war against "Islamic terrorism" without bothering to delve into the roots of support for the terrorists' actions.

The Ayatollah began to face persecution the moment he declared that Iran was in the grip of an oppressive regime headed by the American-backed Shah. His struggle began in the early 1960s and lasted till his death in 1988. But who were his tormentors, and what did they do to him? What eventually became of them? It might be interesting to take a look at the Ayatollah's life and find out.

The Shah

Muhammad Raza Shah Pavlevi was the first of Ayatollah Khomeini's tormentors. The Shah hurt him personally more than anyone else. Khomeini was opposed to the the tyranny of the Shah, who had been installed by the CIA. The Shah tried to bring him to his knees by making his life miserable. He had Khomeini's son tortured and killed. Later the Shah forced Khomeini into exile, thinking his absence from Iran would calm things down. But Khomeini proved to be more than the Shah had bargained for, and it was on account of the Ayatollah's uncompromising, charismatic leadership that the tables were eventually turned: Now it was the Shah's turn to go into exile, and Khomeini's to rule supreme.

But the Shah's exile was no peaceful retirement. He was kicked out of one country after another. Even the Americans whose interests he had served so impeccably begged off from hosting him. He finally bought an island in the Bahamas to find some peace, but peace eluded him. At last he found refuge in Egypt, where his son married Anwar Sadat's insane daughter. The Shah died a few months later. His son migrated to the U.S. and divorced his new wife.

Saddam Hussein

Saddam invaded Khomeini's Iran without provocation, backed by the U.S., Saudi Arabia, Kuwait and the rest of the Gulf sheikhdoms who feared that Khomeini's Islamic revolution might bring down the American-supported Middle Eastern monarchies. The monarchies pumped in billions of dollars to contain Iran, and Saddam used some of that money on chemical weapons that he used against Iranian soldiers and civilians.

Khomeini repeatedly warned the Arabs that Saddam was a Frankenstein's monster that would ultimately turn on his own benefactors. But the Arabs did not heed his warning. Eventually, Khomeini had to accept a ceasefire that he described as a "cup of poison." But his prediction about Saddam proved right. A few years later he turned his guns on Kuwait and threatened to invade Saudi Arabia, causing the Americans to intervene in 1991.

Now the U.S. has destroyed Saddam's regime and occupied Iraq. The Americans killed Saddam's sons last summer while Saddam himself hid in a hole in the ground like a mouse. When the Americans unearthed him, he reportedly surrendered without offering any resistance, disgracing the Arab concept of honour according to which death in combat is the highest virtue, and giving up without a fight is the ultimate disgrace a man can bring on himself and his family name. As he awaits trial by his captors, Saddam stands completely humiliated.

Kind Fahd

For Fahd, Khomeini was a danger because the Ayatollah had called the Saudi monarchy "un-Islamic," though Saudi Arabia was one of Saddam's chief financiers during his war on Iran. Saudi-Iranian relations were never good. Fahd's police kept a close watch on Iranian pilgrims, and in 1987 some of them raised placards criticizing the USA and Israel just outside the House of Allah, the *Ka'aba*, in

Mukkah. It should be mentioned that according to Islamic tradition Allah has absolutely forbidden bloodshed in any form or quantity (*haram*) in and outside the *Ka'aba*. That's why the *Ka'aba* is called *Masjid-e-Haram*, the "Forbidden Place." The Iranian pilgrims were not protesting against Fahd or the Kingdom of Saudi Arabia, but the Saudi police opened fire nonetheless, killing hundreds. King Fahd perpetrated these murders in order to spite Khomeini and to show who was in charge.

To Khomeini, Fahd's massacre was the greatest and most painful blow of his life, even worse than the killing of his own son and hundreds of the thousands of Iranians during the Iraq war. Khomeini used to say that he could forgive Saddam, but not King Fahd for the the sin he had committed in Mukkah. A theologian-jurist *par excellence*, he knew that a sin is worse than a crime: Humans legislate what is criminal, but sins belong to the divine realm.

Khomeini did not long survive the trauma he suffered as a result of the slaughter of the pilgrims. Now, many years after Khomeini's death, King Fahd is scarcely a shadow of what he once was, worn out physically and mentally, hovering between life and death, unable any longer to rule. His brother has in effect replaced him.

General Zia

Soon after returning to Iran from exile in 1979, one of the first statements Khomeini made was concerning General Zia Haq's rule in Pakistan. He called that government despotic, un-Islamic and an American stooge. Whenever he met delegations from Pakistan, Khomeini expressed shock at Zia's captitulation to the Americans and the nature of his administration. Zia responded by creating cadres in Pakistan that killed many Shia Muslims, those most sympathetic to Khomeini, causing the Ayatollah untold grief. Many Pakistani Shias, as well as the Iranians themselves, believe Zia was behind the murder of Allama Arif Hussaini, Khomeini's closest and most trusted Pakistani disciple. The Allama was assassinated just weeks after Khomeini's own death.

A couple months later, Zia was incinerated in a mysterious a plane crash.

Ronald Reagan

It was America's military might and political clout that undermined Khomeini's ideological ambitions. And the man leading the U.S. assault during Khomeini's rule (1979–88) was Ronald Reagan (U.S. President,1980–88). Reagan was the moving force behind Fahd, Saddam and Zia in their anti-Khomeini policies. Reagan surrounded Iran with enemies, even though Iran posed no threat to American interests in the Gulf. But Khomeini had called America "the Great Satan," and that was enough for Reagan to turn a blind eye when Saddam used chemical weapons against Iranian soldiers and civilians. As the leader of the democratic "Free World," it was the American president's moral obligation to see to it that his clients abided by the rules of war. But Reagan chose not to, and under his regime the U.S. opposed every UN action to condemn Iraq for invading Iran.

Reagan also removed Iraq from its list of terror-sponsoring countries, established diplomatic relations and gave it considerable military and other aid. The U.S. sent its navy into the Persian Gulf to protect Iran's interests. American warships destroyed a number of Iranian vessels, killing Iranians who were not technically at war with America. Khomeini could do nothing in response. He died on June 3rd, 1988.

Less than a month later, the *USS Vincennes* shot down an Iranian civilian Airbus carrying 290 passengers. The *Vincennes* was an Aegis-type cruiser with state-of-the-art computerized radar surveillance and missile-weapons systems. Despite eyewitness accounts by naval officers in nearby ships that the plane was ascending and not diving to attack, the captain of the *Vincennes* ordered it destroyed. The Iranian airliner was a regularly scheduled flight using a recognized path recognized by military intelligence. Reagan awarded a medal to the captain of the *Vincennes*.

Today 2004, Ronald Reagan is reduced to a near-vegetative state by advanced Alzheimer's disease.

Anwar Sadat, who gave sanctuary to the Shah and called the

Ayatollah "insane," was killed by his own army.

Khomeini died a besieged, defeated and heart-broken man. But, unlike his tormentors, his end was peaceful. News of his death caused widespread grief in Iran and beyond. His memory is cherished and revered by millions. Even his enemies have not questioned his honesty, integrity or incorruptibility. On the contrary, they refer to his tormentors in terms of their crookedness, duplicity and larceny.

After a life marked by incessant crisis and torment, the Ayatollah may be having the last laugh.

Indelible Imprints
A Review

By Dana De Zoysa
(Sri Lanka)

Indelible Imprints: Daughters Write on Fathers
Edited by Priti T. Desai, Neela D'Souza, Sonal Shukla
Foreword by Neera Desai
Stree Publishers, Calcutta, and
South Asia Books
Columbia, MO 65205 USA

Ann Landers famously summed up her view of boy-girl relationships as, "There are good boys and bad boys, and unfortunately the bad boys are more fun, more exciting and often appear to be more interesting." Apparently fretful of the consequences of this enticing bit of bait, she hastily added, "And in any boy-girl relationship if any one ever suffers it is usually the girl."

Most Asian parents would approve of Landers' words. They do not have to worry about the quality of their daughters' boyfriends, because they choose them. In almost all cases they choose with one goal in mind: strengthened family power through marital alliance. The result is often obsessive restrictions on daughterly freedom, since it is not only the girl who suffers from a trespass, it is her family as well via the mechanics of "honor." Except in a few matriarchal tribes in Indonesia, Malaysia and South India, and despite the persuasive alternatives provided by TV, an Asian girl is still raised to believe submissiveness goes hand in glove with her sex. A daughter is to become a mother, and her upbringing is to prepare her for that. On one side of the marriage feast her role is to submit to her parents; on the other to her husband.

Many Westerners do not realize it, but Western child-rearing and psychological terms are fairly meaningless when applied to Asian behavior. This is especially true in India, whose cultural theatre is far more literate and antiquarian than the costumery provided by psychology. Forget Freud, the fundamental myths aren't the same. Entirely different patterns exist that explain why Indian parents and husbands think so differently about authority, security, responsibility and freedom.

The Indian baby is typically indulged, nurtured and constantly handled. Every sound brings a caring response from the whole family. Infants soon learn that the surest way to get attention is to cry—and later, when they learn the difference, to say something cute. The result is assurance there will be a gratifying response to every wish. In the West this might be called narcissism, but in India it is the natural consequence of having been born. Boys are especially led to feel that they are the center of the universe and deserve to be there. The mother is all-nurturing and all-attending (Indians term their country "Mother India" and symbolize their *bharat,* nationhood, with the sacred cow).

The second baby brings a considerable shock to the first. This typically happens about the age of three, since most mothers breast-feed until then, partly for nutrition and partly for birth control. Being almost totally abandoned for a younger sibling is all the more bitter because the child is simultaneously thrust out into the community—starting with the extended family at first and then school—so the mother can devote her full time to the new one. The first child's specialness evaporates. Clamoring for attention gets nowhere.

The commonest reaction is withdrawal into solitude, which is more bearable than disappointment.. This reaction is reinforced by—or is perhaps the cause of—Hinduism's primordial belief that desire produces suffering. The only worthy goal is to escape desire altogether. The forest hermit and wandering ascetic are partly childhood rejection re-engineered into a quest for enlightenment.

Relations between daughters and fathers are even less satisfying than between sons and mothers. Indian fathers/husbands tend to be demanding, not easily satisfied, critical rather than supportive, remote and authoritarian. The punitive downsides for a daughter not submitting to her father are a powerful force. She might cry around her mother and aunties, but she will not reveal dissatisfaction around her father. Hence, while authority produces escapism in boys, it all but vanquishes girls.

The historical Indian solution has been retreat from reality. If the parental—and later the marital—world is filled with uncertainties, the spiritual world must be where one finds peace and bliss. Indian boys mature yearning for a guide, called a *guru*, who is nurturing, sympathetic and harmonious—everything the father so often is not. The *guru* is a wise and kindly teacher who has himself escaped from the world's turmoil and now reveals how devotees, too, can find their desired inner calm.

No such luck for the girls. As soon as they are able to carry a water pot or whisk away the insects, their days are ever-longer successions of toil. Given the elaborate details that accompany so much of Indian taste, be it food or religious devotion, popular art or the convolutions of family filiality, the girl is trained to exactly adhere to minutia. She knows she had better learn well, for after a relatively forgiving apprenticeship under her mother, she will have to meet the exceedingly rigid, usually waspish and all too often brutal standards of a mother-in-law. The mother-in-law went through this herself and now can hardly wait to extract her revenge. Only after the children are raised and married off does a woman begin to enjoy the fruits of love—from the children, now parents themselves, who gratefully realize what she gave them, and from a husband whose years, if not his attitudes, force him into co-dependence as his body gets frail and tired.

All this is magnified enormously by the lens of arranged marriage. Most young people have no idea who their parents (aided by marriage brokers, astrologers and nosy relatives) will hook them up with. The prospective bride and groom do have the liberty to get to know each other socially and to reject wholly unsuitable candidates, but by and large they haven't a clue about each other's mannerisms and tastes until they have to live with them. Lucky are the marriages that follow the idealized path of "growing to love each other." Countless were the moments when I empathized with my Bombay neighbor's wife, who wept not just grievously but in soul-baring agony under the slights and insults of a husband who even by Indian male-forgives-male standards was a dork. She was seventy-three. This had been going on all her life. She knew no one would care. Until I came along, untouched by local traditions, she gnawed herself near to death with it.

So how to square all this with the supremely self-assertive twenty-something I recently saw jaunting down the Colaba Causeway in Bombay wearing a SUPER-tight T-shirt emblazoned with, "I'm the girl your mother warned you about!"? How to square it with the Indian women's magazines like *Femina* and *Verve*; Indian fashion designers like Hemant Trevedi, Ravi Bajaj, Anamika Khanna and Suneet Verma; and Indian writers like Anees Jung, Anita Desai and even Shoba De, all of whom cut no cloth from either the polyester bolt or the Kanchipuram loom? How to square it with the young women who opt for career instead of husband. Or who, like a gay Delhi artist I know, looked away from my eyes when I suggested she let go of her denial and seek a woman she could love, and finally whispered, "God I'm so glad someone finally said it."

What happened on this behavioral railway from the past to the present tense?

In *Indelible Imprints* we meet twelve women riding those rails. All are middle-class to middle-upper-crust. They span from forty-three to eighty-seven years of age—no T-shirts in *this* lot. Some of their fathers were quite the notables—the artist K. K. Hebbar; Shuksampatrai Bhandari, the compiler of first modern Hindi dictionary; Bimal Roy, an early maker of art films. Some fathers were quite successful in their careers, others not. The daughters are all educated, some of them abroad. Yet Shyamala Ramayya Raman's remembrance "Mixed Signals" hints just how little these factors meant:

There never was a consideration that marriage was a union for the flowering of each partner for the good of the newly created joint unit. It was unilaterally expected that no matter how well the girl was educationally endowed, she was there for the convenience of the ultimate decision-maker—the man. It takes about twenty years into such marriages to realize the unequal nature of the relationship and all the heartache that it entails.

A sentence by Mannu Bhandari in "My Eyes Brim Over" says myriads about marriage in the India of these women's upbringing: "In 1944, right after she passed the Matric (i.e., got her high-school diploma), at the age of sixteen, my sister was married off; the following year both my brothers, who had finished their Master's degrees, got married." Boldfaced between the lines we can read that the parent chose the spouses, but the daughter was perceived as a burden shed and the sons as assets gained. Why waste money educating a daughter who only leaves to support another home?

Each story reveals that the teller was accorded a sense of individuality above the norm. What have they to say about their fathers not as figures but as real people?

For one thing, each father radiated just enough psychic ancestry to march his daughter through tradition before her footprints faded into the present. They were almost all born in the early years of the twentieth century; all but one of the daughters were born between 1931 and 1948. This was a forward-looking time when many were drawn to Gandhian ideals of selfless love of country. Yet it was a political, not behavioral, future. The fathers controlled everything from the household finances to the amount of education a daughter would receive. Mannu Bhandari hints how her father was split between tradition and modernism: "Despite his modernism, he was totally a tradition-bound father, overbearing and commanding, a man of refinement but, nevertheless, a patriarch who distanced himself especially from his daughters." Despite all this, he was proud when she joined a protest movement against British rule.

One doesn't sense the air would have been so cozy around the house had Mannu unfurled the flag of feminism.

Like many of the other authors in the book, Mannu's father rarely revealed feelings of affection. She relates a childhood unfathomable to those who don't comprehend the Asian value that the female be dyspersonal: "Every family had half a dozen children who grew up with each other in their own world, separate from the adults...." The sense of lofty apartness cultivated by so many fathers in this book was replied to in kind: Iqbal Monani's mother "never referred to him except as 'your father.'"

The recipe of paternal aloofness inevitably served up the taste of ideals gone rancid: "Living with my father at the time was a Shah Saheb, one of the wolves-in-saints'-garb, whom my parents, particularly my mother, fell prey to from time to time. The wretched man made advances to me and I was too embarrassed to tell Abba [Father]. Sometimes I wonder how Abba never noticed. I was not yet fifteen and spent the vacation in a turmoil of distress."

Other fathers were honest enough about their maleness to give their daughters some genuinely sage advice. Shyamala Ramayya Raman's "Mixed Signals" is a beautifully written piece describing in part her grandfather's influence on the education of her father. He in turn was fiercely protective—indeed, overly so. Yet he encouraged her to nourish her intellect, take up public speaking, debating, painting and even driving an automobile (unheard of until fairly recently—and then heard very well indeed, as testified to by the legions of young women on motorbikes who give Bombay's taxi drivers a real run for their money to the next stop light). Shyamala describes the lecture delivered by her father on the institution of marriage the day after the wedding:

My father sat me down and told me that marriage was an imperfect institution at best. Therefore, I should not be totally trusting of my spouse; I should always maintain separate financial accounts and develop interests of my own.... It is strange that he said this to me because he certainly did not allow my mother to have her own finances, or for that matter to develop her own interests. On he contrary, he stifled many of her interests and never allowed her to reach her full potential This is still the norm with many of the men in my family.

Irascible mixes of authority versus love, feudal versus modern sensibilities, self-centeredness versus solicitude, male conceits neither gall nor pudding. What to make of these fathers—and much more to the point—not the daughters of the women in this book, but today's daughters?

In the India of *Indelible Imprints*, nearly all marriages were arranged by families in cahoots with matchmakers and astrologers. Today only about seventy percent are. Younger Indians—urban dwellers almost all—more and more insist on partnering their own way. The divorce rate in India is still less than two percent. This sounds lovely to the religious set, but in fact hides many very unhappy marriages that should have ended long ago. Women are rebelling, and the first shots are being fired by novelists and magazines editors.

Over the last three decades India's women writers have moved away from etching the traditional enduring, self-sacrificing wife toward the complex, conflicted woman searching for identity. Compare the servile, suffering unidimensional women in Kamala Markandaya's *Nectar in a Sieve* and Meera Mahadevan's *Shulamith* to the three-dimensional yet still traditional women in works by Chitra Fernando, Anita Desai, Kamala Das, Sara Suleri, and Anees Jung. These new heroines assert themselves, no matter what marriage and family rules say. Chitra Fernando's *Three Women* and Anita Desai's *In Custody* portray women who achieve their individual worth by breaking through the suffering that traditional society dictates to them. Kamala Das's *My Story* and Sara Suleri's *Meatless Days* describe the educated woman's search for identity and meaning in autobiographical form, and Anees Jung's *Unveiling India: A Woman's Journey and Peace in Winter Gardens* do it in both autobiographical and ethnographic form.

India isn't the Taj Mahal and the beggars and the cows any more. Research organizations chart India's social development by looking at what and how much people are purchasing, what they do on holidays, how they adorn their homes. There is an India that is almost totally unseen by tourists despite its staring them in the face even more ubiquitously than the famous old monuments. It is the India that started hardly a decade ago via selling soaps and toiletries by brand name on television, billboards, and in glossy magazines; proceeding upward to basic foods, branching into motorbikes and household appliances and decorator bathroom fixtures and fashionable clothes; and now—advertisements for low-cost divorces.

Still swathed in old merits and scorning the new, the old ways of India are inexorably becoming specks of dust hovering in the air as a great migration now masses and begins to move beneath. The rise of the middle class is dramatically altering the self-image of women—as it has all over Asia. Depending on how one defines the term, between 50 million and 100 million Indians are "middle class." They are becoming the most influential opinion makers in India because of the number of educated, worldly members in the ranks of the media. Forget the Bangalore tech revolution, which is in reality a bonanza of cheap brains for the West, the real revolution in India is the names on the mastheads of the popular magazines and the doors of TV production studios. These make the middle class, and the middle class is becoming a critical mass. Its values are not god-men and grandfathers, but mediagenicity, substance, ideas, realism, unsentimental truth. India's political elders are seen as feudal materialists who have neither a sense of justice nor true belief in the old culture. Young Indians sum up their leaders with a quip: Yesterday All Over Again.

Whatever India's future, its urban middle classes are using the economy and the media to desanctify the sacred cow. Mahatma Gandhi and Jawaharlal Nehru would be appalled to see how much more attractive these things are than the idealistic socialism they thought was the surest way to perpetuate Indian civilization.

Bindu Desai's "Papa on the Swing" ends on a note as touching as the end of a good novel: "The swing fell from its hinges that day. The shuffle of the right foot being dragged, the open window, the familiar figure on the swing at home—all gone."

One could say the same for times past all over India.

Author Bios

Marlene Amero is a Canadian who writes both poetry and prose. "The Donkey-Man" was selected as among the Most Notable short stories published on the Internet in 2005 by the storySouth Million Writers Award.

Anjana Basu's novel *Curses in Ivory* was published by HarperCollins India in January 2003. A second novel, *Black Tongue* is under contract to Rupa. The first chapter of *Black Tongue* that appears in this anthology was selected as among the top ten stories published on the Internet in 2005 by the storySouth Million Writers Award. Her work has appeared in *The Antigonish Review, Wolfhead Quarterly, Amethyst Review, The Blue Moon Review, Kimera* and *Recursive Angel.*

Rumjhum Biswas gave up full-time advertising work "to follow my husband wherever his job takes him, along with my two children." She is currently living in Singapore as a stay-at-home mom and aspiring writer, having finished a novella and a book-length work of fiction. She has written poetry and short stories since her childhood. "If I don't write I'll burst."

Nora Brandon is the pen name of a writer of Irish descent presently living in North America.

Viktor Car currently resides in Great Britain, closer to his native Croatia than where he used to live, in Canada. His short stories have appeared in *Queens Quarterly* (Canada) and other Canadian, British and American literary magazines. His novel *Four Centuries from Zagreb*, from which "Pessoa's Ghost" is excerpted, was recently published by Chameleon Library in the UK.

Richard Czujko was born in Zimbabwe and now lives in South Africa. He has visited Zimbabwe three times since the present crisis began nearly four years ago. "My concern is that if this crisis is not resolved it will have a detrimental effect on southern Africa as a whole."

Dana De Zoysa has a passion for developing-country authors. He commutes pretty much everywhere in Asia, but is happiest at his writer's paradise in Mirissa, Sri Lanka.

James Jay Egan grew up in Minnesota and Wisconsin, and received his education at the University of Minnesota and the Loft Literary Center in Minneapolis. He now lives in Vietnam, where he teaches and writes in his spare time. His stories have appeared in *The Circle Magazine*, *Scrivener's Pen* and *The Antigonish Review*.

Mita Ghose completed her academic career at the Sorbonne and then went on to work as a teacher of French and as a translator. Her travel pieces and book reviews have been published in *The Statesman, The Telegraph* and *The Times of India*. A different version of "Grey White Yellow" appeared in *First Proof, The Penguin Book of New Writing from India* (Penguin Books). The version included in this anthology was selected as among the Most Notable short stories published on the Internet in 2005 by the storySouth Million Writers Award.

Pumla Dineo Gqola lectures in the Department of English and Classical Culture at the University of the Free State in the Republic of South Africa. Her creative writing has most recently been published in *Tyhume* and *Running Towards Us: New Writing from South Africa* (Heinemann, edited by Isabel Balseiro.

Thomas J. Hubschman (tom@gowanusbooks.com) is the author of the novel *Billy Boy* (Savvy Press) and two science fiction novels, *Alpha-II* and *Space Ark*. A collection of his stories, ***The Jew's Wife & Other Stories,*** is scheduled for publication in 2007. His short stories, reviews and articles have appeared in numerous print and online publications and on the BBC World Service.

Abha Iyengar lives in New Delhi, India. She is a writer, traveler and yoga enthusiast. She has studied the practical (Management Studies), the creative (Interior Design) and the spiritual (Yoga). Publication credits include *Femina, Life Positive, Enlightened Practice, Riverbabble, Writers Against War, Insolent Rudder, Raven Chronicles.*

Shireen Joanna is a 29-year-old journalist and writer of poetry and short fiction who is currently at work on a novel. Based in Fairfax, Virginia, she believes in T.S. Eliot's creed of identifying an "objective correlative" for emotion and translating this into pure art.

Diane Johnson is an American academic.

Muhammad Nasrullah Khan is a Pakistani whose work has found critical acclaim in his own country. He teaches English in Saudia Arabia. "The Donkey-Man" was selected as among the Most Notable short stories published on the Internet in 2005 by the storySouth Million Writers Award.

Veronica Khokhlova is a native of Kyiv, Ukraine, but spends much of her time in St. Petersburg, Russia. She'd rather live someplace warm, though, at least in winter. Links to her other work can be found at http://www.euro-correspondent.com/veronica.htm.

Beatrice Lamwaka teaches as well as writes. Her short fiction and poetry have been published in various anthologies. She is one of the pioneers of a British Council writing scheme to link Ugandan writers with established writers in the UK. She is currently working on her first novel.

Andrew McKenna is an Australian writer and journalist. His work has been published in *The Dead Mule School of Southern Literature* (USA), *River Teeth, A Journal of Nonfiction Narrative* (USA), *New Internationalist* (UK), *Carve Magazine* and *the Best of Carve 2002* (USA), *Antipodes*, (Canada/USA) and the *New England Review* (Australia). He has just completed a novel, *The Illness and the Cure,* of which "A Dark Place" is an extract.

Anthony Milne is a professional journalist who worked for several years for *Trinidad Express* in Trinidad & Tobago, and now resides in Canada where he is writing an historical novel about his native Trinidad.

Luis Nieto Degregori, a native of Cusco, is the author the short story collections *Harta Cerveza y Harta Bala, Como cuando Estabamos Vivos* and *La Joven que Subio al Cielo,* all included in *Con los Ojos para Siempre Abiertos.* Nieto has received two of Peru's most prestigious literary awards, El Cope del Cuento and El Cesar Vallejo. Nieto has published a novel *Cusco Despues del Amo"* and is at work on a second.

Crispin Oduobuk is the magazine editor of the *Weekly Trust.* He's a read-a-lot, travel-when-can music and Internet freak. A 1995 best-graduate of Literature-in-English of the University of Abuja, he's been published in BBC *Focus on Africa* magazine, *The Washington Times, Ken*Again,* and *The Ultimate Hallucination.* He can be reached at crispinoduobuk@hotmail.com.

Padma Prasad was born in Chennai, India but now lives and works in Fairfax, Virginia. She has a master's in English Literature and is a writer, painter and graphic artist. Her work has appeared in *Another Toronto Quarterly* and in *Eclectica.*

Lila Rajiva is a freelance writer born in India and the author of *The Language of Empire: Abu Ghraib and the American Media,* (Monthly Review Press). She has written for *India West, Himal South Asia,* the

Baltimore Chronicle, Alternet and *Counterpunch* among others.

Kenneth Ramchand is author of The West Indian Novel and Its Background and other scholarly works as well as numerous introductions to reprints of WI novels and short story collections At present he is working on an extensive collection to be called The Book of the West Indian Story, along with an accompanying critical text. He also serves as Senator in the Government of the Republic of Trinidad and Tobago and as Associate Provost, University of Trinidad and Tobago, directing The Academy at UTT for Arts, Letters, Culture and Public Affairs.

Raymond Ramcharitar earns his living as a journalist in Trinidad and Tobago, West Indies. He has been published throughout the Caribbean and the United States. He has had fiction and poetry published in the US and Caribbean. He can be reached at: raymondramcharitar@yahoo.com.

Rasik Shah (rshah1878@home.com) lives in Vancouver, Canada. He grew up in Kenya and likes revisiting the past through writing fiction. His hobby is taking out groups for trekking in the Indian Himalayas.

Abbas Zaidi <manoo@brunet.bn> was editor of *The Ravi* (1985), Pakistan's premier and oldest academic magazine published by Government College, Lahore. He also edited *Interface* (1990–9191) for the Program in Literary Linguistics, University of Strathclyde, Glasgow. Zaidi has taught English Literature in Bahauddin Zakariya University, Multan, and worked as assistant editor for *The Nation*, Lahore